THE INTELLIGENT
AUSTRALIAN INVESTOR

CHRIS LEITHNER

THE INTELLIGENT AUSTRALIAN INVESTOR

Timeless Principles and Fresh Applications

Wrightbooks

First published 2005 by Wrightbooks
an imprint of John Wiley & Sons Australia, Ltd
42 McDougall Street, Milton, Qld 4064

Offices also in Sydney and Melbourne

Typeset in 11/14 pt ITC New Baskerville LT

© Chris Leithner 2005

National Library of Australia Cataloguing-in-Publication Data:

Leithner, Chris 1963—
The intelligent Australian investor: timeless principles and fresh applications.

Includes index.
ISBN 0 7314 0303 7.

    1. Investments—Australia. 2. Investment analysis—Australia.
    3. Saving and investment—Australia.
    4. Financial services industry—Australia. I. Title.

332.6722

Cover design by Rob Cowpe

Printed in Australia by Griffin Press

10 9 8 7 6 5 4 3 2 1

Disclaimer

The material in this publication is of the nature of general comment only, and does not represent professional advice. It is not intended to provide specific guidance for particular circumstances and it should not be relied on as the basis for any decision to take action or not take action on any matter which it covers. Readers should obtain professional advice where appropriate, before making any such decision. To the maximum extent permitted by law, the author and publisher disclaim all responsibility and liability to any person, arising directly or indirectly from any person taking or not taking action based upon the information in this publication.

Tu ne cede malis, sed contra audentior ito.

TO EDDA

ACKNOWLEDGMENTS

This book has benefited greatly from others' advice and encouragement.

David John Gow, a co-director of Leithner & Co. and Leithner Investments (the latter company is the manager of the Western Pacific–Leithner Value Fund), read successive drafts, offered many wise suggestions and, as always, provided an invaluable sounding board.

David Guy, the chairman of Western Pacific Group of companies and ably assisted by Danah Smallwood, is an island of calm wisdom in an investment sea that often exhibits frenetic and seemingly foolish tendencies. The more Western Pacific people I meet, the more impressed I become.

Len Coote (who also read several drafts), Robert Gee and Kevin Holman have long encouraged me to turn materials originally intended for a private company's shareholders into a book for a general audience; Sandra Haswell is a model of grace and dignity under pressure; and Ian McAllister is a model of efficiency.

Anthony Stone, the acquisitions editor at John Wiley & Sons Australia, kindly invited me to write this book and offered several worthy suggestions.

I also thank three impressive but unduly modest people who choose to remain anonymous.

Most of all, Edda Leithner has offered much encouragement and identified numerous errors of omission and commission. More than anyone—and probably without realising it—she inspires me to keep my standards high. Whenever I ponder an investment I ask myself: *would it be good enough for her portfolio?*

TABLE OF CONTENTS

Foreword

◇◇◇◇◇◇◇◇◇◇◇◇◇◇◇◇◇◇◇◇◇◇◇◇◇◇◇◇◇◇◇◇◇◇

At the 2004 annual general meeting of Wesco Financial Corporation, the company's chairman, Charles Munger, summarised what both Wesco and Berkshire Hathaway, chaired by Warren Buffett, consider to be their 'investment philosophy'. Simply put, he said, they endeavoured to engage in 'enlightened opportunism'. At the 2005 AGM, Munger expanded upon this theme, attributing Wesco's success to two qualities: patience and 'aggressive opportunism'.

So to achieve unparalleled investment success, such as that of Wesco and Berkshire Hathaway, one need only have patience and enlightenment and act opportunistically? Sadly, for us mere mortals this is not always easy. Patience is in the main a matter of one's personal temperament, and even the keenest opportunist must wait for those opportunities the market throws up from time to time. Enlightenment, on the other hand, comes from learning and is most certainly something that can be achieved by the individual.

Dr Chris Leithner, the author of this book, is that rare kind of intellect, who, in undertaking his investment operations, reverts to timeless principles rather than creating ever more esoteric, and ever more inaccurate, models of how investments *should*, rather than do, work. The principles Chris Leithner relies on are those of Ben Graham, which truly qualify as timeless.

That Graham's teachings have been largely discarded by mainstream investment management firms and business schools is lamentable, considering the obvious practical success that first Graham and then his students (including his most celebrated student, Warren Buffett) have had in implementing his principles. In the rollcall of the world's greatest investors, those who have been influenced by Graham are conspicuous by their disproportionate presence. Internationally, the names Buffett, Munger, Ruane, Neff and even Lynch spring to mind, while in the Australian context, Maple-Brown, Morgan, Metanomski, Tagliaferro and Leithner have similarly borne the torch for Graham investors.

It is my ardent hope that the Graham/Buffett school of investment management continues to be disregarded by the mainstream; it makes it easier for the remainder of us! It is my expectation, however, that the clear and concise manner in which Chris Leithner has outlined how Graham's principles can (and I believe, should) be applied to the Australian market will likely lead to an increase in the number of 'value' investors in this part of the world. We will grudgingly welcome readers to the value school!

In conclusion, if I had been asked to select someone to write this book for the Australian market, Chris Leithner would have been my first choice. In our numerous business dealings he has displayed incredible patience; his 'enlightenment' or intelligence continues to astound me and his eye for a good opportunity is increasingly evident as he successfully negotiates the difficult investment environment we are rapidly entering.

I recommend all parties interested in investment read and learn from this book. I know that my near and dear will be receiving copies as presents for the foreseeable future.

David Guy
Chairman
Chief Investment Officer
Western Pacific Group of companies
<www.westernpacific.com.au>
July 2005

Introduction

In the courts of princes, in the drawing-rooms of the great, where success and preferment depend, not upon the esteem of intelligent and well-informed equals, but upon the fanciful and foolish favour of ignorant, presumptuous and proud superiors; flattery and falsehood too often prevail over merit and abilities ... This disposition to admire, and almost to worship the rich and the powerful, and to despise or, at least, to neglect, persons of poor and mean condition ... is ... the great and most universal cause of the corruption of our moral sentiments.

Adam Smith
The Theory of Moral Sentiments (1759)

This book presents some principles and applications—an investment philosophy, if you will forgive the rather pompous phrase—that intelligent and diligent Australians can use either to invest their own money or to select, interrogate and keep on a short lead those who do it for them. It is certainly not a 'how to make a million' book: instead, it attempts to be a 'how not to lose money' book. It shows that the investment losses many amateurs and professionals incurred between 2000 and 2003 were self-inflicted. Simple yet rigorous reasoning, plus information readily available to the general public during these years, could have produced (and, for the people who availed themselves of these things, did lead to) the conclusion that during these years the purchase of most stocks, whether 'hot techs' or 'blue chips,' was a speculation rather than an investment. I believe that this is still true today.

I have tried to steer a middle course between two unappealing features of Australia's financial services industry. On the one hand are large and brazen advertisements that say, in effect, that if you pay a small fortune for somebody's 'secrets' (or software or seminars or whatever), you can make money quickly and easily. On the other hand, some major financial institutions imply that investment is too difficult for laypeople. The benighted should therefore abandon any attempt at investment and simply forward their funds to the anointed experts. Much less prevalent is the middle-ground opinion: sound investment is much less arcane than some financial institutions might want you to think; but it is also much harder than the 'secrets of the rich' brigade would have you believe.

It seems to me that the average Australian adult has more than enough brainpower, if she or he chooses to use it, to withstand both kinds of spruikers. The trouble, of course, is that many people—professional investors included—dislike reading and thinking. These days, it is also hard to create the large blocks of time required to learn about investment and to conduct one's own investment research. I have therefore written this book with two types of people in mind. The first have the time and the inclination to think hard and dig deep. These people might use this book to help guide their own cautious and conservative style of investment. The second prefer to devote their time to other important things such as gardens or grandchildren, but they are willing and able to think. In short, they want both free time and sound sleep. Accordingly, in conjunction with their advisers, they might use this book as a template with which to select—and sternly judge—the stewards who invest their capital on their behalf.

Four grounds have prompted me to write this book. The first is the conviction that the ideas and methods of Benjamin Graham, widely regarded as the founder of modern investment analysis, are just as valid in today's Australia as they were in the United States during Graham's heyday in the 1930s, 1940s and 1950s. In 1999 I founded Leithner & Co. Pty Ltd, a private investment company based in Brisbane, as a didactic as well as a capitalistic enterprise. I sought to demonstrate that a firm modelled upon Graham's vehicle, Graham-Newman Corp., and adapted to Australian conditions, could serve its shareholders well. Five years later, its cumulative results have been satisfactory by Grahamite standards—despite the aborted deflation of the Great Bubble, a sharp upturn and—who knows?—perhaps the onset of the bear market we have to have. This book is an opportunity to present to a wider audience the principles that guide Leithner & Co.'s investment operations.

Secondly, I seek to highlight some glaring and insurmountable weaknesses of mainstream finance and investment. To put it brutally frankly, the standard—and effectively the monopoly—approach to these subjects that is taught in universities in Australia and other English-speaking countries makes my job much easier than it should be. The legions who emerge from the academic degree factory possess flawed conceptions about fundamental things. They tend to discount or ignore the distinction between investment and speculation and believe that mathematical proficiency trumps rigorous thinking, thus becoming speculators-who-think-they-are-investors; they regard value and price as synonyms, and consequently understand neither; they obsess about irrelevant details, yet blithely ignore significant risks; and their conceptions of interest and inflation are, I believe, dangerously wrong and will eventually lead many to grief. I have therefore written this book to draw attention to new (that is, old and mostly forgotten) approaches and their fresh application to commonsense, conservative investment. It remains perfectly possible for the laity to reason simply but rigorously to conclusions that dispute and perhaps refute some of the financial priesthood's most fervently held doctrines.

Thirdly, this book is contrarian in the sense that it draws attention to the important similarities between minority groups of investors and economists. Grahamite investors and

Austrian School economists hold compatible views about a range of fundamental things. Indeed, each may have more in common with the other than with the mainstream of its respective field. It is perfectly possible to live a long and fulfilling life, love your spouse and children and live peaceably next to your neighbours without the slightest knowledge of Grahamite investing and Austrian School economics. Yet to value investors, the economics of Carl Menger, Eugen von Böhm-Bawerk, Ludwig von Mises and Murray Rothbard should be compelling because it uses justifiable laws of human action to explain real commercial and financial events. Unlike the mainstream, Austrians not only acknowledge but also celebrate individuality and entrepreneurship. Both Austrians and Grahamites also recognise that investment acumen, whilst hardly widespread, can and likely does exist.

These groups' contributions are occasionally remembered and—once in a blue moon—even praised by the financial and economic mainstream. However, for decades their methods have seldom been practiced, and their advocates are usually either denigrated or ignored—until, that is, some crisis or unexpected occurrence embarrasses the mainstream and angers the public.

The fourth and most important motivation I had in writing this book is implicit in the first three: I believe that private property, shackled governments and unchained people are crucial to Australia's moral and material future. Alan Kohler noted in *The Australian Financial Review* on 5 February 2002 that:

> very few people actually preach capitalism in public, especially CEOs. Mostly they preach its antidotes and constraints: regulation, triple bottom line, corporate governance, auditing, checks and balance, corporate citizenship, leadership in the modern age, transparency.

In my opinion, this reticence to praise the gift of laissez-faire capitalism is unfortunate. I also think these antidotes and constraints are misguided and probably dangerous.

Introduction

The mechanism of natural liberty is fragile and third-party decision-making—that is to say, decisions that are removed from the hands of the individuals concerned and hijacked by people who have no incentive to act prudently—results in all manner of debacles.

Only individuals can act. Any statement about a group of people, such as a committee or a crowd, is no more and no less than a statement about the individuals comprising the group. There is, for example, no 'economy' or 'market' apart from the individuals who comprise it. Nor is there any 'market sentiment'—there are simply the many and varied attitudes and actions of the individual buyers and sellers who comprise the market. Accordingly, in an economic setting action takes one of only four possible forms:

- You can spend your money on yourself.

- You can spend your money on someone else.

- You can spend somebody else's money on yourself.

- You can spend somebody else's money on somebody else.

If you spend your own money on yourself, you tend to seek the best value—a subjective thing that only you can determine when it comes to your wants and needs—at the best price. You seek to stretch your money as far as it will go and thereby to meet as many of your desires as possible. Under this scenario good things, morally and materially, typically occur. (This last assertion is supported by an extended example provided in chapter 6.)

If you spend your own money on other people, you still seek the best price. The problem with altruism, though, is that you may not know—or care—what other people want, and will tend to give them what *you* think they *should* want. This shortcoming is minimised when people spend money on their family members. They tend to know their close relatives' wants and needs reasonably well (or at any rate better than strangers would); and parents' vicarious self-interest is usually a reasonable proxy for their children's long-term welfare.

In order to spend other people's money on yourself, you must first beg, borrow or steal their money. Once you have it, you are intensely concerned about subjective value—about getting what you want—but have much less incentive to obtain a good price. Rather than stretch each dollar as far as it will go, it will probably be easier to extract more dollars from your host. And if you spend other people's money on other people—that is, if you are a politician—then you must confiscate from Peter and meddle in the affairs of Paul. As such, you have no incentive to care about either value or price: anything that brings you votes today will do, and hang the costs that others will eventually have to bear. Clearly, then, as third-party decision-making rears its ugly head, moral as well as economic constraints weaken, probity evaporates and perversities and pathologies proliferate. (It is beyond the scope of this book to go into this argument at length, but books included in the reading list in chapter 14 provide many depressing examples.)

As night follows day, in other words, and in addition to their innate immorality, politicians are inherently incompetent and their interventionist policies necessarily fail. Without a direct link between the subjective values underlying the choices of consumers and the objective prices used by both producers and consumers to make economic calculations—without, in short, a free market—waste, corruption and chaos inexorably result. No matter what task politicians remove from individuals and arrogate to themselves, they will do it improperly, inefficiently and ineffectively. They are a disgrace to all that is good and true, and their activities constitute an unreformable axis of plunder. Take a man who is a saint and a genius, put him into politics and he inevitably—and quickly—becomes a sinner and a drongo.

Whether Australians like it or not (and I suspect that most won't like it one bit), politicians' inescapable outrages and blunders will one day oblige ordinary people to take charge of their economic and financial affairs. Hence the sooner Australians realise the truth about their 'leaders' the better: politicians are roughly one-third dreadful, two-thirds (more or less) laughable and precisely three-thirds contemptible. To protest this iron law of nature is akin to criticising the 'unfairness' of the tides or bewailing the 'injustice' of the periodic table of elements.

The greatest risk to Australians' moral and material standards of living, apart from their delusions about politics and government, is therefore the aggressive and noxious interventionism that oozes from Commonwealth and state governments into every aspect of their lives. In diametric contrast, there is nothing so charming, uplifting and beneficial (to themselves and others) as a man or woman in hot pursuit of an honest dollar. Entrepreneurs—and value investors—exemplify the positive results that individual effort and the harmonisation of enlightened self-interest can achieve. The countless follies of governments and mainstream economists often prompt both Grahamites and Austrians to adopt dour short-term outlooks, but despite this they remain long-term optimists. To adopt their approaches is ultimately to affirm a basic faith in human nature, unfettered markets and capitalism, one's country and a future that will be at least as prosperous as the present.

To read general business and specialist trade publications, the daily newspaper and so on is occasionally to discern a valuable insight or nugget of information. Accumulating them, adding them to one's own ideas and using justifiable principles to sift and subsume them into coherence will, over time, provide a firm basis for decisions. At any given point in time, however, few of the reports, articles, email messages and other ephemera that typically clutter one's desk should be taken seriously. The vast bulk of the stuff that an intelligent investor peruses, in short, is not worth reading. What will repay painstaking study, however, are the principles and methods that over the decades have helped to identify sound businesses whose prices are lower than their values. Benjamin

Graham and Austrian School economists, it seems to me, provide a moral and logical radar system. Using this radar, the investor tends less often, in a figurative sense, to trip over chairs and nightstands. The future is always unlit and so we must all work in the dark. But with a sound framework, solid information and a calm temperament, we can anticipate where the furniture might lie and (more often than not) step aside. Armed with valid logic and reliable evidence, plus a sceptical and humble disposition, intelligent Australian investors can protect themselves against the daily deluge of part-information, misinformation, misconception, outright falsehood and mass delusion.

Part I

◇◇◇◇◇◇◇◇◇◇◇◇◇◇◇◇◇◇◇◇◇◇◇◇

Six foundation stones

Speculation is an effort, probably unsuccessful, to turn a little money into a lot. Investment is an effort, which should be successful, to prevent a lot of money from becoming a little.

Like all of life's rich emotional experiences, the full flavour of losing important money cannot be conveyed by literature. Art cannot convey to an inexperienced girl what it is truly like to be a wife and mother. There are certain things that cannot adequately be explained to a virgin either by words or pictures. Nor can any description that I might offer here even approximate what it feels like to lose a real chunk of money that you used to own.

Fred Schwed
Where Are the Customers' Yachts?
Or, a Good Hard Look at Wall Street (1940)

Chapter 1

<><><><><><><><><><><><><><><><><><><><><>

Distinguish investment
from speculation

*In the past, the speculative elements of a common stock resided
almost exclusively in the company itself; they were due to
uncertainties, or fluctuating elements, or downright weaknesses in
the industry, or the corporation's individual setup. These elements
of speculation still exist, of course; but it may be said that they have
been sensibly diminished by a number of long-term developments ...
But in revenge a new and major element of speculation has been
introduced into the common-stock arena from outside the companies.
It comes from the attitude and viewpoint of the stock-buying public
and their advisers — chiefly us security analysts. This attitude may
be described in a phrase: primary emphasis upon future expectations.*

Benjamin Graham
'The New Speculation in Common Stocks'
The Analysts Journal (June 1958)

A NATION OF INVESTORS OR SPECULATORS?

These days in Australia, the words *investor* and *investment*
are used very loosely. Judging from the business sections

of newspapers, the glossy pages of business magazines and the chatter of finance programs, an investor is practically anybody who buys and sells stocks, bonds or real estate, and an investment is virtually anything whose purchase price is expected to rise. The Australian Stock Exchange (ASX) seems to agree. In a press release dated 25 February 2005, announcing the results of the 2004 ASX Share Ownership Survey (SOS), it stated:

> respondents ... expressed the view that shares have 'come good' in the last twelve months or so. They understood that the market goes in peaks and troughs, with property being seen to have had its day for now. Many said that shares have taken over as the stronger performer. A strong economy and good company profits were cited as factors behind the performance of shares.

(The respondents' expectation is probably mistaken. See chapter 7 for further discussion of this issue.) Similarly, on 3 February 2004 the ASX announced:

> Australians are maintaining their reputation as a 'nation of shareholders' ... The 2003 [SOS], the latest in an ASX series stretching back to 1986, showed that Australians not only follow the market more closely than ever, they are more committed and increasingly active participants.

According to the 2004 SOS, 55 per cent of adult Australians—eight million people—own shares. They own them either in their own names or indirectly through a superannuation or managed fund. Further, 'these investors ... are increasingly using the Internet to research their investments, buy shares and track their holdings—and they are monitoring those investments far more often.' They are also trading more frequently. The 'average investor' trades seven times per year, compared with six times in 2003 and five in 2002. 'The value of the average portfolio is $41,400, an increase of around 1 per cent. Both of these [changes] probably reflect the entry of new investors, reducing the extent of the average increase.'

The ASX's press releases resemble the advertisements of the many firms that sell financial products and services. Some firms urge people to focus upon the long term, and others claim that they can teach them to trade securities quickly, safely and profitably. The advertisements differ in many ways, but when they are considered as a group, they tend to convey a standard two-part message: first, 'invest your money with us or through us'; and second, 'either trade it constantly or let us churn it on your behalf'.

The trouble with this loose usage of the word 'invest' is that it obscures and often eliminates the critical distinction between investors and investments on the one hand and speculators and speculations on the other. To blur this distinction is to create two problems. First, it encourages people to indulge their innate leaning towards the excitement—and hazards—of speculation without being aware that this is what they are doing. However, not everybody who buys stocks, bonds and real estate is an investor. Indeed, many people who think that they are investors—including funds managers at many major institutions—are actually speculators. The second problem is that often (I am tempted to say inevitably) the first problem induces severe financial and psychological pain. The line that separates investment and speculation, which is never bright and clear, becomes even more blurred during booms; and speculation is most dangerous at precisely those times when it looks easiest. The trouble with booms, gilded prosperity and bull markets, in other words, is that they cause busts and bear markets.

Our first task, then, is to define key terms. Benjamin Graham's classics, *Security Analysis* and *The Intelligent Investor*, provide the firm foundation we require. (A list of Graham's major works, together with other essential reading, appears in chapter 14.) Following Graham, let us define an *investment* as an asset that, on the basis of thorough analysis, is likely to provide safety of principal (that is to say, the money originally exchanged for the asset) and an adequate return (that is, a stream of income generated by the asset). An asset that does not have these attributes is therefore a *speculation*. For our purposes, it is useful to regard an *asset* as a legal title that confers rights to, or ownership of, specified resources or property. To buy a company's stock, for example, is to become one of the company's owners and therefore to possess a pro rata right to any profits that the company might generate; and to buy a bond is to acquire the right to receive interest payments as specified in the product's prospectus. An *investor* uses plausible yet cautious premises, reliable evidence, valid patterns of reasoning and a businesslike and sceptical disposition in accumulating assets. By Graham's definition, then, the distinguishing characteristic of investors is their ability to use logic and prudence to guide and justify their actions. The person who buys and sells assets on some other basis — whether or not they are investments — is a *speculator*.

Benjamin Graham

Benjamin Graham (1894–1976) was a businessman and investor, and is regarded as the founder of modern security analysis. His books *Security Analysis* (co-authored with David Dodd) and *The Intelligent Investor* provide the moral and intellectual foundations of 'value investing'. For many years, Graham taught at Columbia University, and Warren Buffett is one of his most prominent former students.

GRAHAMITE INVESTORS V. SPECULATORS

The remainder of this chapter is devoted to the differences between investors and speculators according to 'Grahamite' definitions of investors and investments. However, before embarking on a discussion of these differences, it is important to make a few observations, bearing in mind the positive image Grahamites have of 'investment' and the often pejorative connotation given to 'speculation'.

First, the dividing line between investing and speculating is hardly crystal clear. For this reason, perhaps it is better to think of a continuum with investment at one end, speculation at the other and various shades of grey in the middle.

Second, although for most people it is not financially fattening, speculation is neither illegal nor immoral. Indeed, in a general economic sense speculation is necessary and beneficial. Speculators can help the prices of stocks, securities and commodities to tend towards their values more quickly than they otherwise would. (The difference between price and value will be discussed at length in following chapters.) Speculators also present people who wish to mitigate the level of risk they carry (for example, farmers who wish to receive a set price for a crop that has not yet been sown, or has been sown but not yet harvested) with an opportunity to transfer this risk to those who, in exchange for the perceived likelihood of a commensurate reward, are prepared to bear it.

Finally, just as there are intelligent investors there are also intelligent speculators. The fact that it is much more difficult to speculate intelligently and profitably than it is to invest astutely and successfully (see chapter 2) does not deny the existence of able speculators and profitable speculations: it simply reminds us that successful speculators are far less numerous than successful investors.

In that respect, then, the following general discussion unintentionally snubs talented speculators. Accordingly, it should be read as a contrast between an unusual investor (that is, a Grahamite) and a typical speculator. Its injustice to a few is outweighed by its salutary message to the many: of the numerous forms of unintelligent speculation, perhaps the most pervasive—and harmful—is risk-fraught speculation by people who mistakenly believe that they are safely investing.

Table 1.1 sets out the differences between the Grahamite approach and that of the typical speculator.

Table 1.1: comparing investors and speculators

Criterion	Grahamite investor	Typical speculator
Primary objective	Avoiding the 'downside'	Grasping the 'upside'
Secondary objective	Adequate return	Excellent return
Time frame	Medium-term (5 years+)	Short-term (less than 1 year)
Unit of analysis	Companies and their operations	Markets, prices, charts and trends
Key focus	Discrepancies between value and price	Price fluctuations
Self-image	Part-owner of a portfolio of businesses	Trader of pieces of paper
Primary measure of results	Dividends and interest payments	Capital gains
Actual result	Tends to make money	Tends to lose money

The primary objective

The Grahamite investor is a cautious investor. She[1] seeks first and foremost to avoid losing money, and takes multiple steps to protect herself against serious and irreparable losses. In practice, the Grahamite strives to preserve the purchasing power of her capital by compounding it at a rate that compensates for the effects of consumer price inflation (CPI). Only when investment operations give her grounds to believe that she can preserve her wealth does she attempt to build it.

The Grahamite's primary objective, then, is to 'protect the downside' (guard against the occurrence of bad things) and let the 'upside' take care of itself (see chapters 12 and 13 for further detail).

The typical speculator, on the other hand, seeks first and foremost to 'beat the market'. If the Grahamite is a tortoise, then the speculator is a hare. If he can grasp the upside then the downside need not concern him. The investor strives to accumulate a portfolio of companies with strong track records, and is prepared to put in the time it takes to do so. She therefore waits until genuine investment opportunities appear, and uses savings—and rarely debt—to finance these investments. The speculator, in contrast, cannot wait. Impatient to participate in the next big thing, and perhaps even to find the 'next Microsoft', he is attracted to the new and the unproven, exciting prospects, 'hot stocks', emerging trends and 'celebrity CEOs'. His lack of sufficient cash to finance these purchases is no object. Firms compete for the pleasure of lending him the money, and he is happy to borrow it.

If the speculator who does these things recognises that he is a speculator, then that is his business and good luck to him; however, if he is under the impression that he is an investor, he should think again. In Graham's opinion, every non-professional who borrows in order to buy stocks, bonds and real estate is *necessarily* speculating—and it is his broker's or adviser's duty to advise him accordingly. Further, anybody who buys a 'hot stock' or similar security because it is popular is, by definition, speculating.[2]

The Grahamite investor protects herself against permanent loss by figuratively kicking the tyres, checking under the bonnet and buying nothing without a thorough—and time-consuming—analysis. She learns the most salient characteristics of the business she analyses, and is able to compare it to its peers and against more general criteria. She knows that risk inheres in any investment; she has a clear conception of risk and a reasonable idea of her attitude towards it. The investor builds her portfolio of assets taking these factors into account. The speculator, on the other hand (because he lacks the ability, patience or time required to conduct an appropriate analysis), usually wants to know little about the economics of a particular business or the industry in which it operates. Yet he is still prepared to 'take a punt' on a 'sure thing'—a judgment he has made on the basis of his own intuition, an article in a newspaper or magazine, a mate's 'tip', or even an anonymous tip. He is likely to agree that his actions are potentially risky—but hastens to add that his intuition or sources are reputable and therefore that he is confident that his 'picks' will 'do well'.

The Grahamite investor, in contrast, seeks a margin of safety. She draws upon relatively simple but rigorous reasoning and hard data. Given the tools at her disposal, she flatly refuses—because she simply has no need—to take her chances. The typical speculator lacks these tools and is thus game to try his luck. He is likely to believe that time is on his side and that he is able to 'read the market'. On these grounds, he believes that the odds are in his favour. Such claims did not convince Graham. They do not draw support from any coherent line of reasoning or reliable body of evidence. Graham said that he very much doubted whether anyone staking money on a personal belief that the market was heading up or down could ever be said to be protected by a margin of safety in any meaningful sense of the phrase.[3]

Adequate versus excellent results

As a cautious investor, the Grahamite aspires to obtain adequate—and not extraordinary—results. Just as children's eyes are bigger than their tummies, adults' aspirations usually exceed the effort they are prepared to exert in order to achieve them. The results to which an investor can reasonably aspire do *not*, in other words, depend upon the amount of risk she is prepared to accept. Instead, they vary according to the amount of continual and intelligent effort she is willing and able to apply to her investment research. Few people can devote themselves on a full-time basis to the analysis and selection of investments, and most people, it is reasonable to suppose, prize safety and freedom from undue worry. Normal people want free time and sound sleep. Accordingly, and to use Graham's terms, most people should aspire to be 'defensive' investors; the relatively few who have the requisite stoic temperament and who possess (or can find or develop) the necessary time, energy and skills may aspire to become 'enterprising' investors.

The minimum results belong to the defensive investor, and the maximum normally accrue to the enterprising investor. In either case, the Grahamite investor aspires to and contents herself with results that are no more than average for her profile. Unlike the speculator, in other words, the investor makes no attempt to exceed long-run averages or to beat the market. Investment might be easier to understand than 'experts' say—but it is nonetheless much harder and more time-consuming than it might look. Graham was sceptical of defensive investors' ability to generate superior results—and his scepticism extended to large funds managed by experts. The enterprising investor can reasonably aspire to *somewhat* better results than her defensive companion, but it is arguable, Graham cautioned, whether these enterprising results will be sufficient to compensate for the considerable extra time and effort required to produce them. In any case, the enterprising investor must first take steps to ensure that her results are not *worse* than those of her defensive counterpart. This is easier said than done. Graham noted that it was not unusual to see talented, energetic individuals come to Wall Street, only to end up with losses instead of profits. Study and native ability were virtues, he said, but if channelled in the wrong directions, they became indistinguishable from handicaps.[4]

What, then, are 'adequate' results? Over the years, an average annual result that exceeds the rate of inflation by roughly 1 to 3 percentage points should satisfy the defensive Grahamite; and an average yearly result that exceeds inflation by 3 to 5 percentage points should gratify her enterprising counterpart.

(See chapter 10 for details about the results an intelligent investor might reasonably expect over the medium term.) Striving for more, the speculator tends to take unintelligent risks—and invites not just disappointment but also permanent loss of capital. Graham might have added that to plough and maintain one's fields in order to reap reasonable but sustainable long-term results (relative to those desired by the speculator) is often to garner an unexpectedly bountiful harvest.

The medium term versus the short term

The Grahamite investor is not just cautious; she is also patient. Because she is patient, she has a medium-term focus. That is to say, she invests with a time frame of five years (and often much longer) in mind. The typical speculator, in contrast, is impatient and therefore demands short-term results. In practice, the 'short term' generally refers to a period of a year or less, but some speculators consider 'short term' to mean weeks or even days; 'day traders', as their name implies, mark time in terms of hours and minutes.

The economics of a business or industry do not change daily, from week to week or one month to the next; and mature industries do not change significantly from year to year. From this point come two implications. First, the shorter the period of time upon which one concentrates, the greater focus one must necessarily have on short-term fluctuations of prices. Therein lies a problem. Major financial institutions devote much time, energy and money to the selection of stocks or industrial groups whose prices they believe will shortly rise more than the rest of the market. (Yes, that is right: many prominent and major institutional 'investors' are actually speculators—and have been so for decades.) This activity suits neither the needs nor the temperament of the true investor. Many institutional analysts analyse the same securities and are trying to do the same thing. Accordingly, the results of clients who follow their short-term recommendations tend to be 'zero-sum'—that is to say, the gain of one client is perfectly matched by the loss of another. This activity is thus not just self-neutralising: given brokerage and other costs, over the months and years it is self-defeating. (I will explore this point fully in chapter 2.)

The second implication is that the greater one's interest in fluctuations of prices, the more one tends to take seriously forecasts about these prices. This, too, from Graham's point of view, is absurd. Forecasting, in short (and as demonstrated in chapter 7), is a mug's game. Yet forecasts and market timing are very important to the typical speculator — indeed, few things are more important to him — because only on these bases can he hope to produce his results quickly. Companies' operations and analyses thereof are useless to him, because in the short term they seldom change enough to cause any significant volatility of stocks' prices.[5] Buying a stock or a bond today and then waiting several years before receiving a commensurate reward for his patience is simply not an option.

An extended waiting period does not trouble the Grahamite investor as it troubles the speculator. Quite the contrary, it whets her appetite. Because the speculator is unwilling to wait, he is unlikely to buy an asset whose fruits require several years to ripen. (Or, at any rate, if he does, it is likely that reasons other than its quality as an investment will induce him to buy it.) Speculators, then, often ignore or avoid the very types of assets that most interest Grahamites. And because many 'investors' are actually speculators, or at least part-speculators, under certain circumstances the demand for the assets desired by Grahamites is low. Reflecting their general unpopularity, these securities occasionally become available at particularly attractive — that is to say, low — prices. Hence, the investor's basic advantage vis-a-vis the speculator: by waiting patiently, she is occasionally able to buy quality assets at bargain prices. Having done so, time is on her side: she can allow the economics of the business of which she is now a part-owner — and not the whims of speculators — to push its price towards its value. The investor thus makes no attempt to buy and sell at propitious times; instead, she strives to buy and sell at attractive prices.

Companies and owners versus markets and traders

It is important to emphasise that a company's underlying operations are usually reasonably stable in the short term and evolve gradually over longer periods of time. Accordingly, these operations seldom cause significant short-term fluctuations in the price of a company's stock. A company's economics and operations, in other words, change much less from day to day, week to week and month to month than does the price of its stock. During the medium term, however, a firm's revenues, profits and the like exert a substantial influence upon the price of its securities, and over the years a company's operations will tend to push and pull the price of its stock towards its value. From this point spring two implications. First, the Grahamite investor focuses upon the economics of a given industry and the operations of the companies that comprise it, and she pays relatively scant attention to short-term fluctuations of prices (except to the extent that these fluctuations occasionally enable her to buy and sell assets at advantageous prices). Second, the typical speculator takes relatively slight notice of these economics and operations; instead, he obsesses about the short-term fluctuations of the prices of particular assets or of some general level of prices ('the market').

The investor, then, thoroughly analyses a company before she buys and sells its securities. The speculator does not. The investor studies many companies' financial statements and occasionally buys and sells. The typical speculator buys and sells much more frequently than the investor, and is guided by intuition, 'tips', charts, charting software or other means that purportedly determine appropriate times to buy and sell. In the supermarket or at the petrol pump, both the investor and the speculator economise when prices rise and attempt to shift expenditures from dearer to cheaper items. However, in financial markets, the speculator uses—and his sources advise—an utterly different set of principles. Nearly all of these so-called technical approaches conclude that the speculator should buy because a stock or bond or the overall market has risen, and that he should sell because the security or the market has declined. As Graham notes, this is the polar opposite of sound business practice and common sense. For that reason, it is most unlikely to lead to lasting success. In over fifty years of observation, Graham said, he had never known a single individual who had 'consistently or lastingly' made money by following the market. He felt no compunction in declaring that this particular approach was as 'fallacious as it was popular'.[6]

The typical speculator, then, buys a security because he believes, on whatever grounds, that somebody else will shortly offer to pay a higher price for it. An investor buys a security because she concludes, on the basis of cautious and thorough analysis, that its price is significantly lower than its value. She does not buy with the immediate intention to sell; she does not know—and probably does not care—whether she will be able to do so.

The purchase of an 'illiquid' security does not trouble the Grahamite investor. (An illiquid security is one for which there are relatively few buyers and sellers, or few or small transactions, in the market.) In fact, if the stock market closed for several years, the Grahamite would be troubled only to the extent that she would be unable to buy assets at prices below her estimates of their values or to sell them at prices above their subjective values. The investor, in other words, does not need the incessant blizzard of market quotes to validate her decisions. The operating results of the companies of which she is a part-owner provide all the validation she requires. If there is no basis upon which to analyse a company reliably—if, for example, a new firm has no financial statements or just a few years' worth, or if these statements indicate that its operations are forbiddingly complex or erratic—then its purchase is a speculation. Indeed, from Graham's point of view many companies cannot be reliably assessed—whatever the mathematical and verbal sleights of hand of those who purport to 'analyse' them. These securities are speculations rather than investments.

Although she is at all times free to do so, the investor is seldom forced to sell her securities. She is free to disregard the current price—and usually does. She need pay attention to it and act upon it only where it is favourable enough to justify buying or selling. According to Graham, the investor who allows an unjustified decline of the market prices of her holdings to worry her—or, even worse, to stampede her into selling—transforms her basic advantage into a disadvantage. Under these circumstances, it would be better if her securities had no market quotation at all—she would then be spared the mental anguish caused by others' mistakes.

Estimating values versus second-guessing other speculators

An investor analyses a business. Sometimes, but by no means always, the results of that analysis enable her to derive a justifiable estimate of its value. She compares her estimate of the value of the company's shares to their present price; buys when her estimate significantly exceeds price; and sells when price considerably exceeds estimated value. The typical speculator, in contrast, attempts to intuit or anticipate the attitudes of other speculators. He compares a security's present price to his assessment of (or intuition about) what others will shortly be prepared to pay for it. He compares his assessment of future price to the present price; buys when the assessment is greater than the price and sells when the price exceeds his assessment. The investor compares an estimate of present and future value to present price; and the speculator compares present price and assumed future price. For the speculator, then, an unending supply of security prices and their fluctuation is vital: without prices and fluctuations the speculator cannot speculate. For an investor, prices and price movements are much less relevant.

The investor who has accumulated a portfolio of sound securities knows that (if they are listed on a public market) their prices will fluctuate, but she is neither worried by substantial falls nor enthused by considerable rises. She does not allow bear markets to depress her spirits. Quite the contrary, she welcomes them as potential opportunities to purchase attractive assets at attractive prices. Having done her homework and accumulated cash during the boom, she is able to act decisively when speculators are fearful. During bull markets, when the tide lifts all boats and prices rise beyond reasonable assessments of value, she declines to form an inflated opinion of her investment prowess. At all times, then, the investor understands that market quotations exist for her convenience and not her survival. At no time does she equate value and price. Unlike the speculator, she never buys a security simply because its market price has increased; nor does she sell one just because its price has fallen. She pays little attention to 'the market' and concentrates upon her dividends and the operating results of 'her' companies.

Streams of income versus lumps of capital gain

The investor exchanges one kind of asset (usually cash) for another (say, a stock or bond). She does so because she expects this security to generate a reliable stream of income over an extended period of time. The speculator, on the other hand, spends a lump of cash today and in return expects to receive a bigger lump of cash (that is, a realised capital gain) in the near future. It is true that capital appreciation can be converted into a cash flow, but short-term price fluctuation is not a *reliable* source of cash flow. Rents from good tenants; profits and dividends from sound and well-established businesses with extended track records of generating profits and paying dividends; interest payments from secure notes—all of these things are much more reliable than day-to-day, week-to-week and month-to-month fluctuations of stock prices.

Accordingly, assets that generate these sorts of cash flows are investments, and assets that do not are speculations. Indeed, it often transpires that speculations generate expenses rather than income. To invest, then, is to purchase an asset that generates a relatively reliable stream of income; and the cost of that investment (that is, the value of the tap from which flows the stream) tends to be roughly proportional to the quality, breadth, depth and duration of the stream. Speculation is the attempt to purchase a (relatively unreliable) lump of capital gain. Reflecting its unreliability, the cost of the speculation tends to be much less directly proportional to the size of the eventual lump.

One way to decide whether a given opportunity to exchange cash for a particular security is an investment or a speculation is to judge whether the cash flows that the security can reasonably be expected to generate over the medium term can justify its current price. The greater the extent to which the current price exceeds the justifiable price, the greater the risk that inheres in the purchase of the security; and the lower the purchase price relative to the justifiable price, the greater the security's margin of safety. How to foretell changes in opinion is the speculator's central challenge; how to ascertain streams of dividends and payments of interest is the object of the investor's analyses. Investors, as we will see in subsequent chapters, sit a difficult but nonetheless much easier test than speculators.

John Burr Williams noted that the longer a buyer holds a stock or bond, the more important are the dividends or interest payments she receives while she owns it — and, for this reason, the less important is the price when she sells it. To the speculator, dividends and interest are relatively insignificant because the length of time he holds a stock or bond is too short to receive cash flows that are significant in relation to the capital outlay. For a security that is held by the same family for several generations, the selling price in the end is a relatively minor matter.[7] For this reason, Williams defined an investor 'as a buyer interested in dividends, or coupons and principal, and a speculator as a buyer interested in resale price. Thus the usual buyer is a hybrid, being partly investor and partly speculator. Clearly the pure investor must hold [a] security for long periods, while the pure speculator must sell promptly, if each is to get what he seeks.'[8]

Making versus losing money

Although there are undoubtedly some individual exceptions, speculators as a class are almost certain to lose money. They strive mightily to profit from an endeavour whose logical and mathematical laws virtually condemn them to lose. In contrast, Grahamite investors as a class are very likely to maintain the purchasing power of their capital, although again there will always be some exceptions. Grahamites also have a reasonable chance to increase their wealth modestly and steadily. Investors tend to make money because their operations conform to certain laws of economics and human action. The next chapter shows why speculation almost inevitably ends in tears; and parts II and III demonstrate why the odds ultimately favour investors.

NOTES

1   Throughout this book I will deliberately use the feminine pronoun 'she' to refer to the investor. Women are more likely to invest, and to invest successfully, than men. Women get better results than men—on average, 1.4 percentage points better. Single women do even better—achieving 2.3 percentage points a year more than single men. On that basis, single women should stay single, and married women should block their husbands' access to financial websites on the internet. Women tend to be less arrogant and overconfident, and are not as likely to be infatuated with charts and charting software. They are therefore less prone to trading and other boneheaded activities. These are of course generalisations—because they are human, both men and women continuously devise imaginative ways to drain money from their own pockets. Still, given the 'investment gender gap', I think it is appropriate to associate the feminine pronoun with the intelligent investor (and her traits of caution, common sense, rationality, modesty and patience) and the masculine pronoun with the typical speculator (and his extremes of emotion, fondness for babble and esoterica, overconfidence, rashness and serial stupidity). For arguments supporting this position, see in particular Brad Barber and Terrance Odean, 'Boys Will Be

Boys: Gender, Overconfidence and Common Stock Investment', *The Quarterly Journal of Economics*, vol. 116, no. 1, February 2001, pp. 261–292.

2   Benjamin Graham, *The Intelligent Investor: A Book of Practical Counsel*, rev. ed. with preface and appendix by Warren Buffett and commentary by Jason Zweig (HarperBusiness Essentials, 2003) p. 21. (This and subsequent citations refer to the 2003 edition.)

3   *The Intelligent Investor*, pp. 519–520.

4   *The Intelligent Investor*, pp. 28–29.

5   Keep this point in mind as you confront the blizzard of babble in the mainstream financial media. The daily ups and downs of a particular stock or bond, or of the All Ordinaries or other index, are not completely random; but it is safe to say that the shorter the duration of time, the more random the fluctuations of prices tend to be. You would never know this from the after-the-fact 'analyses' that follow every day's trading. Commentators use a reliable cast of characters to 'explain' any daily rise or fall: there is 'profit taking' or 'confidence' or—a perennial favourite—'uncertainty'. Once, just once, I would like to hear a commentator say something like: 'Today on the stock market was much like any other day: there were as many reasons to buy or sell as there were buyers and sellers. We cannot know these individuals' motivations, but we can say that, statistically, the changes in today's prices were basically random. This statement of fact will probably apply tomorrow, too.'

6   *The Intelligent Investor*, pp. 2–3.

7   According to professors Elroy Dimson, Paul Marsh and Mike Staunton of the London Business School, if you had invested $1 in a representative sample of American stocks in 1900 and spent all your dividends, your portfolio's market capitalisation would have grown to $198 by 2000. But if you had re-invested all your dividends, it would have grown to $16,797. According to *The Wall Street Journal* (4 January 2002), the 10.7 per cent average annual percentage gain that the S&P 500 has recorded since 1926 falls to 6.3 per cent without dividends. Expressing this result in dollar amounts, consider the number of dollars you would have today if one of your ancestors had invested $100 in the S&P in 1926: compounding this sum and reinvesting dividends, this kitty would have grown to $253,000 in 2002; without the reinvestment of dividends, it grows to just $10,500.

8   John Burr Williams, *The Theory of Investment Value* (North-Holland, 1938), p. 4.

Chapter 2

◇◇◇◇◇◇◇◇◇◇◇◇◇◇◇◇◇◇◇◇◇◇◇◇◇◇◇◇◇◇◇◇◇◇

Speculation almost always ends in tears

The distinction between investment and speculation in common stocks has always been a useful one and its disappearance is a cause for concern ... The stock exchanges may some day be blamed for heavy speculative losses, which those who suffered them had not been properly warned against. Ironically, once more, much of the recent financial embarrassment of some stock-exchange firms seems to have come from the inclusion of speculative common stocks in their own capital funds.

Benjamin Graham
The Intelligent Investor (1949)

This chapter demonstrates that, as I stated in chapter 1, it is much more difficult to speculate profitably than it is to invest successfully. It does not deny the existence of able speculators and profitable speculations; rather, it explains why successful speculators are few and far between. It is an irony: opportunities to speculate are vast but the number of people who can take consistent advantage of them is very small.

I have already noted that in practice it makes sense to think in terms of a continuum with investment at one end, speculation at the other and shades of grey in the middle. Because there is no such thing as a 'pure' investment, even the strictest investor must recognise that her actions will have speculative aspects. Few investors are strict investors, and many Australians who think they are investors are actually hybrids who possess some of the attributes of the investor and many of the characteristics of the speculator. The real-world challenge is therefore to think and act as much as possible like an investor and as little as possible like a speculator, and to locate those opportunities that most resemble investments.

CAN 'JUNK BONDS' BE INVESTMENTS?

The following analogy is useful in exploring the idea of the investment–speculation continuum. Imagine that three people wish to borrow $100,000:

- The first is a medical specialist who lives and works in your suburb. You do not know her, but you have heard from reliable sources that her professional standards are high and that her practice is financially sound.

- The second aspiring borrower is a middle manager, employed by a large local organisation, who also lives and works in your neighbourhood. You do not know him, but you have heard that he is generally regarded as competent and that his finances are in acceptable shape.

- The third borrower is a young freelance writer whose income is modest and irregular. Although he is not a friend, he is an acquaintance whom you have known for years. You know that he comes from a well-respected family, that his ethical standards are very high and that he is talented but that his talents are not widely recognised.

Each of these people receives a loan. However, the source of each loan is different, and so too are its terms. A loans officer at a bank decides that the medical specialist will almost certainly be able to repay the $100,000 without difficulty. She therefore receives the loan at an attractive rate of interest and is not asked to pledge collateral. A loans officer at another bank decides that the manager is very likely to repay the money, although at times he may struggle to do so. In order to receive the loan, he must therefore pay a higher rate of interest and pledge his house as collateral. No bank is willing to lend to the writer, but a wealthy private citizen is—provided that the writer pays a very high rate of interest and pledges future royalties as security.

Now imagine that the medico and manager service their loans as agreed with their banks, but the writer encounters difficulties. The writer does not repudiate the debt, but rather defaults (that is, informs the private citizen that he is unable to repay according to their agreed schedule). Some of his writing projects do not pay as much as he anticipated, some are delayed and a few are cancelled. In order to avoid expensive and time-consuming litigation, to salvage something now and avoid losing even more later, the private citizen offers to sell the writer's debt to you for $50,000. Given the terms of this debt (which you study carefully), what you know about the writer's character and talents and your estimate of the likelihood that he will make good the missed payments and repay the remaining interest and principal, do you accept this offer? Can the purchase of the writer's debt be regarded as an investment?

Stripped of its many complexities, the world of corporate borrowing and lending is not unlike this simple scenario. A company borrows money by issuing bonds to lenders. It receives the money it seeks today, agrees to repay it at a specified point in the future and in the interim pays interest of specified amounts at pre-agreed intervals. Clearly, however, some companies are sounder than others; accordingly, some can borrow large amounts of money on attractive terms (that is, for long periods and at lower rates of interest), and others can only borrow small amounts over shorter periods and on strict terms.

Companies that assess other companies' creditworthiness use the terms 'investment grade' and 'speculative grade' to describe the ratings they assign to bonds. In particular, bonds rated lower than 'BBB' by Standard & Poor's (or lower than 'Baa' by Moody's) are frequently dubbed 'speculative' (or 'junk' or 'high-yield') bonds. A bond's rating refers to its issuer's capacity to pay interest and repay principal in accordance with the bond's terms. When it assigns a rating, an agency does not intend to imply anything about an appropriate price at which the bond should be bought or sold. Similarly, an agency's rating is not a recommendation with respect to either the bond's value or whether anybody should buy or sell it at any particular price.

Clearly, a junk bond is not necessarily an investment. Given the new or strained or parlous or perhaps even bankrupt condition of the company that issued it, safety of principal (that is to say, the money originally exchanged for the bond) is hardly assured. For the same reason, neither is an adequate return (that is, a stream of interest income on the terms set out in its prospectus). But is the purchase of a junk bond necessarily a speculation? If not, under what circumstances might it constitute an investment? A junk bond's yield is usually much higher than that offered by bonds with an investment-grade rating, but the probability that interest will be paid and the principal repaid is usually much lower than that for investment-grade bonds. If, when these factors are considered, the bond's yield compensates more than adequately for its relatively high risk of default, then it *may* be appropriate for *some* investors. The greater the yield that a junk bond offers to compensate for its risk of default, the closer it approaches the hazy conceptual line distinguishing investment from speculation. Nevertheless, unless there are compelling reasons to do otherwise, the safest thing is to assume that a junk bond is a speculation, and that it approaches the conceptual line from the speculation end of the investment–speculation continuum.

To a Grahamite investor, these potential rewards seldom overcome the actual risks. Hence the purchase of 'second grade' or 'lower grade' bonds, as Graham called them, by a non-specialist is usually a speculation. Only in exceptional circumstances might the purchase constitute an investment (namely, when the investor possesses enough up-to-date and reliable information to analyse a given bond particularly thoroughly, and its yield rises sufficiently to compensate for the risk of default). It is, therefore, only in unusual circumstances that an enterprising investor should consider them. The defensive investor should never do so.

Returning to our example, the purchase of the writer's debt from the private citizen might thus conceivably qualify as an investment. If on the basis of thorough research you can assure yourself that the writer is very likely to honour his obligations, the 50 per cent discount offered to you—and the doubled yield you will thereby receive—may be attractive relative to the credit risk you are purchasing. Your decision would be based upon your longstanding knowledge of his character, and thorough research into his financial condition and prospects, as well as additional information about these matters obtained from the writer, his family, fellow writers and clients. Given that the basis of credit is character, where the purchase price is sufficiently low and additional reliable information is obtainable, what has hitherto been a speculation might plausibly be considered as an investment.

CAN THE FAMILY HOME BE A SPECULATION?

Now imagine four people who undertake separate purchases of real estate:

- Mr Typical Home Buyer learns that during the past thirty years the prices of houses in a particular neighbourhood have increased by approximately 1 to 2 per cent per annum in real terms; that is, at an average annual rate that is slightly above the rate of consumer price inflation. He assumes this trend will continue, more or less, into the future and on that basis he buys a house in this neighbourhood as his principal place of residence.

- Mr Resumption buys a parcel of land in a remote location because he has heard a rumour that a major arterial road will soon be built through it.

- Ms Positive Gearing seeks to buy a house and then rent it. She finds and buys a house which generates rental income exceeding its operating and financing expenses (including depreciation).

- Ms Property Developer buys a dilapidated and mostly vacant shopping centre. She intends to renovate it so that it becomes attractive to a larger and more stable mix of tenants. She has bought it because she has heard from a friend, who is a reputable commercial estate agent in the area, that a national retailer has purchased the lot next door and will use it to construct a major warehouse outlet.

Are these transactions investments or speculations? Ms Positive Gearing and Ms Property Developer seem to be motivated primarily by the desire to purchase reasonably secure and predictable cash flows. If so, then in these respects their transactions are investments. Given the time and trouble which would be required to sell their holdings, it is reasonable to suppose that they intend to hold them for at least several years. Clearly, they will sell if the price is right. However, if their cash flows eventuate as planned, then they have no *need* to sell—and so if they do, the price they are offered must be attractive. It is also reasonable to suppose that these women regard these transactions as opportunities to acquire cash-generating 'businesses' (Ms Positive Gearing may regard this house as a 'profit centre') rather than simply paper titles to real estate. In this sense, too, assuming that they bought at a sensible price, they are investors.

Mr Resumption, on the other hand, seems to be a speculator. He is not motivated primarily by the desire to generate regular income or cash flow. Indeed, given its remote location, his parcel of land may have no medium-term ability to generate a stream of income. Instead, the desire for a lump of cash significantly bigger than the one used to buy the parcel underlies the transaction. He also seems to be in a hurry. He has not purchased after extensive and time-consuming research, but rather on the basis of a rumour that a particular event will soon occur. If so, then he may indeed reap a handsome profit; but if not, the price of the parcel may fall and leave him with a loss of capital. Mr Resumption, then, is chasing the upside rather than trying to protect the downside. His transaction is a speculation.

Mr Typical Home Buyer's transaction lies in the grey area between an investment and a speculation. It is a speculation in the sense that it will generate no regular income or cash flow. It is true that his purchase of the house obviates his need to pay rent, which improves his cash flow, but the cash costs of home ownership are usually greater than renting. On balance, then, and particularly during the early years of his mortgage and until he sells, this transaction is likely to decrease Mr Typical Home Buyer's cash flow position; and in that respect it is a speculation. His transaction is also a speculation in the sense that its results depend upon the house's eventual selling price. The primary measure of the results of his transaction, in other words, is realised capital gain. The longer he owns the house, the safer (on the basis of the historical record) is the assumption that its market price will eventually rise, and hence the safer his speculation. But a speculation it remains.

Yet Mr Typical Home Buyer's time frame and self-image resemble those of an investor. The average Australian lives in his or her principal place of residence roughly seven years. During these years Mr Typical Home Owner is more likely to regard himself as a homeowner than the owner of a piece of paper whose market price constantly changes. It is fortunate that there is no website that he can visit several times daily to request a quote of the current market price of his house. Whether his transaction is an investment or a speculation depends more than anything upon his purchase price and the quality of his research. As with a few junk bonds, so too with many families' primary place of residence: what in some hands might be a reckless speculation can in many (and perhaps most) others be a safe investment.

'PURE' SPECULATION

Bearing in mind that the real world of practice is much messier and more complicated than the simple and tidy world of principle, we are now in a position to demonstrate two fundamental points. First, the results of investment operations virtually always exceed the returns from speculative operations; second, investors tend to make money and speculators tend to lose it.

To understand this, recall that the purpose of 'pure' speculation is to anticipate the direction of price trends and the magnitude of fluctuations around these trends. If we were omniscient and able to predict these things perfectly accurately, buying at a low price and selling shortly afterwards at a higher price, we would clearly reap huge profits. It is precisely this tantalising prospect—together with their confidence that they can divine the future—that tempts so many people to speculate. Alas, as alluring as this sounds, in practice it is extraordinarily difficult, if not impossible, to time one's purchases and sales to the standard of precision required to beat the buy-and-hold investor.

Three simple examples show us why. Figures 2.1 and 2.2, opposite, and figure 2.3, overleaf, are graphs depicting the prices of two stocks at twelve equally spaced points in time. In each example, a speculator has multiple opportunities to buy low and sell high. In figure 2.1, the two stocks' trends are identical: prices increase from $1.00 at time 1 to $1.50 at time 12. However, movements around this trend differ: stock 1's pattern is consistent (that is, a rise of 15¢ tends to be followed by a fall of 8¢) and has relatively small price fluctuations; the price of stock 2, however, fluctuates more widely and erratically. In figure 2.2, the trends are again identical; this time, however, the trend is for a constant price of $1.00 over the twelve time periods. Again, stock 1 has relatively small fluctuations (that is, a rise of 8¢ is followed by a fall of 8¢) and stock 2 has larger fluctuations (that is, a rise of 16¢ is followed by a fall of 16¢). In figure 2.3, price trends decrease from $1.50 at time 1 to $1.00 at time 12. Stock 1 falls consistently (that is, a fall of 15¢ tends to be followed by a rise of 8¢) and with relatively small fluctuations; stock 2 decreases more erratically and with larger fluctuations.

Figure 2.1: two rising stocks

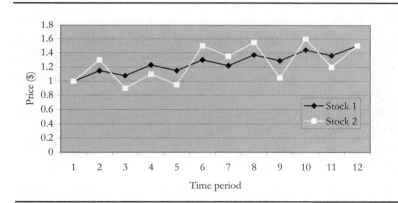

Figure 2.2: two stagnant stocks

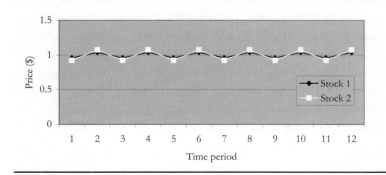

Figure 2.3: two declining stocks

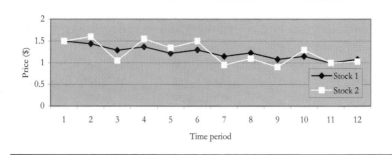

In each of these three pairs of examples, the results of a buy-and-hold investor are easy to calculate. If either stock is purchased at $1.00, held until the price reaches $1.50 and then sold, then (assuming a brokerage rate of 0.1 per cent of proceeds and ignoring capital gains tax) a capital gain of 50¢ per share is earned, brokerage of 0.25¢ is incurred and a return of 49.75 per cent results. If either is bought for $1.00 at time 1 and sold for $1.00 at time 12, then there is no capital gain, brokerage is 0.2¢ and the return is −0.20 per cent. If either is bought for $1.50 at time 1 and sold at time 12 for $1.00, then a capital loss of 50¢ per share is suffered, brokerage of 0.25¢ is incurred and a return of −33.5% results.

How would a speculator's performance compare to the buy-and-hold investor's? To answer this question we need to make several assumptions. For the sake of simplicity, assume again that brokerage is 0.1% and there is no capital gains tax. Assume as well that there are three varieties of speculator: the first can identify a price trend correctly and predict perfectly all deviations from the trend. The second is almost perfectly omniscient, but can predict deviations from trends only to within 5% of the actual prices. And, least unrealistically, the third is still very accurate but least omniscient, predicting trends and each of the twelve prices to within 7.5% of the actual prices (that is, to within 10¢ at prices of $1.30).

These assumptions, it is important to note, impose a slight penalty upon the investor. Her preference, assuming that the operating results of 'her' companies remain satisfactory, is to buy and hold indefinitely. She is seldom forced to sell; the sale of these securities after one year is purely for the purpose of illustration. Many investors would not sell after a year and would not thereby incur brokerage expenses. As a result, their returns are slightly understated here. These assumptions also load the dice extraordinarily heavily in the speculators' favour. Assume there is one-in-four chance of ascertaining when a price is near a local high or low point, and to make money, a speculator must make two accurate guesses: one to buy low and the other to sell high. The chance of a 'perfect' speculation, one where the speculator perfectly guesses the low buy and high sale price, is no more than one-in-sixteen or 6.25 per cent. The chance of two perfect speculations in a row is no greater than 0.0625×0.0625 or about one in three hundred; and clearly the chance of doing it perfectly twelve times in succession is, for all practical purposes, zero.

Table 2.1: comparing investors' and speculators' returns

	Rising (reg.)	Rising (irreg.)	No trend (reg.)	No trend (irreg.)	Falling (reg.)	Falling (irreg.)
Buy and hold	+50%	+50%	0%	0%	−34%	−34%
No error	+94%	+665%	+54%	+134%	+40%	+255%
5% error	+13%	+202%	−16%	+30%	−23%	+97%
7.5% error	−15%	+112%	−38%	−5%	−44%	+42%

Table 2.1 sets out the results generated by our investor and types of speculator under these assumptions, rounded to the nearest percentage point. Not surprisingly, the perfect speculator obtains the best results, ranging from a minimum

+40% to a maximum +665%. Further, the greater the extent of price fluctuations, the greater the perfect speculator's results. Obviously, perfectly omniscient speculators should concentrate their attention upon those securities whose prices fluctuate most.

Much more surprising is the finding that *in four of the six scenarios the 'dumb' buy-and-hold investor* (dumb in the sense that she claims no ability to foretell prices at any particular point in time) *beats at least one — and sometimes both — of the extremely 'smart', very accurate, but imperfectly omniscient, speculators.* Most notably, in the first scenario the investor's return of 50 per cent greatly exceeds both of these speculators' results—indeed, the least omniscient speculator achieves a *negative* return. And in the third scenario, where the trend is stable and prices fluctuate little, the investor's marginal loss is clearly preferable to the speculators' much more considerable losses.

PURE SPECULATORS ARE BROKERS' BEST FRIENDS

To a broker, an investor is a useful adjunct to business. Investors buy and sell infrequently, so under normal circumstances they are a minor source of brokers' revenue. However, in some circumstances—most notably, when market participants are either euphoric or despondent—investors figure more prominently in brokers' lives. It is from investors that brokers obtain disproportionate amounts of the securities demanded by the euphoric crowd during bull markets; and it is to investors that stockbrokers despatch disproportionate amounts of the securities that the despondent crowd clamours to unload during bear markets. To an investor, in turn, a broker is a useful resource. Under normal circumstances, brokers place orders in a timely fashion and provide information about the orderliness and liquidity of the market for a particular security. It is with respect to smaller and less liquid stocks that they really earn their keep: they conduct enquiries and utilise their networks of contacts in order to locate large blocks of stocks or bonds to buy or sell.

For speculators, on the other hand, the commissions of a stockbroker—whether full-service or (more likely these days) discount—compound their losses. Speculators, in short, lose money not just because they cannot predict prices with any useful degree of accuracy, but also because they trade—and hence incur brokerage costs—so frequently. Even allowing the extraordinarily generous assumption that a speculator's losing trades equal their winning trades, they will constantly leak a cumulating percentage of their capital to commissions. For both reasons, then, and for most people, speculating is a 'loser's game'. Charles Ellis uses this term in a very specific way:

> Most institutional investment managers continue to believe, or at least say they believe, that they can and soon will again 'outperform the market'. They won't and they can't ... The belief that active managers can beat the market is based on two assumptions: (1) liquidity offered by the stock market is an advantage and (2) institutional investing is a Winner's Game. [My] unhappy thesis can be briefly stated: owing to important changes in the past ten years, these basic assumptions are no longer true. On the contrary, market liquidity is a liability rather than an asset, and institutional investors will, over the long run, underperform the market because [conventional] money management [that is, speculating] has become a Loser's Game.[1]

Ellis showed that frequent trading and the desire to register short-term (typically quarterly) results *necessarily* lead a conventional funds manager to generate substandard results. Assume that an Australian manager's goal is to exceed the ASX/S&P 300 index by 5 percentage points per year and that his firm's strategists expect this index to increase 10 per cent during the next twelve months. Assume as well that the manager 'churns' his portfolio every fifteen months (that is, on average, he sells any security in the portfolio within fifteen months of its purchase) and charges an average combined commission and management fee of 1 per cent to his fund's assets. If so, then given Ellis's model, this manager would have to deliver gross returns (that is, before transaction costs) 1.71 times or 71 per cent better than the market.

Given these costs, in other words, this fund's manager must deliver a gross return that is 8.55 percentage points better than the market in order, after costs are deducted, to beat the market by the desired 5 percentage points. By trading so frequently, the manager increases his transaction costs and thereby raises the bar he must surmount to achieve his goals; the more he trades the higher his hurdle and the harder he must run. In this instance, this manager's portfolio must rise by 1.71 per cent simply in order to keep pace with every increase of 1 per cent in the ASX/S&P 300.

The moral of the story:
invest and don't speculate

Why should a normal person eschew speculation and stick to a Grahamite philosophy of buying quality securities at attractive prices and then holding them as long as their fundamentals justify doing so? The answer is simple: even when one loads the dice very heavily in speculators' favour and attributes them with superhuman powers of prediction, speculative errors of even small magnitudes lead to results which are often well below those achieved by buying-and-holding. These errors, compounded over time, can also produce significant losses.

In practice, and for the vast majority of speculators, poor timing and cumulatively large transactions costs will eliminate any gains that might emerge from speculation. If we accept that very few people can time their purchases and sales on anything remotely resembling a consistently profitable basis, then we must conclude that poor results—and potentially large losses—are a virtually inevitable consequence of speculation.

NOTES

1   Charles Ellis, 'The Loser's Game', *Financial Analysts Journal*, vol. 31, no. 4 (July–August 1975), p. 95. See also Charles Ellis, *Winning the Loser's Game* (4th ed., McGraw- Hill, 2004).

Chapter 3

<><><><><><><><><><><><><><><><><><><><><><>

What is value anyway?

Value is ... nothing inherent in goods, no property of them,
but merely the importance that we first attribute to the satisfaction
of our needs. The value of all goods is merely an imputation of
this importance to economic goods ... [Hence] value does not exist
outside the consciousness of men [and] the value of goods is entirely
subjective in nature.

Carl Menger
Principles of Economics (1871)ʹ

'Value' and 'price' are not synonyms; and the value and
the price of a stock, bond or block of real estate are not the
same thing. To be an intelligent investor is to recognise this
distinction; and to understand it is to possess a coherent and
justifiable conception of value. This is a very severe criterion: if
it is taken seriously, surprisingly few participants in Australian
financial markets are as adept as they think. Even fewer
qualify as intelligent investors. Many—particularly funds
managers, analysts, strategists and commentators—regularly
express the opinion that this security or that sector or the
market as a whole is 'undervalued' or 'overvalued'. Value is
an integral part of their vocabulary, but it seldom underlies
their thinking. The prominence of value in their view of the

world, in other words, is much more apparent than it is real. A careful reading of their reports and quotes in the media makes plain that their focus—indeed, their obsession—is not value. Instead, it is 'the market' and short-term 'performance.'[1] From this fixation spring many misconceptions; and from these confusions costly mistakes flow.

How's the market doing today? Most people use a shorthand to think about investments; and one of the most ubiquitous forms of shorthand is the All Ordinaries Index (or some related index); that is, a weighted average of the current prices of a group of securities. People who use this shorthand tend to regard a stock not as a title to part-ownership of a business but rather as a piece of paper whose price fluctuates over time. 'Performance' is defined as the extent to which the price changes from one point in time to another (usually expressed in percentage terms). The more an index increases (or the greater the rise of a particular asset's price), and the more quickly it rises, the better its performance. Conversely, the smaller the increase (or the greater the decrease) the more negative the interpretation. And if index A (say, Jack's portfolio) increases relative to index B (Jill's portfolio or some overall market index), then A has 'outperformed' B.

Three questionable assumptions — many harmful consequences

Participants in markets, ranging from the humblest individual to the funds manager at the largest institution, are creatures of habit; as such, they seldom subject their thinking to searching scrutiny from first principles. The pressure of time and the crush of events distract them from this difficult and labour-intensive activity. And so they rarely recognise that three fundamental assumptions underlie their glorification of price, index and performance. The first assumption is that there is a one-to-one correspondence between the price and the value of a good, service or security. To most people, value is basically exactly the same thing as the quoted price. If the price of a steak or a haircut or a stock is $20.00, then its value is also $20.00 — no more, no less and no doubt about it; and if this price changes by some amount, value changes by an identical amount. For this reason, when a typical market participant — that is, a speculator — says that something is 'undervalued', he means that he expects that its price will shortly rise; and when he says that something is 'overvalued', he anticipates that its price will soon fall..

The second assumption is that goods and services possess an intrinsic and objective property; that their prices — and thus, given the first assumption, their values — can be determined by their cost of production. Classical economists from Adam Smith to David Ricardo, as well as Karl Marx, defined a good's cost of production in terms of the land and labour required to produce it. Adam Smith, for example, tells us in *The Wealth of Nations* that 'labour is the real measure of the exchangeable value of all commodities'. Karl Marx agreed.

The third assumption is that equality of value is a necessary condition of the proper exchange of some amount of one given good or service for some amount of another. If their values are not equal, they should not (on moral and economic grounds) change hands.

It follows from the first and second assumptions that the values of different quantities of certain goods can be declared equal to one other. If the price of good X is three times the price of service Y, for example, then by definition the value of one unit of X equals three units of Y.

From the second and third assumptions, it follows that the prices of goods or services should equal what they cost to produce — and that if they do not, any exchange is 'unfair', because one of the parties is 'exploiting' the other. Further, if 'fair' trade occurs only when the values of the goods and services being exchanged are equal, then any exchange in which one party is deemed to receive more value than he gives must be dishonest or otherwise illegitimate — and therefore deplorable and, it is almost invariably alleged, best resolved by legal sanction and government regulation. Given these assumptions, to say that something is 'overvalued' is usually to say (if only implicitly) that consumers or workers are receiving too few of the benefits of its production and consumption — and that owners and capitalists are living too high on the hog and need to be taken down a peg or two.

From these assumptions spring a wide range of absurd and harmful consequences. Prominent among them are not just the dry syllabus and lifeless catechism of contemporary finance (see chapter 8), but also what I consider to be destructive organisations such as the Australian Competition and Consumer Commission and the Productivity Commission.[2] The notion that price should approximate cost plus some margin permissible by government has been used to justify the 'cost-plus' pricing mechanisms and 'competitive' arrangements that fix many contracts, utility rates, insurance premiums, tolls on roads, bridges and tarmacs, wages and terms of employment and myriad other things regulated by governments. Among its unpleasant consequences, the 'cost-plus' system invites producers to use resources less efficiently than they otherwise might (for example, to lift the managerial nose from the grindstone, allow costs to rise and thus 'justify' requests to the government regulator to increase prices). It thereby allows producers to incorporate perks for managers and workers into these higher costs.

These three assumptions are deeply ingrained. Indeed, they boast a lineage that extends back to Aristotle, who argued that money, 'acting as a measure, makes goods commensurate and equates them; for neither would there have been association if there were not exchange, nor exchange if there were not equality, nor equality if there were not commensurability'.[3] Above and beyond their troubling practical consequences, they also employ circular logic. If, for example, the value of a personal computer depends upon the labour and materials required to construct it, and if the value of these materials depends upon the labour and other materials required to produce them, then how does one determine the value of that labour? If the value of a kilo of apples depends upon the value of the labour and land that produced it, then how does one ascertain the value of farm labour and land?

Classical economists implicitly recognised but ultimately failed to resolve this difficulty. According to Marx, only 'socially valuable' labour determines the value of goods and services. By what criterion do Marxists characterise labour as 'socially valuable'? The 'social value' of the goods it produces! Hence the vicious circle the classical economists could not resolve (and which continues to bedevil large swathes of contemporary mainstream economics and finance): the value of goods and services derives from the value of the capital, labour and land required to produce them; and the value of that capital, labour and land depends upon the value of the goods and services they produce. Given this circularity, it is no wonder that the typical funds manager, analyst or strategist is happy to talk interminably about the price of a security — but has little to say when asked to define and justify its value from first principles.

Carl Menger (1840–1921)

Carl Menger was an Austrian finance journalist, academic and civil servant, and for two years was a tutor of Crown Prince Rudolf of Austria-Hungary. During the 1870s he climbed the academic ladder at the University of Vienna, and in 1879 was appointed by Emperor Franz Josef, Rudolf's father, to the Chair of Political Economy in its Law Faculty. His appointment was to a significant extent a result of the impact of his book, published in 1871, entitled *Principles of Economics*. It revolutionised economists' thinking about value and their comprehension of the formation of prices and the operation of markets.

The founder of the Austrian School of economics, Carl Menger, demonstrated that the conceptions of value and price adopted by Aristotle, the British Classicists and Marx (and also, alas, by much of today's mainstream) are muddled and mistaken. So too, in important ways, are present-day views about 'the market' and the exchange of goods and services in the market. To regard value and price as synonyms is to introduce a circularity into one's reasoning that leaves these concepts unexplained — and may render estimates of value and negotiations of price prone to costly error. Menger hardly intended to overthrow classical economics. Quite the contrary: he applauded its emphasis upon universal and immutable economic laws and the laissez-faire conclusions derived from these laws. Menger sought to reconstruct classical economics by grounding the laws of supply and demand in the choices of individual consumers.

It is interesting that Menger and two of his contemporaries (William Stanley Jevons in England and Léon Walras in Switzerland) discovered similar principles, such as the law of diminishing marginal utility, independently but almost simultaneously. The 'neoclassical' school of economics builds upon the foundation laid by these three economists; yet the 'efficient markets hypothesis' (EMH), modern portfolio theory (MPT) and the like, which are close relatives of mainstream neoclassicism, utterly ignore Menger and the Austrian School. It is also interesting to note that the followers of Benjamin Graham, dissenters from the contemporary mainstream, pay much more attention to value — and possess a much more refined and justifiable conception of value — than does the mainstream. Value investors think about value in terms that are not consciously 'Austrian' but are nonetheless much closer to Menger than Aristotle.[4]

John Burr Williams came close when he said that real worth and market price were 'separate and distinct things not to be confused, as every thoughtful investor knows'. Graham held that price is what is paid and that value is what is received. He observed that over time price and value tend to gravitate towards one another, but that at any given point in time they may diverge (sometimes by a wide margin). He lamented that very few people recognise the fundamental difference between value and price.[5] It is this quasi-Austrian conception of value and price that ultimately distinguishes Graham and his successors from the contemporary mainstream.

SUBJECTIVE VALUE, MARGINAL UTILITY AND CRUSOE'S ISLAND

The value of a good or service does not inhere in the good itself; rather, it resides in each individual's perceptions, judgments and calculations about the good and the various ends it might serve. These perceptions vary from one person to another, and for any given person they also vary from one time and place to another. Value, then, is an attitude or disposition that a person adopts towards a good or service—and, by implication, towards a stock, a bond or a block of real estate. An individual chooses whether to value something; and if so, she chooses what value to place upon it. *Value, in short, is subjective; accordingly, there is simply no such thing as 'intrinsic value'.* John Burr Williams approached this view (but did not shake himself completely from the notion that value is an innate characteristic of what is being valued) when he said 'concerning [a stock's] true worth, every man will cherish his own opinion.'[6]

To say that value is subjective is not to say that it is arbitrary. Quite the contrary: rigorous statements can be derived from first principles about the process individuals use to ascribe value to goods, services and securities. Most notably, an individual's valuation of a given amount of a particular thing derives from his or her assessment of its *marginal utility*. The greater an individual's assessment of the utility an extra unit of the good provides or the urgency of the need it meets, the greater that individual's valuation of that unit. *The value of any single unit of a stock of identical goods in an individual's possession is that person's perception of the least important or least urgent use to which the unit can be put.* Individuals strive to place the limited resources at their disposal to the most highly valued uses. Once those most highly valued uses are met, each additional unit of a stock of identical goods will be allocated to a lesser valued use than was previously possible, and the value attached to each additional unit will be lower than that assigned to previously held units.

Consider, for example, a Robinson Crusoe who discovers three fertile fields on his island. Imagine that each field is identical to the others. One will be assigned to the fulfilment of what Crusoe regards as his most urgent want (say, the cultivation of foodstuffs essential to his survival). Assuming that the first field satisfies this want, the second will be used to satisfy what Crusoe assesses to be his most urgent desire that has not yet been met (say, the cultivation of foodstuffs not essential to his survival but of which he is very fond). Crusoe clearly ranks — that is, values — the want that field 2 satisfies below the want that field 1 has satisfied. Similarly, field 3 might be capable of fulfilling the same desires as the others, but it will be used to satisfy the highest remaining desire satisfied by neither field 1 nor field 2 (say, the cultivation of colourful and aromatic flowers). Under these conditions, the value to Crusoe of any one of his three equivalent fields is equal to his assessment of his least urgent or 'marginal' desire; that is, the cultivation of colourful and aromatic flowers.

As the number of units of an identical good in one's possession decreases, on the other hand, they can fulfil fewer desires; and the value to the individual of the least important (marginal) use to which this decreased available stock can still be applied will increase. If a landslide destroys field 2, for example, then Crusoe will be able to satisfy fewer of his wants. Given his ranking of wants (assuming it remains unchanged) and the two remaining fields' ability to satisfy them, he will therefore cease the cultivation of flowers and shift field 3 to the cultivation of crops not essential to survival but of whose taste he is very fond. Under these conditions the value to Crusoe of either of his two remaining fields is his assessment of the least-urgent wants which they are able to serve; that is, the provision of non-essential foodstuffs. *Crusoe has fewer fields, they can fulfil fewer of his desires and thus their value to him has increased.*

A necessary condition for exchange is that the two goods being exchanged have *reverse valuations* on the respective value scales of the parties to the exchange. If Jones possesses a certain amount of good X and Smith possesses a certain amount of good Y, and if each is to exchange some of his good for some of the other, then two conditions must obtain. To Jones, the marginal utility of an added unit of Y received from Smith must be greater than the marginal utility of the unit of X traded to Smith; to Smith, the marginal utility of an added unit of X received from Jones must be greater than the marginal utility of the unit of Y traded to Jones. It is flatly wrong, in other words, to assert that Smith and Jones place the same value upon X and Y: it is the very inequality of Smith's and Jones's valuation of these things that motivates them to trade. As long as these conditions continue to hold, they will exchange additional units of X and Y. They will continue to trade as long as both perceive that they receive more value than they surrender to the other.

In any exchange, the *price* of one commodity is simply its expression in terms of the other. The price of a unit of X, for example, is the amount of Y that Smith is willing to exchange for it; and the price of a unit of Y is the amount of X that Jones is willing to exchange for it. Subjective utilities (that is, the value scales of particular individuals in certain places with respect to marginal amounts of particular goods at a given time) determine the prices and quantities of the goods that are exchanged. Clearly, these utilities change constantly as individuals' wants and assessments of their circumstances change; and therefore, so do prices. Prices, then, do not depend upon costs of production (which, as Menger showed, are also subjective). Menger established a link between the *subjective* values underlying the choices of consumers and the *objective* prices used in the economic calculations of consumers and businessmen. A price is objective in the sense that it is interpersonal (that is, agreed by two people), but its purpose is to facilitate exchange resulting from the disparity of individuals' subjective valuations rather than the equality of labour or other costs.

THE PASSAGE OF TIME AND THE IMPUTATION OF VALUE

To Menger, the starting point both of the character and the value of goods is subjective. The very conception of a good, in other words, begins in the minds of thinking and acting human beings, and it radiates outwards to their physical surroundings. Until the mid-nineteenth century, for example, crude oil was usually regarded as a 'bad' rather than a 'good', because its presence rendered agricultural land less suitable for cultivation—and therefore, in a primarily agricultural society, less valuable. If Crusoe discovers oil in one of his fields and it renders that field unsuitable for cultivation, then that field ceases to be identical to the others. The oil-laden field lacks any ability to produce goods and services that Crusoe desires; consequently, its value to him plummets. Crusoe, in effect, has fewer remaining fields; they can meet fewer of his needs and so their value to him increases.

It was only when individuals devised means to transform crude oil into fuel, with which to power machinery to produce the goods and services valued by consumers, that oil-laden land was recognised as valuable. In this context it is important to emphasise another of Menger's principles: human action is purposeful and thus tends to concentrate upon the establishment of the 'goods-character' and value of things that most directly satisfy consumers' wants. Menger categorises these things, including food, clothing, shelter, convenience, leisure and entertainment, as *consumers' goods*. They are also known as *lower order goods* and *goods of the first order*. More generally, lower order goods are goods that are consumed by their final users.

Clearly, consumer goods must be produced before they can be consumed. They cannot be conjured out of thin air.

What is value anyway?

It takes time and capital to produce them. Menger dubbed the intermediate (that is, capital) goods required to make consumer goods as *producers' goods* (also known as *higher order goods* or *goods of the second and higher orders*). Steel is an example. Consumers neither desire nor consume steel per se, and so they do not value it. Instead, they desire, value and consume certain goods and services of which steel is a component. Consider a consumer good, such as a motor car, which contains much steel. The machines required to assemble a car's steel components, as well as the components themselves, can be regarded as second-order producers' goods. The machines, machine tools and materials required to produce the components (such as moulds, blast furnaces and prefabricated steel) can be conceived as third-order producers' goods. The materials required to produce these goods (such as processed iron ore and coal) are fourth-order producers' goods, and so on.

Menger's insight is that the 'goods-characters' of consumers' goods radiate outwards from human beings and their subjective wants towards external things ever more remote from the direct satisfaction of those wants. The value of a particular supply of iron ore, for example, will increase in proportion to the value consumers place on goods whose manufacture requires iron. Further, the greater the value imputed to the iron ore, the greater the incentive to transform a given thing (such as a newly discovered deposit of ore) into higher level producers' goods such as mined ore, processed ore, iron or steel, and ultimately into lower level consumers' goods such as motor cars, refrigerators and washing machines.

Assume again that Crusoe discovers oil in one of his fields and that it renders that field unsuitable for cultivation. Once again, that field ceases to be identical to the others. But now assume that Crusoe has devised means to transform crude oil into fuel. Assume as well that Crusoe possesses oil-powered machines that vastly increase his ability to produce the lower order goods (say, food) and services (say, heating) that he desires. If so, then he will regard the oil as a higher order

47

good and the oil-laden land as valuable. Indeed, depending upon the uses to which he can put the oil (that is, the value to Crusoe of the consumer goods that the oil can help to produce), he may regard the oil-laden paddock as more valuable than his two remaining agricultural fields.

By means of this process of *value imputation*, then, the prices of producers' goods are derived from the prices of consumers' goods; and the prices of consumers' goods are derived from their ability to satisfy consumers' subjective wants. In the view of Menger (which modern Austrian School economists have extended and elaborated), the *technical process of production* proceeds forwards; that is, from goods of higher order to goods of lower order; and at each stage there occurs a transformation of the good into another good which more directly satisfies consumers' wants. For this reason, the creation of value is envisaged at each stage. Production thus proceeds from goods relatively remote from the direct satisfaction of human wants and towards goods relatively close to the satisfaction of those wants. The *economic process of valuation*, on the other hand, proceeds backwards; that is, from goods of lower order towards goods of higher order. The imputation of value, in other words, proceeds from more refined goods back to the less refined goods required to produce them.

CARL MENGER AND THE VALUE INVESTOR

Menger bequeathed to us a fundamental and mostly forgotten insight: unfettered market prices (in other words, prices that are not manipulated by governments) provide the only *objective* means whereby individual buyers and sellers can make rational calculations about their *subjective* wants. From this insight follow others that are invaluable to, though, alas, typically forgotten by, buyers and sellers in financial markets.

Prices are set 'at the margin'

A price is a ratio at which the most eager buyer(s) and most eager seller(s) voluntarily exchange some specified good or service. A buyer is 'most eager' in the sense that she or he is willing to purchase the good for the greatest amount of some other good, such as money. A seller is 'most eager' in the sense that she or he is prepared to accept less money for the good or service offered than any other seller. In the case of a stock or bond, its least optimistic present owner and most optimistic non-owner determine its price. In John Burr Williams's words, 'the margin will fall between owners and non-owners, the ins and outs, the ayes and nays; *and at this margin, opinion, mere opinion, will determine actual price*' [italics added].[7] Note, then, that if the greediest buyer and most depressed seller set the price, then it is hard to maintain—although many academics do—that market prices are invariably 'rational' prices that encapsulate all that is known about the good, service or security in question.

The price of a stock, bond, or other good at a given instant is determined by 'marginal' opinions *at that instant.* It follows that a particular price is unique to one or more given buyers and sellers, the security being exchanged, the information they possess about it and their evaluation of that information. These determinants of a security's price will vary from one individual and circumstance to another and are subject to constant change. Accordingly, so too is its price. A stock's price may, in other words, imply something about the values imputed to it by a particularly eager buyer and a particularly eager seller at, say, 11.00 am on Monday, 14 March 2005. But this price tells us nothing about the values attributed to it by other owners and by non-owners; still less does it tell me personally the value that I should impute to it.

A stock's price and the value individuals subjectively attribute to it, then, are distinct things: in any given exchange the one will not equal the other, and its current price may well differ greatly from my estimate of its value or yours or blind Freddy's. Only if the current price differs considerably from my assessment of its value, and no better opportunity presents itself, do I have an incentive to act. According to Warren Buffett (*Forbes*, 4 January 1988), 'the market is there only as a reference point to see if anybody is offering to do anything foolish'. Buffett added in *The New York Times Magazine* on 1 April 1990 that 'for some reason, people take their cues from price action rather than from values. What doesn't work is when you start doing things that you don't understand or because they worked last week for somebody else. The dumbest reason in the world to buy a stock is because it's going up.'[8]

Warren Buffett

Warren Buffett (born 1930) is Benjamin Graham's most famous student, employee and torchbearer. He studied under Graham at Columbia University in 1950 and 1951 and a few years later worked for him at Graham-Newman Corp. in New York. In 1955 he formed his own investment partnership (based at his place of birth in Omaha, Nebraska). In 1965, the partnership acquired a controlling stake of a struggling textile manufacturer, Berkshire Hathaway, Inc. When the partnership closed in 1969, Buffett retained control of Berkshire. During the 1970s, Berkshire evolved into a diversified holding company with particular expertise in insurance and other financial services. Since the 1980s, it has become widely recognised as one of America's best managed companies. It is also an investment powerhouse that has made Buffett the world's second-wealthiest man.

Prices are neither omniscient nor prescient

The price of a stock or a bond is determined by marginal opinions. However, opinions are not facts, and the opinions of the most enthusiastic buyers and depressed sellers are not necessarily informed opinions. Participants in financial markets, in other words, are neither omniscient nor prescient—and neither are the prices of the securities they buy and sell. To suppose, as much of the research of mainstream academics seems to do, that the price of a stock accurately reflects all that is currently known about the company is to forget that not all information is accurate and relevant, that people respond differently to information and that they do not always interpret it accurately. 'Informed' people have repeatedly stormed to war on false pretences. A few have passionately defended Joseph Stalin, and many believed Orson Welles when he told them over the radio that the Martians had landed—even though he also told them several times that he was presenting a radio drama and not a news broadcast.

Like human beings more generally, funds managers, brokers, advisers and speculators are a very varied lot. They are occasionally prone to extremes of emotion, so the prices they pay for stocks and bonds can be as fallible as they are variable. Indeed, the market's function as a mechanism by which value is evaluated and re-evaluated assumes that miscalculations and changes-of-mind—and mistakes—will be commonplace. Buyers may, for example, realise retrospectively that they have received less value than they 'paid for', even though sellers had no intention of deceiving them. Many buyers of tech stocks learnt in 2000 and 2001 that they had made such miscalculations. Conversely, buyers make a more fortunate error when (despite no sign of any obvious ignorance on the seller's part) they discover after the transaction that they have received far more value than they paid for. In this respect, both the buyers and sellers of Berkshire Hathaway shares miscalculated throughout the 1960s, 1970s and 1980s. Sellers unwittingly sold a goldmine for a pittance; and unsuspecting buyers bought one for pennies on the dollar.

Price changes and the false imputation of wealth

Assume that the economics and operations of a business—call it X Ltd—change little from day to day. If so, then the short-term volatility of its stock tells us nothing about these economics and operations. This volatility might indicate something about marginal buyers' and sellers' malleable perceptions about its economics and operations. Clearly, some changes of price stem directly from the appearance of genuinely new information about the business, but most fluctuations, and particularly short-term ones, bear little or no direct relation to the company's long-term operations. If this is so, the absurdity of defining the 'performance' of a security, a bundle of assets or an overall market in terms of day-to-day or even month-to-month price changes becomes readily apparent. (As a rough and ready rule of thumb, the 'expert' who uses the word 'performance' to describe the short-term ups and downs of a security is unwittingly advertising the fact that he or she knows little or nothing about the vital distinction between value and price.)

For the same reason, an increase of a security's price per se does not signify the creation of wealth; and a decrease of its price need not imply its erosion. If you believe that a higher price necessarily means more wealth and vice versa, then ask yourself: do the hefty increases in the prices of most residential houses in recent years *necessarily* mean that they now produce more housing services than they did previously? Analogously, does the increase in the price of a factory *inevitably* mean that it can produce more widgets per day or that it can produce them more cheaply?

If your answer to these questions is 'no', consider its implication: just as a nation's wealth depends upon the quantity and quality of the capital goods within its borders, an individual's wealth depends upon the quantity and quality of the capital goods he owns. Wealth has everything to do with the ability of higher order goods and services to produce the lower order goods and services that people want at the prices they are prepared to pay. *Wealth, then, has nothing directly to do with the market prices of capital goods and securities.* Rather, the linkage between wealth and these prices is indirect: the better a collection of capital goods serves consumers' wishes, the greater the value that consumers impute to it; and the

52

greater the imputed value, the higher, on average, the stream of income it emits and the prices of those capital goods will eventually be. As Carl Menger showed, a short-term change of price indicates a change in marginal market participants' subjective preferences for one thing (say, cash) vis-a-vis another (say, a share in X Ltd, or a particular house). It does not necessarily imply any long-term change in the company's or the house's ability to serve consumers' wants.

As a rule, distrust media commentators

It is frequently assumed in financial markets that a change in price is necessarily a change in value and that a change in value is necessarily a change in wealth. Using Menger's insights into value and price, it becomes clear that this standard boilerplate about buying and selling is misleading—and that several of the claims commonly advanced by 'experts' in media reports are patently false. When tumult is observed in financial markets, reporters typically draw erroneous conclusions. In the US on Friday 14 April 2000 (the wee hours of Saturday 15 April in Australia) the Dow Jones Industrial Average decreased by 618 points (5.7%), from 10924 to 10306; the Nasdaq Composite fell 355 (9.7%) from 3676 to 3321; and the S&P 500 dropped 84 (5.8%) from 1441 to 1357. In absolute (as opposed to percentage) terms these three decreases were collectively among the biggest ever recorded on a single day. For this reason, and also because changes in the All Ordinaries Index tend to correlate roughly with changes in its American counterparts, these events received extensive coverage in Australian tabloid newspapers over the weekend of 15 to 16 April and on Monday 17 April.

Tabloid reports sought to convey a crisis-laden atmosphere that posed grave and imminent dangers to owners of stocks. Brisbane's *Sunday Mail* of 16 April, for example, ran the front-page headline 'BLOODBATH', set out in massive letters so that nobody could miss it, and under it stated that 'Australian investors are expected to lose up to $18 billion [in] the aftershocks from Wall Street's most spectacular crash …' It added that 'United States markets plummeted by a staggering US$1 trillion in just seven hours' and this was 'the largest sum of money ever lost in a single day'. Feature articles emphasised that 'massive plunges' in markets had occurred, that 'indexes [had] suffered record-breaking falls' and that 'most stocks were battered'. Similarly, the front-page lead story of Sydney's *Sunday Telegraph* repeated that 'Wall Street investors lost a staggering US$1 trillion (A$1.7 trillion) in just seven hours as the stock market suffered its biggest crash ever', and concluded that 'trading on the Australian Stock Exchange is expected to be frantic tomorrow as equally terrified Australian investors try to get out of their high-tech holdings.' (On 17 April 2000, the All Ordinaries Index fell from 3096 to 2920, a fall of 176 points or 5.7%. In percentage terms, this was one of the five biggest daily falls that have occurred in Australia since the 1987 crash.)

This tabloid coverage, considered as a whole, was (no doubt unintentionally) deeply misleading and several of its individual claims were simply false. According to *The Wall Street Journal,* approximately 1.2 billion shares changed hands on the New York Stock Exchange on 14 April 2000; however, by my (admittedly very rough) calculations, there were approximately 240 billion shares registered on the exchange on that day. In what was described as a selling frenzy, fewer than one-half of one percent of those shares actually changed hands. (This daily turnover of 1.2 billion shares on the NYSE, by the way, was not dramatically greater than that prevailing since the beginning of 2000). As in New York, so too in London, Toronto and Sydney: from one day to the next, week after week and month to month, most investments stay invested.

It is also false to talk, as journalists and others typically do when prices fall suddenly and precipitously, about 'a rush to get out of the market.' Under these circumstances, reporters imply that the market comprises only one party—namely sellers. However, it takes two to tango and every market transaction requires a buyer as well as a seller. Every stock that is sold, in other words, is a stock that is simultaneously bought. If a sale is to take place, there must necessarily exist, for every person who wishes to exchange a share of X Ltd for some amount of cash, another person who is prepared to exchange that amount of cash for the share. In other words, for every person who wishes to 'exit the market' at some price, there must be another prepared to 'enter the market' at that price. At the end of a day's trading 'the market' contains the same number of shares that it did at the opening bell (excluding floats, rights issues and share 'buybacks'). At the close of trade, then, it has neither shrunk nor grown and the 'exits' are perfectly matched by the 'entries.' This argument should also dispel the old, absurd and damaging chestnut that 'the market' is some sort of 'collective mind' or 'social intelligence' that exists apart from the actions of the many and varied individuals who constitute it.

The bizarre cult of unrealised capital gain and 'phantom wealth'

It is also false to assert, as people incessantly do, that, on a particular date and in response to a rise or fall of the All Ordinaries or other similar index, market participants 'made' or 'lost' money. This assertion, like so many others commonly voiced in the mainstream media, misconceives the nature of price and value. It conflates (and thus confuses) 'paper' gains and losses, adjustments of sentiment and changes in wealth. It also claims knowledge that one cannot easily possess, namely the prices at which those who sold their shares in X Ltd on a particular day originally bought those shares.

Dividends and interest payments on the one hand and unrealised capital gains on the other are fundamentally incommensurate things. Dividends are 'endogenous'—they are generated within a company. They are tangible outcomes of its operations and earnings. Because dividends are usually paid in cash, and because the value of cash cannot be manipulated (except by a central bank), once they are declared their worth cannot be questioned. Dividends are also permanent: once they are paid they cannot be revoked. Unrealised capital gains, in sharp contrast, are neither endogenous nor necessarily permanent. They are 'exogenous'—they do not spring from the company or its operations, but arise indirectly from outsiders' perceptions of the company and its assets, earnings, prospects and so on. The extent of an unrealised capital gain depends upon the price that subsequent marginal buyers and sellers are prepared to pay for a company's stock. Because this willingness changes from day to day, until they are realised, these gains are usually volatile, and can often be ephemeral. Dividends and unrealised capital gains, then, are measured in terms of a common metric: dollars and cents. However, in many respects, they are incommensurate. Like wallabies and road trains, it may sometimes make sense to count each separately, but it rarely makes sense to combine these counts.

An unrealised capital gain—or what Thornton Parker dubs 'phantom wealth'—is created or destroyed when a market transaction establishes a new price for a given company's shares.[9] As we have seen, a market transaction is a 'marginal' transaction, in the sense that it involves the most eager buyer and the most eager seller. The parties to a typical transaction on the ASX are a very small fraction of 1 per cent of all of the owners of the security in question. Yet on the basis of that marginal transaction, *all* of the company's shares are treated as if they are 'worth' the new price. For example, if a company has issued 100 million shares, and if in a transaction involving 100 shares the price per share rises by $1, then the value of each of the 100 million shares is conventionally deemed to rise by $1. Although only a miniscule fraction (one out of every million) of the shares has been traded, each of the 100 million shares is now 'valued' at the new market price, and an unrealised capital gain of $100 million has been created out of thin air. But where did that money come from? Nobody knows. And if on the next day the price slips by a dollar, the $100 million vanishes. Where did it go? It was never there in the first place—it was simply a phantom.

Unrealised capital gains comprise a major component of most conceptions of private 'wealth'. Given this misconception, the major reason to buy stocks (and residential real estate) is the expectation of capital gain at some point in the future. To a greater and greater extent, then, today's portfolios (whether private or institutional) are perceived as inventories of things that are bought and held in the expectation that they will later be sold at higher prices. As we saw in chapters 1 and 2, this is a speculation. Yet standard accounting practice requires that virtually all inventories of things bought for resale should be valued at cost or market price—whichever is *lower*. If anything, international accounting standards that come into effect in the 2005–06 financial year reinforce this practice. Hence the book values of 'inventories' may be revised downwards, but rarely upwards, and profits are not recorded until the items have been sold. Portfolios of financial securities appear to be the major—and glaring—exception to that practice. As far as funds managers are concerned, whenever the prices of 'their' shares rise, 'profits' are recorded, even though these profits have not been—and may never be—realised.

Can 'phantom wealth' really be realised?

The sale of shares whose market price has increased above their purchase price is usually assumed to be easy; but it need not be so, and at critical historical junctures has not been so. Consider as an example the changes, measured annually between 1926 and 1979, in the share prices of companies listed on the New York Stock Exchange.[10] For each five-year period during these years, companies were placed into five equally sized groups (quintiles) on the basis of their market capitalisation (that is, their number of shares times the market price per share). For the entire period, the average annual total return for companies in the smallest quintile was 11.6 per cent; and the average for companies in the largest quintile was 8.8 per cent. The analysis also concluded that the owners of small companies reaped stunning capital gains from the nadir of the Great Depression through to the late 1930s. More generally, it concluded that outsized capital gains can be reaped by purchasing small cap stocks at the troughs of recessions. Most notably, between 1930 and 1935, owners of these stocks reaped annualised capital gains of up to 120 per cent. This path-breaking study, and others inspired by it, provided an impetus for the investment of billions of dollars by hundreds of thousands of investors in 'small cap' funds.

David Dreman, a prominent funds manager and investment writer, has shown that studies of this 'small cap effect' overlook the relative illiquidity of small companies, the frequently very low prices of their shares and the dormant state of the NYSE (in terms of the volume of shares traded) during the Depression. In the 1930s, most of the small company shares in question sold at a fraction of a dollar (many sold for 25¢; and some for as little as 6¢ per share). Further, many of these companies' shares were so thinly traded that appreciable numbers could be neither bought nor sold. Any hypothetical purchaser in 1930 would have been unable to buy more than a handful of shares: the average daily volume of companies in the smallest quintile was 240 shares per day during the entire 1930–1935 period, and the median volume in 1930 was 95 shares. Similarly, the hypothetical seller who sought in 1935 to sell the shares purchased in 1930 would have encountered considerable difficulty selling even a handful. Given the very small number of shares involved, any unrealised capital gain incurred would have been quite modest; furthermore, the gain would have been very difficult, if not impossible, to realise.

So what, then, is 'value'?

It is clear that value and price are not identical. Price is what is paid and value is what is received. In an unfettered market in which many people are reasonably informed, it is true that price and value will tend over time to gravitate towards one another, but at any given point in time they may diverge (sometimes by a wide margin), and they may require an inconveniently long time — perhaps years — to converge.

The value of a good, service or asset is subjective in the sense that it will probably differ, perhaps markedly, from one person to another. Further, an individual's valuation of a given asset will also differ, perhaps greatly, from one time to another. Value, it is vital to emphasise, is thus a matter of individual estimation and not of collective 'consensus'. According to Benjamin Graham, investors are neither right nor wrong because the crowd disagrees with them. Rather, they are right because their data and reasoning are right.[11]

The better a business serves consumers' wishes:

- the more highly consumers value its goods and services

- the greater the value consumers impute to the capital goods used to produce these goods and services

- the higher, on average, the price the business's stock will *eventually tend* to be.

The value of a company (or its stock), then, is a subjective assessment that is greater than the objective price an informed, experienced, cautious and savvy businessman is typically prepared to pay. So, the next time somebody tells you with a straight face that value can be objectively assessed; that there is such a thing as intrinsic value; that all investors have the same information, expectation and time horizon; that markets are very liquid, making transaction costs so small that they can be ignored; or that value and price are synonyms, the sane response is simply to laugh.

Given this conception of value, the core of value investing, in Graham's words, is the belief that 'investment is most successful when it is most businesslike'. This focus upon *businesses* and their economics, operations and results—and not *'the market'*—permeates value investors' assumptions, reasoning and behaviour. It also forms the basis from which they gauge the results of their investment decisions. Value investors think long and hard about value and only incidentally about price. While they do so in terms that are not 'Austrian', they are nonetheless much closer to Carl Menger than to Aristotle. Value investors carefully and cautiously estimate value and then compare their estimate to current price. If their estimate of value is significantly greater than the current price, and if no better opportunity presents itself, then value investors act. Otherwise they sit and wait.

The short-term fluctuations of the price of a company's stock typically have little (and often nothing) to do with the company's operations and financial results. For this reason, price and oscillations of price play no part in any rational assessment of a company's value. Yet for the vast majority of funds managers, analysts, strategists, advisers and speculators-who-think-they-are-investors, prices and short-term fluctuations are the be-all and end-all. The greater the short-term increase in a security's price, the more favourable their evaluation of its 'performance'; and the more fervently they believe that its price will shortly rise further, the more 'undervalued' they believe the security to be. Conversely, the smaller the rise or the greater the decrease, the more negative their interpretation. And if asset A or index A increases relative to asset B or index B, then A has 'outperformed' B. From the point of view of a value investor, this pervasive foolishness is not just counterproductive—at times it is also dangerous. It encourages people to check stock quotes every day, to rejoice when prices rise and fret when they fall. It also prompts institutions with responsibility for billions of dollars of other people's savings constantly to buy and sell, to churn assets at dizzying rates and to generate significant transactions costs—that is, to do everything except act as sober businesspeople making cautious, justifiable estimates of value.

The financial mainstream's tendency is to neglect value and glorify price, index, short-term performance and unrealised capital gain. This is one of the principal reasons why exuberant speculation is typically far more prevalent than cautious investment on financial markets. This disposition has its origins in the philosophy of Aristotle and ultimately culminates in what Charles Munger, Warren Buffett's vice-chairman, rightly denounced as the 'twaddle' and 'dementia' of contemporary mainstream finance. The conflation and misconception of value and price eventually generates tears.

Many learnt this lesson between 2000 and 2003, but, perhaps because humans are genetically predisposed to this frenetic and pointless behaviour, it is a lesson many may have to relearn before long.

NOTES

1   Much the same point applies to academics. According to Lawrence Summers—a prominent finance academic and, as the 'CEO' of Harvard University, surely a powerful one—mainstream finance is simply uninterested in securities' values. As he wittily put it, academics obsessively check that the price of two eight-ounce bottles of tomato sauce is 'efficiently' close to the price of a single 16-ounce bottle. But it never occurs to them to ask what determines the price of the big bottle; still less do they have any coherent conception of value. See Summers's 'On Economics and Finance', *Journal of Finance*, vol. 40 (1985), pp. 633–635.

2   See in particular the research of Dominick Armentano: 'A Critique of Neoclassical and Austrian Monopoly Theory', in Louis Spadaro, ed., *New Directions in Austrian Economics* (Sheed Andrews & McMeel, 1978); *Antitrust and Monopoly: Anatomy of a Policy Failure* (Independent Institute, 1996); *The Austrian Economics Newsletter* (vol. 18, no. 3, 1998); and *Antitrust: The Case for Repeal* (Ludwig von Mises Institute, 1999).

3   *Nicomachean Ethics*, book 5, chapter 1, available at <http://www.constitution.org/ari/ethic_05.htm>. See also Gene Callahan's 'Carl Menger: The Nature of Value' (Daily Article, Ludwig von Mises Institute, 17 October 2003) and Hans Sennolz's preface to Eugen von Böhm-Bawerk's *Value and Price: An Extract from Capital and Interest* (Libertarian Press, 1960, 1973).

4   See Chris Leithner, 'Ludwig von Mises, Meet Benjamin Graham: Value Investing from an Austrian Point of View' (paper presented to the Austrian Economics and Financial Markets Conference, Las Vegas, Nevada, 18–19 February 2005).

5   See John Burr Williams, *A Theory of Investment Value* (North-Holland, 1938), p. 3 and Benjamin Graham, *Security Analysis: The Classic 1940 Edition*, (McGraw-Hill, 1996), particularly chapter 50

('Discrepancies Between Price and Value') and chapter 51 ('Discrepancies Between Price and Value Cont'd'). Unless otherwise stated, all subsequent citations of *Security Analysis* refer to its 1940 edition.

6   *The Theory of Investment Value*, p. 11.

7   *The Theory of Investment Value*, p. 12.

8   Both of these quotes are cited in Janet Lowe, *Warren Buffett Speaks: Wit and Wisdom from the World's Greatest Investor* (John Wiley & Sons, 1997), pp. 96–97.

9   Thornton Parker, *What If Boomers Can't Retire? How to Build Real Security, Not Phantom Wealth* (Berrett-Koehler, 2001). See in particular chapter 5 ('Stocks, Wealth and Phantom Wealth') and chapter 7 ('Why Stock Prices Don't Create Real Wealth').

10   See David Dreman, *Contrarian Investment Strategies: The Next Generation* (Simon & Schuster, 1998), chapter 15.

11   *The Intelligent Investor*, p. 524.

Chapter 4

<svg>◇◇◇◇◇◇◇◇◇◇◇◇◇◇◇◇◇◇◇◇◇◇</svg>

Coping with risk and managing Mr Market

Sometimes risk and reward are correlated in a positive fashion ...
[But] the exact opposite is true with value investing. If you buy a
dollar bill for sixty cents, it's riskier than if you buy a dollar bill for
forty cents, but the expectation of reward is greater in the latter case.
The greater the potential for reward in the value portfolio, the less
risk there is.

Warren E. Buffett
'The Superinvestors of Graham-and-Doddsville' (1984)

There is no way to eliminate risk, so the intelligent investor
accepts the stark reality: *risk inheres in any and every investment
operation.* To cope successfully with risk, an investor must first
properly understand risk; and to understand it, she must
clearly define it. Just as the intelligent investor knows that the
price and the value of a security are distinct things, she also
knows that risk and price volatility are not synonyms. Indeed,
she knows that risk, like value, is a subjective phenomenon.
Risk, in other words, does not reside in the stocks, bonds, real
estate and so on that an investor buys and sells. Instead, it lies in
the investor's temperament, the reliability of her assumptions
and the validity of her reasoning. The more dispassionate her

disposition and the better her reasoning, the more satisfactory the results of her investment operations are likely to be. To be an intelligent investor, then, is also to have a coherent and justifiable conception of risk. The problem is that surprisingly few participants in Australian financial markets are as cautious and risk-averse as they might like to think. Moreover, many routinely take risks of which they are unaware.

Investment is a process whereby one incurs short-term inconvenience in order to enjoy long-term benefits. The investor saves some of this year's harvest and sows carefully today so that she can reap bountifully into the future. Expressed less metaphorically, to invest is to forgo some current consumption, accumulate savings and exchange these savings for titles to certain types of property. The investor exchanges cash for these titles because she expects that they will generate a stream of income that:

- is greater than the one that cash can generate

- will help to finance her desired level of consumption in the future.

To invest is to outlay money now in order to receive more money in the future — more money in real terms, after taking the central bank's inflation into account.

The investor exchanges cash for stocks, bonds, real estate and the like not because they will certainly generate some minimum anticipated stream of income, but because she has grounds to expect that they will probably do so. Like much else in her life, investment operations conform to laws of probability, which are inexact in the short-term but very powerful over more extended periods. Although poor processes will periodically produce good outcomes and good decisions will occasionally beget poor results, superior processes will, over time, probably generate superior results. If someone repeatedly tempts fate (crosses the Nullarbor without water in January, climbs Mt Kosciuszko in shorts in June and so on), plays unfavourable games (buys lottery tickets, for example, or plays in casinos or speculates in stock or real estate markets) or engages in unethical or illegal practices, then a 'bad' outcome will eventually occur—even though the result on any single occasion is uncertain and need not be a loss. Conversely, if one repeatedly engages in 'good' practices (consumes a healthy diet, exercises regularly, dissipates life's tensions and pressures, saves and invests diligently, and so on), over the years, desired results—namely, health, wealth and perhaps even wisdom—will likely be achieved and the losses borne along the way will tend to be tolerably small.

Historically, when an investor's patience and perspective extend over years and decades (as value investors' tend to do), the ownership of businesses has generally produced a somewhat larger stream of income than has ownership of real estate. (See chapter 10 for details.) It has also generated a much larger stream than has the ownership of bonds. Further, the stream of income derived from the ownership of real estate and corporate bonds has generally and usually significantly exceeded the interest payments paid by governments on their bonds or banks on their cash deposits. On the basis of the twentieth-century historical record, one inference is very clear: at most milestones in the investment marathon, cash has run last and by a country mile, largely due to the persistent consumer price inflation that has cumulatively devastated the purchasing power of most currencies. For this reason, the investor strives to convert cash into other, more productive kinds of asset.

'RISK-FREE' INVESTMENTS AND OTHER FANTASIES

The investor might embrace, discount or ignore long-term historical tendencies. She might posit that these tendencies will continue, strengthen, weaken or be displaced. Regardless of these specific decisions, to invest is necessarily to make some assumptions about the future. That some or perhaps even many market participants' assumptions are only implied and unspoken does not alter this fact. But the future is uncertain, and one's views about it will never correspond exactly to what transpires. What actually happens often deviates drastically from what is expected.

Hence a fundamental point about the nature of investment risk: a 'risk-free' investment is a logical absurdity. Assets like bank deposits and Commonwealth Government bonds are typically regarded as risk free in at least two senses. First, the likelihood that the bank or government defaults and the depositor or bondholder permanently loses her capital is, for all practical purposes, nil. Second, the interest these assets pay is, for all practical purposes, assured.[1] Both the payment of interest and the return of capital are considered to be extremely highly probable and therefore almost perfectly predictable.[2] For these reasons, the stream of income generated per dollar invested in bank deposits and government bonds tends to be relatively small.

But what assumptions might the investor make about the future? Here is one candidate among the vast number of possibilities: the risk-free characteristics typically attributed to government bonds may not continue into the indefinite future. Indeed, if certain long-term trends persist, within the next generation the sovereign debt of major western nations will lose its investment-grade status. (Sovereign debt is the money that politicians borrow today and taxpayers have to repay at some point in the future.) If so, then both the payment of interest and repayment of principal will no longer be assured—and these assets will hardly be considered risk-free.

In a research report released on 22 March 2005 and entitled *In the Long Run, We Are All Debt: Aging Societies and Sovereign Ratings*, Standard & Poor's (S&P), a major debt ratings agency, concluded that unless the world's richest industrialised countries move quickly and forcefully to balance their budgets and reduce their spending, spiralling pension and medical expenditures will reduce their sovereign debt to 'junk' debt status within thirty years. If current policies remain unchanged, French government bonds, presently rated AAA (the highest possible rating), will plummet to a sub-investment grade of BBB minus or less by the early 2020s; those of the US and

Germany will do so before 2030 and the UK's bonds will follow by 2035. If so, then for the first time in roughly 200 years, the American and British governments will be persona non grata in investment-grade debt markets.

Another major ratings agency, Moody's, sees the situation differently. In a report dated 2 June 2005 and entitled *United States Has Yet to Reach Excessive Debt Levels*, Moody's analysts concluded that although the US government faces long-term concerns about its debt and social spending obligations, assertions that it faces a looming debt crisis are unfounded:

> Moody's expects that US government debt will remain well within a range consistent with its Aaa rating, and that only if no action is taken over the next decade or so will the US's rating face downward pressure ... While there is cause for long-term concern, it is misleading to indicate that the US government has a debt problem at this time.

In fairness, it should be pointed out that S&P's report emphasises that the scenario it describes is not intended to be understood as a prediction, but rather as a projection.

> It is a simulation that highlights the importance of age-related spending trends as a factor in the evolution of sovereign creditworthiness. In reality, it is highly unlikely that governments will allow debt and deficit burdens to spiral out of control. The example of Italy in the past two decades is instructive: once governments are confronted with unsustainably rising debt burdens they do react, however reluctantly, by tightening [their] fiscal stance.

Well, maybe. As the report itself acknowledges, ageing is only one factor that imperils western governments' solvency. Their presently feeble fiscal position, above and beyond the pressures of age-related spending, is another. If American, British, French and German governments balanced their budgets in 2005 and then kept them in balance over time, their projected debt ratios in 2050 would on average only be about one-half as great as they would otherwise be—even without squeezing age-related outlays. This 'forcefully underlines the need to embark on a prudent fiscal stance as early as possible to be able to better absorb the surge of entitlements ahead.'

Still, there is precious little evidence that these governments are heeding this message. The question is thus, do you believe that major western governments will improve their appalling finances sufficiently to avert the slump in their credit ratings that S&P projects will occur if they do not? Which report, S&P's or Moody's, is more plausible? People aged sixty-five and above can safely ignore this looming potential train crash (if that is what it is); those aged between twenty and sixty-five might take steps to shield themselves; and those aged under twenty (to say nothing of the unborn) could, for once, have real grounds to resent their elders. Nobody should simply and blindly assume that governments' debts—long regarded as the safest of investments—will continue indefinitely to be risk free.

SO WHAT IS INVESTMENT RISK?

Commercial and residential real estate presently tends to be regarded as a 'riskier' asset than investment-grade government debt because the likelihood of bankruptcy, liquidation or other similar scenarios, while generally very small, is not negligible. Further, rental income has historically been more variable, intermittent and less assured, and thus less predictable, than interest payments on bank deposits and government bonds. To compensate for these greater uncertainties, streams of rental income per dollar invested in real estate tend to be greater than those produced by so-called risk-free assets. Ownership of businesses and corporate bonds tends to be still riskier, because a particular business is far more likely to fail than the Commonwealth Government is to default on its financial obligations. Further, the ability of businesses (as opposed to bonds and real estate) to generate earnings and make interest payments is most variable, least predictable and least assured. In order to compensate for these additional uncertainties, investors demand an even larger stream of earnings per dollar invested.

Clearly, then, businesses, real estate, debts and deposits have possible advantages and disadvantages and potential risks and rewards. It is therefore imperative that the investor recognise two unpleasant possibilities. The first is that the return on the investment does not transpire as envisaged — that is, the stream of income generated by the investment is significantly lower than expected. The second is that the return of the investment does not transpire as anticipated: the money that is lent is not returned (in the case of a bond) or the original amount that is paid for an asset cannot subsequently be sold for a greater amount (in the case of a share or piece of real estate). To say that risk inheres in any investment operation is thus to recognise that two unpleasant outcomes can emerge from any such operation. *Risk — that is, the chance that certain desirable events do not occur, or that undesirable events actually do occur — unavoidably accompanies any investment operation.*

In addition to these two general risks, Grahamite investors single out four specific risks that they consider particularly noteworthy. They acknowledge the possibility that an investor might:

- misjudge, such that a business which seems on the basis of its past and current operations to be sound ceases in the future to be sound

- miscalculate, such that an unreasonably high price is paid for a sound business or such that unduly optimistic assumptions are made about its prospects

- mistake a mediocre or poor business for a sound one, perhaps as a result of inaccurate or insufficiently thorough research

- receive widely accepted fallacies and falsehoods as facts.

Clearly, then, risk is subjective; it is determined by the attitude, disposition and behaviour of the *investor* — and not by the characteristics of the *investment*. One investor (call her Investor 1), using faulty assumptions and invalid reasoning, undertakes an investment operation (say, the purchase of shares in X Ltd) that ends poorly. Investor 2, in contrast, using more robust premises and reasoning and taking advantage of more favourable circumstances—such as much lower prices—buys shares in X Ltd and does well. Two different investors who purchase shares in the same company (albeit under different circumstances) may accept very different risks and thus generate very different results. Risk is subjective, not only because it resides in the investor rather than the security, but also because perceptions of risk will differ from one investor to another and because a given investor's perception of risk will differ from one time to another. With the benefit of hindsight, what was risky for Investor 1 was not risky (or was much less risky) for Investor 2.

It is equally clear that short-term (that is, day-to-day, week-to-week and month-to-month) volatility of market prices is not a risk to investors, despite frequent assertions that this is so. Quite the contrary: if understood properly, short-term price volatility presents great opportunities to investors.

The investor and 'Mr Market'

It is important to emphasise again that a basic difference between investors and speculators lies in their attitude towards current market prices. To the limited extent that he thinks about value at all, the speculator regards the 'value' and the 'market price' of a security as synonyms, and, regardless of the (probably slight to non-existent) degree to which he thinks about value, the speculator tries to anticipate and profit from short-term fluctuations of market prices. In contrast, the investor draws a clear distinction between objective price and subjective value, and pays attention to prices and their short-term volatility only to the extent that they enable her to acquire the securities of sound companies at reasonable or bargain prices. To keep the distinction between value and price constantly and automatically in mind is to possess a distinctly calm and dispassionate temperament. Whatever their business and accounting abilities, individuals who cannot master their emotions seldom invest successfully.

Benjamin Graham used a simple allegory to explain these points.[3] Imagine that you and a good friend, 'Mr Market', are partners in a private business. Assume also that each and every business day, without fail, Mr Market quotes to you a price at which he is willing either to buy your interest in the business or to sell his to you. Your business has steady and reasonably favourable economic characteristics. Cautious premises and rigorous reasoning clearly yield the conclusion that reasonable profits are likely to occur as the years pass. Your business, in short, is relatively stable; but Mr Market's price quotations are quite erratic—indeed, they are unpredictable from one day to the next. On some days his quotes seem to be justifiable in light of the firm's characteristics and a reasoned assessment of its prospects. On other days, however, he is exuberant about the business and can see only warm breezes, sunshine and smooth sailing ahead. On these days, fearing that you will try to snap up his interest and deprive him of imminent and substantial gains, he insists upon a very high price for his share; however, on yet other days, seemingly without rhyme or reason, Mr Market is despondent about the business and its prospects. Seeing nothing but clouds and rough seas ahead, and fearing that you will attempt to unload your interest in such a wretched enterprise upon him, on these days he quotes a very low price.

For all his instability and possible irrationality—by the way, what on earth were you thinking when you formed the partnership with him?—Mr Market takes no offence if you ignore him. Any transaction is conducted solely at your discretion and if you snub him today, there is no problem: he will unfailingly return tomorrow with a fresh price. If you are a prudent investor–business owner, you are extremely unlikely to let Mr Market's daily quotations influence your estimate of the firm's worth. Notice, though, that the more manic-depressive his behaviour—and hence the more volatile his quotes from day to day—the greater the opportunities that he presents to you. Clearly, you possess something that Mr Market does not: a reasoned estimate of the firm's value. You will therefore be happy to sell to him when he quotes to you a ridiculously high price, and you will be equally happy to buy from him when he quotes a foolishly low price. In this hypothetical world, you would engage in many transactions over time: whenever he quoted an absurdly high price, you would sell to him; and whenever he offered an absurdly low price, you would buy from him. In this world, Mr Market would be your best friend, because he would allow you to accumulate shares in a sound company at what are — given your analyses — unreasonably low prices.

The moral of Graham's parable is powerfully clear: the prudent investor–business owner must remain detached from and dispassionate about the market's always erratic, seldom sensible and sometimes manic-depressive gyrations. The investor must keep her own counsel, form her own ideas and conduct her own analyses. Intelligent investors appreciate the full importance of this implication; it forms a cornerstone of their investment operations. Graham warned that Mr Market's pocketbook is useful, but that his emotions and personality never are. Mr Market's role is to serve rather than to guide investors. If he is in one of his crazy moods and quotes a foolish price, then investors can either ignore or take advantage of him, but disaster will ensue if they succumb to his influence.

GRAHAMITE AND MAINSTREAM CONCEPTIONS OF RISK

Graham not only denied that price and value are synonyms, he also rejected the financial mainstream's conviction that the more volatile a security's price, the 'riskier' it is. To the mainstream, the conception of risk refers to the possibility that a security's price will shortly decline — even though the decline may be of a cyclical and temporary nature, and even though the long-term holder under these circumstances has no need to sell. Graham's followers, in contrast, understand that they do not 'lose money' merely because the prices of their holdings decline. They avoid the common confusion between risk and price volatility by restricting their conception of risk to the loss that occurs either through the actual sale of a security or through a significant deterioration in a company's operations. In both cases, the loss occurs not as result of price volatility but as the result of the payment of an excessive price in relation to value. These risks are real, but Graham showed that an investment in common stocks, if properly executed, does not carry any significant risk of this sort. Such investments, he argued, should not, therefore, be labelled 'risky' on the basis of this element of price fluctuation alone.[4]

Grahamites have taken these admonitions to heart. They look at market prices not to affirm the wisdom of their investment operations, but only to see whether others—namely speculators—are doing something foolish. In Warren Buffett's words, 'if you aren't certain that you understand and can value your business far better than Mr Market, you don't belong in the game.'[5] Graham concluded that in order to be successful, an investor requires no more than average intelligence and judgment. However, it is critical that she have a much better than average ability to remain detached from the emotional whirlwinds, sometimes manic and other times despondent, that Mr Market regularly unleashes. In order to remain level-headed and insulated from the constant emotion and occasional silliness that occurs in financial markets—to cope with risk and to manage Mr Market—the intelligent investor keeps Graham's allegory firmly in mind.

NOTES

1   Many Australians seem to assume—incorrectly—that bank deposits in this country are guaranteed. This is false in a legal sense: there is no counterpart in Australia to the Federal Deposit Insurance Corporation in the US. However, in a practical sense, reliance upon government is so deeply ingrained in this country

that Australians are probably correct to assume that governments would respond to any bank failure by compensating the vast majority of depositors 100 cents on every dollar deposited, with the exception, perhaps, of the largest and foreign depositors.

2   The purchasing power of interest payments and capital repaid at the termination date of the deposit or bond is, of course, much less predictable. These assets are not a surefire means of protecting purchasing power over the decades—ask anybody who bought bonds in the 1950s and 1960s and suffered gut-wrenching losses during the 1970s. Long-term government (or other) bonds are *not* a risk-free investment. Quite the contrary: during extended periods of time they have proved 'loss-guaranteed'.

3   *The Intelligent Investor*, pp. 204–205. See also pp. 213–225.

4   *The Intelligent Investor*, pp. 121–122.

5   Quoted in Janet Lowe, *Benjamin Graham on Value Investing: Lessons from the Dean of Wall Street* (Pitman Publishing, 1995), p. 84.

Chapter 5

<><><><><><><><><><><><><><><><><><><><><><><><>

Irrational exuberance revisited: lessons from the Great Bubble

The growth premium you are being asked to pay for Telstra now does not take into account any of the goodies in the pipeline that are likely to start appearing over the next couple of years. We have a target price of $20 on the stock by 2003, but all that assumes is above average earnings growth and continual expansion in the ... price–earnings ratio the market is prepared to pay ... The risk/reward profile is better than you will get anywhere else ... and the likelihood of Telstra outperforming the market over a longer period is very, very good.

'Why Telstra's a Real Humdinger'
The Weekend Australian (26–27 June 1999)

The Grahamite investor knows that in principle investors and speculators are very different animals, but that in practice the distinction between them is not always obvious. She recognises that in the real world there are many speculators but relatively few investors, and, moreover, that while opportunities to speculate are limitless, investments are usually hard to locate. The value investor knows that it is much more difficult to speculate intelligently and profitably than it is to invest astutely and successfully, and that successful speculators are far thinner on the ground than successful investors. She possesses a coherent and justifiable conception of value, understanding that the value and the price of a security are different things. She does not conflate risk and volatility and remains detached from the tempests of euphoria, anxiety and despondency that Mr Market regularly unleashes. Her nature and her approach protect her to some extent from the vagaries of the market. She knows that value, like risk, is subjective. It resides not in the stocks, bonds, real estate or other assets that an investor buys and sells; instead, it inheres in the investor's temperament, the reliability of her assumptions and the validity of her reasoning.

The criteria that distinguish a value investor from the vast majority of market participants are strict. If they are applied diligently, regrettably few participants in Australian financial markets, including analysts and managers at major institutions, are as adept as they believe. Moreover, few are as conservative as they might like to think and many harbour various misconceptions and take risks of which they are unaware. This general shortcoming has frequently had melancholy consequences in the past, and unless appropriate lessons are identified and learnt they will recur in the future. An examination of typical aspects of the Great Bubble (Warren Buffett's term for the mania that developed in many financial markets, particularly in the US, during the mid-1990s and which reached a crescendo early in 2000) provides an excellent means by which to elaborate these points.

The lesson of this and the next chapter is that the investment losses incurred between 2000 and 2003 were self-inflicted. That is to say, simple yet rigorous reasoning applied to information readily available to the general public at the time could have produced (and, for people who availed themselves of these things, did generate) the conclusion that during these years most securities were demonstrably unsafe. The purchase of shares in many of Australia's largest and most exciting companies and seemingly best securities—the 'hot stocks' and 'blue chips' of that era—at prices that prevailed at the time did not provide a margin of safety. I am not implying that the prices of these securities were foreordained to fall when they did: at no time has any value investor been blessed with a reliable crystal ball. Rather, I am cautioning that the purchase of securities at prices that are demonstrably higher than what a Grahamite investor would pay constitutes a speculation rather than an investment. As such, it is unlikely to produce desirable results in the long term.

Those who succumbed to the Great Bubble—and those whose confidence has grown as a result of successes in the 2003–2005 period—would do well to ponder something that has happened repeatedly over the decades. Encouraged by the recent past and extrapolating it into the indefinite future, the buyers of so-called hot stocks and growth stocks lose their sense of value and pay excessive prices. Investors should recognise that it usually takes an extended period of time for the value of even an outstanding company to rise sufficiently to match these excessive prices. Perhaps that is what certain politicians (together with many stockbrokers, funds managers, financial advisers and media commentators) meant when during the Bubble they chanted incessantly that one of the hottest blue-chip stocks, Telstra, was a 'long-term investment'—more about this later.

SOME VERY DANGEROUS WORDS: 'IT'S DIFFERENT THIS TIME'

Value investors generally welcome gloom, doom, pessimism and despondency—not because they are closet Lutherans, but because they seek to buy sound assets at bargain prices, which are most likely to become available under these conditions. As investors, they may well have been disturbed by the upbeat mood and seemingly unshakeable faith in growth that were discernible in Australian financial markets during the first half of calendar 2000. An analysis of reports in the financial media at the time makes these themes quite clear.

Although journalists are obliged as professionals to present stories which are fair, balanced and accurate, business media tend to publish and broadcast what their audiences want to hear. During the Great Bubble, Australians wanted to hear that the financial grass was lush and green, that the sky was sunny and blue and that an unprecedented stretch of fine weather was forecast. Indeed, they wanted to hear this and nothing else. Humans' innate disinclination to hard work also plays a role here: it is alarming how often the media make little or no attempt to verify the facts presented in a press release before printing or broadcasting it as 'news'.

The first theme apparent was widespread optimism among market participants. Significant numbers were in fact extremely optimistic; and most believed that as long as they stuck with selected blue chips (such as the '100 Hottest Stocks' selected by 'Australia's business experts' in *The Australian* on 5 June) they would do just fine.

The Australian Financial Review (AFR) (27–28 May) reported that 'investor confidence regarding returns over the next twelve months [did] not appear to have been dampened too much by the April 17 sharemarket fall'. (See chapter 3 for a summary of the events of 17 April 2000.) On 6 June, one of *The Australian*'s columnists prophesied:

> during the next three years we are going to see some of the greatest productivity increases ever recorded in the history of the U.S. With the cost reductions will come some very big profit rises for those companies that can hold their prices ... Many long-term [American] investors say that ... the coming productivity revolution will boost share profits and share markets.'[1]

That columnist acknowledged that bumps might occur along the way. But no matter: 'in Australia we will experience a similar medium-term trend'. More specifically, it was stated that 'most enterprises in Australia can reduce their operating costs by 20 per cent to 30 per cent over the next three years by embracing the new technology systems' (5 June 2000), and that accordingly, 'analysts are optimistic about established [Australian] companies because of the cost reductions that are coming via the new technologies' (27–28 May).

A survey conducted by a major Australian bank found that, notwithstanding the volatility of market prices, almost two-thirds of people who borrow money in order to buy shares intended to buy more stocks during the next twelve months.

If the first trend was giddy optimism, the second was invincible faith. An article in *The Weekend Australian* (27–28 May), entitled 'Tech Check Reveals Value,' distilled its essence. 'The force of the new technology paradigm that has driven growth during the past three months should ensure the latest correction will be temporary.' Further, 'the underlying information technology growth story and its impact on the new economy remain as pervasive today as they did a year ago'. It therefore concluded not only that 'sound technology stocks [will] remain in favour because of their underlying growth potential, coupled with fundamental market position and management strength', but also that 'the dotcom and technology sector will probably provide better capital returns to the discerning investor than the equivalent small cap old technology stock'.

GRAHAMITE REASONING IN THE MIDST OF MANIA

How did value investors react to statements such as these? By keeping their heads while other people were apparently losing theirs. And how did investors retain a sense of perspective? By reasoning from first principles. One principle is that the investor foregoes jam today because she expects that her investments will generate helpings of jam in the future. If this is to occur, then an investment must not only produce a stream of earnings, it must also outpace the effects of inflation and other taxes. Accordingly, at least two motivations underlie the decision to invest: the desire to maintain the purchasing power of one's capital and the desire to receive a reasonably secure and growing stream of earnings.

Another principle is that the stream of earnings an investment generates need not pass immediately or directly to its owner. A stock's dividends and a bond's payments of interest are paid to their owners today. In contrast, a company's retained earnings are returned indirectly, over time and—if the company does not subsequently erode or destroy them—in the form of higher dividends. The expected value of an income stream—which depends upon its size today and the likelihood that it will continue into the future and grow over time—is thus a key criterion by which one can evaluate a particular security's potential as an investment. Clearly, given the risks of erosion or destruction of investment capital and its income stream, a direct and immediate stream of earnings is preferable to an indirect and delayed one. Equally clearly, the investor seeks to purchase assets that will provide streams of future earnings that:

- are reasonably secure

- are available at prices significantly below their expected value.

Purchases that meet these criteria tend to compensate for the risks that inhere in the decisions to exchange cash for assets. As an example, consider a corporate bond. Assume that a corporation sells it for $100, pledges to pay its purchaser $6 per year for five years, and that at the end of the fifth year it will pay the last instalment of interest and repay the $100 initial capital. The bond thus generates an annual interest stream of $6 (usually called its 'coupon') and has an initial annual yield of 6 per cent (that is, $6 divided by $100). No matter how many times or at what price the bond subsequently changes hands, the $6 coupon remains fixed. Accordingly, the higher the price at which the bond is sold, the lower its yield, and vice versa. The price any subsequent purchaser will be willing to pay for the bond depends upon at least three things:

- the purchasing power of the Australian dollar during the bond's term, which depends upon the rate of consumer price inflation during the bond's remaining life

- the yield of risk-free Commonwealth Government bonds maturing at the same time

- the 'risk premium'; that is, the additional return in the form of higher yield which the bondholder requires in order to offset the risk that inheres in the bond's ownership relative to government bonds.

Similarly, the 'coupon' of a company's shares is its earnings per share (EPS); and its yield is the EPS divided by the shares' purchase price. As an example, consider a company that earns 10¢ per share. Imagine that an investor purchases shares in this company at $2.00 per share on the assumption that its earnings will grow at a rate of 25 per cent per year over the next five years. If this assumption is correct, in the first year she will receive a coupon of 10¢ per share (either as a dividend, as earnings retained and re-invested in the company or some combination of the two). This represents an earnings yield of 5 per cent on the initial investment of $2.00 per share (that is, 10¢ ÷ $2.00). In the next year the coupon grows to 12.5¢ per share. This represents a yield of 6.3 per cent on the investment of $2.00. If the coupon continues to grow at the assumed rate, the earnings yield will increase year by year such that, at the end of the fifth year, it reaches 12.2 per cent. Clearly then, if a company is able to increase its earnings, the yield on one's initial purchase will also increase over time. This attribute distinguishes ownership of a company's equity (shares) from ownership of its debt (bonds). It is this compounding which makes the ownership of good businesses so rewarding— *if they can be bought at a sensible price*—because the price of equity will tend over long periods of time to rise in tandem with the growth of its earnings.

EVALUATING A SECURITY USING A COMMONWEALTH GOVERNMENT BOND AS A BENCHMARK

We can apply this same logic to determine whether a relatively risky asset, such as a particular company's bonds or common stock, offers a better or worse potential return than a purportedly risk-free asset such as a Commonwealth Government bond. Generally speaking, shares are more attractive when their earnings yields and streams are significantly greater than those of bonds. (There is a vital exception to this rule that we will note in chapter 11.) Conversely, bonds are more attractive when their yields are equal to or greater than those of stocks. All else being equal, the higher a share's (or a corporate bond's) sustainable yield relative to that of a risk-free bond, the greater its attractiveness to the investor. Please note that these rules of thumb should be regarded as just that: rules of thumb. The techniques used in examples in this and the next chapter are not purported to replace a thorough and systematic analysis of a company's financial statements.

Example 1: a (fallen) tech market darling

Shares of Solution 6 Ltd (ASX code SOH) were selling for more than $18.00 late in 1999, but had fallen to approximately $3.00 by 1 June 2000. Did this latter price represent a bargain? To decide this question, roll the calendar back to 1 June 2000 and assume you have the choice of buying either one share of Solution 6 at $3.00 or a hypothetical five-year $3.00 Commonwealth Government bond with a yield of 6.1 per cent (the yield of five-year Commonwealth bonds on 1 June).[2] You have no crystal ball and so cannot know what will transpire during the next five years. Assume as well that whether you choose the share or the bond, you are a long-term investor and will retain your choice until at least 1 June 2005.

Even though you cannot foresee the future with any reliable degree of accuracy, you do have access to an historical record that illuminates the past and might help you to navigate your way through the present and provide rough clues about the future. You know that no Commonwealth Government bond has ever defaulted, so you have strong grounds to expect that if you buy the bond you will have earned 90¢ in coupons by mid-2005, having received an income stream of 18¢ per year for five years. There is also good reason to believe that during its life the bond will return to you a total of $3.90 (the $3.00 principal plus 90¢ in interest payments).

If the 'risky' Solution 6 share is to be a better investment than the risk-free Commonwealth bond, then it must return to you at least $3.90 over the five-year period. Given that the commentary about the company's operations was generally very favourable on 1 June 2000, this seemed to many observers to be a very easy hurdle to jump. Perhaps most notably, the company's senior managers regarded a very strong rise in the price of SOH shares as a foregone conclusion. Solution 6's chief executive officer was very warmly received at the company's annual general meeting in November 1999. Noting that its shares had risen from $1.80 to as high as $18.00 during the previous twelve months, he opined that this was only the beginning. He famously added that there was no reason why the stock's price could not reach $100 in a year's time! However, when you look at hard figures rather than soft PR, and adopt the perspective of an investor (the owner of a share in a business) rather than a speculator (the owner of an interest in a wager), this $3.90 hurdle becomes much more formidable.

Table 5.1, overleaf, makes several deliberately generous assumptions about the operations of Solution 6 for the five years to 1 June 2005. These assumptions are made on the basis of information readily available to the general public on 1 June 2000.

The first assumption is that SOH shares will earn 10.4¢ per share during the financial year to 30 June 2001. This assumption is very generous because in mid-June 2000 Solution 6 had never earned more—and had usually earned considerably less—than 10.4¢ per share. Indeed, from the time it was first listed on the ASX in the mid-1990s until the middle of 2000, SOH earned an average of exactly $0.00 per share. It never earned more than 10.4¢ per share and lost money as often as it turned a profit—losing as much as 34.8¢ per share. To assume that the shares will earn 10.4¢ per share during the financial year to 30 June 2001 is thus to assume that SOH's earnings will improve dramatically and to an unprecedented level during the next twelve months.

Table 5.1: a thumbnail evaluation of Solution 6

Year	Coupon	Cumulative coupons	Yield on $3.00
2001	10.4¢	10.4¢	3.5%
2002	12.0¢	22.4¢	4.0%
2003	13.8¢	36.2¢	4.6%
2004	15.8¢	52.0¢	5.3%
2005	18.2¢	70.2¢	6.0%

Table 5.1 also sets out a second assumption: Solution 6's coupon will increase each year over the next five years at a rate of 15 per cent per annum. Again, this assumption is extremely generous, because SOH has hitherto never been able to increase its earnings per share from one year to the next. However, we are assuming not only that it will do so five years in succession, but also that it will do so at a rate more rapid than that which most other large Australian companies had managed to achieve during the period 1995–2000.

These generous assumptions have a startling implication: if all goes to plan in the first four years, and 18.2¢ per share is earned in 2005, at the end of the fifth year cumulative earnings of only 70¢ will accrue to the Solution 6 shareholder— *considerably less than the Commonwealth Government bond's cumulative earnings of 90¢*. Even in the fifth year, SOH's projected yield fails to exceed that already available in the first year from the risk-free bond (6 per cent versus 6.1 per cent).

To buy Solution 6 at $3.00 per share on 1 June 2000 was thus to assume—whether knowingly or not—that its operations would immediately improve to an unprecedented extent and unfold exactly in line with these very generous assumptions throughout the full five-year period, thereby providing a return in 2005 which nevertheless only approaches that guaranteed from a five-year Commonwealth bond. What are the chances that generous and optimistic assumptions such as these transpire? Should the intelligent investor accept them?

An unrealistically exuberant answer to the first question and an affirmative answer to the second provided many market participants the rationale for the purchase of SOH at the prices available on 1 June 2000. It is true that, when compared to 1999 prices, SOH shares' price in mid-2000 was drastically reduced, and yet, if their return was to exceed that offered by the bond, one of two things had to occur: either the very generous assumptions outlined above had to prove to be conservative, or Solution 6's share price had to increase much more rapidly than its earnings. (For this latter result to occur, somebody even less rational than the person who bought SOH at $3.00 per share had subsequently to buy its shares.) Solution 6's operations from 1995 to 2000 justified neither of these very ambitious expectations. Clearly, then, even at the 'low' price available in the middle of 2000, to the value investor, Solution 6 Ltd represented a risk-fraught speculation rather than a sensible investment. So much for one of the Australian market's most prominent fallen tech angels.

Example 2: three blue-chip behemoths

Let's look now at some of the largest, most prominent and prestigious 'blue-chip' companies. On 1 June 2000, three of Australia's five largest companies by market capitalisation were Broken Hill Proprietary Co. or BHP (as it then was, before the Billiton merger), News Corp. and Telstra Corp.

Travel back in time, as we did in the last example, and consider BHP. Assume that on 1 June 2000 you have the choice of buying either one share of BHP at $17.80 (its closing price on that day) or a hypothetical five-year $17.80 Commonwealth bond with a yield of 6.1 per cent (the yield of five-year

Commonwealth bonds on that date). Assume as well that you are a long-term investor and that you will hold onto the share or the bond for the five years to 1 June 2005. If so, then by mid-2005 you will have earned $5.45 in coupons from the bond (that is, a stream of $1.09 per year for five years). If the BHP share is to be a better investment than the Commonwealth bond, then clearly it must return at least $5.45 in the form of dividends, retained earnings or some combination of the two during the next five years. Results are set out in table 5.2.

Only if two assumptions prove correct can it do so. The first is that BHP's earnings per share will recover smartly from the loss of $1.34 recorded in 1999 to a gain of 87¢ in 2001 (a 15 per cent premium on its average of 77¢ during the nine years preceding the disaster in 1999). The second assumption is that BHP's earnings per share will grow at a compound rate of 15 per cent per annum until 2005. This assumption is extremely generous: even excluding the loss of $1.34 in 1999, BHP's EPS grew at a compound rate of only 1 per cent during the 1990s. These assumptions produce cumulative earnings (whether retained or distributed as dividends) of $5.90 and an earnings yield of 8.6 per cent over the five-year period. The owner of the BHP share would have to wait three years before the share's *projected* earnings yield could match that guaranteed *today* from the bond. Only if we assumed (speculated?) that BHP's operations would improve dramatically and produce historically unprecedented results could we justify the purchase of its common stock at prices prevailing in mid-2000.

Next, consider Telstra (ASX code TLS). Imagine that on 1 June 2000 you can buy either one TLS share at $6.92 (the closing price on that day) or a hypothetical five-year $6.92 Commonwealth bond with a yield of 6.1 per cent. Again, you are a long-term investor and will retain the share or the bond for five years. By mid-2005, you will have earned $2.11 in coupons from the bond (that is, a stream of 42¢ per year for five years). If the TLS share is to be a better investment than the Commonwealth bond, then clearly it must generate at least $2.11 during this five-year period.

Table 5.2: thumbnail evaluations of BHP, News Corp. and Telstra

	BHP ($17.80)	TLS ($6.92)	NCP ($19.49)
Assumed coupon in 2001	$0.87	$0.31	$0.42
Assumed coupon in 2005	$1.53	$0.55	$0.73
Expected cumulative coupons 2001–2005	**$5.90**	**$2.10**	**$2.83**
Earnings yield 2001	4.9%	4.5%	2.2%
Expected earnings yield by 2005	8.6%	7.9%	3.8%
Earnings from risk-free 5-year bond with 6.1% yield	**$5.45**	**$2.11**	**$5.95**

Assume that TLS's earnings per share will increase at a rate of 15 per cent per year until 2005. This is somewhat generous, because TLS's EPS grew at a compound rate of 13 per cent between 1996 and 2000, a time of unusual prosperity in the telecommunications industry. Your expectation is that the TLS share will produce cumulative earnings of $2.10 and an earnings yield of 7.9 per cent over the five-year period (whether these are retained or distributed as dividends). Like the owner of the BHP share, the owner of the Telstra share will have to wait at least three years before its *projected* earnings yield will match that guaranteed *today* from the risk-free Commonwealth Government bond. Only if we are willing to postulate (speculate?) that TLS's operations are going to improve even more considerably than our already-generous estimation could we justify the purchase of its common stock at the prices prevailing in mid-2000.

Finally, consider News Corp. (Its ASX code at that time was NCP). Assume that on 1 June 2000 you have the choice of buying either one share at $19.49 (its closing price on that day) or a hypothetical five-year $19.49 Commonwealth bond with a yield of 6.1 per cent. As a long-term investor you will hold your chosen investment for at least five years. By mid-2005, you will have earned $5.95 in coupons from the bond (that is, a stream of $1.19 per year for five years). If the NCP share is to be a better investment than the bond, then clearly it must return at least $5.95 during this five-year period.

Alas, it does not come remotely close to doing so, even on the basis of very generous assumptions, far exceeding expectations arising from News Corp.'s actual operations during the 1990s. Assume that NCP's earnings per share will increase 15 per cent per annum each year for five years, even though the company's EPS only grew at a compound rate of 10 per cent between 1990 and 2000. On this basis of these assumptions, investors could expect the NCP share to produce cumulative earnings of only $2.83, almost all of which will be retained—NCP pays notoriously miserly dividends. This sum represents *less than half the risk-free bond's earnings.* Not even in five years' time will the share's *projected* earnings yield come close to matching the guaranteed yield available *immediately* from the bond. Only if we are willing to speculate that we could pass this hot potato to somebody who is even sillier than we are could we justify the purchase of News Corp. stock at the prices available in mid-2000.

GRAHAM SAW IT ALL LONG AGO

Warren Buffett has used a baseball metaphor to illuminate the sensible allocation of investment capital. Don't swing at a bad throw, Buffett counsels: wait patiently for a good one. Hold cash or lend it to a bank you trust until a sound business or other asset becomes available at a compelling price. But judgments are difficult. Is Mr Market presently throwing strikes? In mid-2000, a calm demeanour and publicly available information would have yielded the conclusion that Mr Market was pitching high and erratically.

It made little sense to purchase the securities of tech darlings and blue chips at anything approaching their prices in mid-2000, because their returns—even when boosted by some very generous assumptions—could not be expected to surpass the return of a risk-free Commonwealth Government bond. People who chose to do so were not allocating investment capital on the basis of a justifiable assessment of these companies' past present and future operations; rather, they were gambling that the prices of these securities would continue to increase (thereby becoming even further detached from business fundamentals). In addition, they were gambling that it would be possible to flip these securities to other speculators at even more inflated prices. The Grahamite value investor's investment philosophy precludes speculation, and would therefore prohibit the purchase of these securities at these prices.

It is important to emphasise that very few people took a Grahamite view. Telstra provides a good example. A 'leading telecommunications analyst', quoted by Brisbane's *The Courier-Mail* on 6 May 2000, described TLS as 'a $10 stock pricing comfortably in the low $7 range.' The article continued:

> in a weak market, Telstra's share price is likely to fall further. Anticipating this, leading broking firms, including some close to the company, have been downgrading their recommendations from buy to hold, despite the fall in prices.

A second analyst was quoted in *The Australian Financial Review* on 12 May 2000: 'Telstra is a long-term buy but that doesn't mean that you should buy it today'. This logic, to put it mildly, is curious: given the fall in its price, if Telstra were really a '$10 stock' and a 'long-term buy' then surely this *was* the time to increase one's holdings?

Recommendations to this effect appeared in the *AFR* on 13 and 14 May 2000. 'Market experts suggest that those who don't own T2 [Telstra's instalment receipts] may see this as a buying opportunity ... and if the experts know their stuff it will only get better.' One 'expert' was quoted as saying, 'I'm telling people they should be buying Telstra with their ears pinned back.' Another stated, 'this is a stock that's going to show 10 percent growth in earnings before interest and tax for a number of years to come, and that's not bad ... Investors should feel very comfortable with it.' A third 'expert' added, '[Telstra is] very cheap and presents a good buying opportunity ... For those who have only a handful of T2, it's even better value to buy more and top up.' Finally, the 3 June issue of *The Courier-Mail* told readers that 'brokers are bullish on the Telstra price outlook'. One stated: 'we think Telstra is very good value and we have a valuation on the stock of $7.90.'

Perhaps the strongest indicator of the conventional wisdom regarding Telstra appeared in *The Australian* on 5 June. Its '100 Hot Stock Picks', made by its six 'experts', were displayed in the form of a bullseye. On it were arranged 100 darts, each pinning to the board a Post-it note containing a company name and a justification for its purchase. 'The closer the dart to the bullseye, the more favoured [the company].' Among the four closest to the bullseye were Telstra common shares (TLS) and Telstra instalment receipts (TLSCB). The justification? 'Australia's best tech stock. Growing markets and technological developments in the pipeline will boost earnings going forward; but held back by remnant government stake.' BHP appeared halfway between the bullseye and the dartboard's outer edge ('petroleum offers most earnings growth potential'). News Corp. ('growth lies in levering into e-commerce') and Solution 6 ('has had a rough time but underlying business delivers solid cash flows') appeared on its outer edge.

All investment decisions must necessarily rest upon premises based on the past and the present and on assumptions about the future. Justifiable decisions stem from cautious assumptions and explicit analyses; conversely, what turn out to be grave mistakes can often be traced to overly optimistic assumptions and the abandonment of analysis. Although Benjamin Graham formulated his views during the 1930s, they apply equally well to many Australians' unfortunate experiences during the Great Bubble. Graham noted that the 'new era' commencing in 1927 'involved at bottom the abandonment of the analytical approach; and while emphasis was still seemingly placed on facts and figures, these were manipulated ... by a sort of pseudo-analysis to support the delusions of the period. The market collapse in October 1929 was no surprise to such analysts as had kept their heads.' Graham warned that the 'new-era' doctrine that 'good stocks' (blue chips) were solid investments no matter how high the price paid for them 'was at bottom only a means of rationalising under the title of "investment" the well-nigh universal capitulation to the gambling fever.'[3]

NOTES

1   Although I have relied heavily in this chapter on extracts and quotes from *The Australian* and *The Australian Financial Review*, it is not my intention to criticise either of these newspapers or any of their journalists. During and after the Great Bubble they embarrassed themselves no more or less than other major media outlets (or other market participants); and analogous snippets could also have been selected from other Australian newspapers, business magazines and business programs—to say nothing of their counterparts in America, Britain, Canada and New Zealand. It is precisely because the '*Oz*' and the '*Fin*' are among this country's most widely read daily business publications that their reports are important and worth revisiting.

2   This bond is hypothetical because on 1 June 2000 there existed no Commonwealth debt instruments with precisely these attributes (namely this particular price, coupon and date of redemption). As a result, this and the following examples are not completely realistic. They are intended only to exemplify the thought experiments that value investors devise in order to test their assumptions and reasoning.

3   *Security Analysis: The Classic 1934 Edition* (McGraw-Hill, 1996), pp. 11 and 14.

Chapter 6

◇◇◇◇◇◇◇◇◇◇◇◇◇◇◇◇◇◇◇◇◇◇◇◇◇◇◇◇◇◇◇◇◇◇

The policy of
reasoned scepticism

Most people get interested in stocks when everyone else is. The time to get interested is when no one else is. You can't buy what is popular and do well.

Warren Buffett
Newsweek (1 April 1985)

The prices of most Australian stocks, including blue chips and 'hot tech stocks', were prohibitively expensive at the apex of the Great Bubble. To purchase these stocks, as thousands of Australians ranging from humble individuals to powerful investment institutions did, was (probably unwittingly) to speculate rather than consciously to invest. The underlying cause of this speculation was unwarranted optimism—and in some instances irrational exuberance—about these companies' ability to generate rapidly growing streams of earnings into the future.

This chapter uses the same logic as chapter 5, but employs sceptical rather than optimistic assumptions. By no means does it purport to conduct a systematic investigation of a company and its operations and a thorough scrutiny of its financial statements. It does, however, provide grounds to believe that reasoned scepticism produces better long-run investment results than uncritical optimism. It also shows that the trade-off between risk and return is the polar opposite of that which is virtually always supposed. The commonly held belief is that the higher the risk, the higher the potential return, whereas I believe that the *lower* the likelihood that the purchase of a particular asset will cause a substantial and permanent loss of capital, the *greater* its potential return (that is, the expected value of its stream of future earnings). Unwarranted optimism—and, in extreme instances, irrational exuberance—fuels speculation; a policy of reasoned scepticism underpins investment.

MAKING SCEPTICAL ASSUMPTIONS

Consider again our basic starting point. The choice is to buy either a hypothetical five-year Commonwealth Government bond with a yield of 6.1 per cent (the yield of these bonds prevailing on 1 June 2000) or one share in a hypothetical company called X Ltd. Assume for simplicity that the price of both securities is $1.00. Assume as well that X Ltd is 'sound', having an established (five- to ten-year) track record with respect to three criteria. The first criterion is *effectiveness*—the generation of a real and growing stream of earnings. The second is *efficiency*—the use of modest amounts of capital to generate these earnings. And the third is *managerial rationality*—the wise use of those earnings which management has retained within the company rather than paid to its owners as dividends. Rational managers do not squander these earnings; rather, they use them to generate higher earnings in subsequent years.

As in chapter 5, assume again that the year is 2000. Whether you choose the bond or the stock you are a long-term investor, and you will hold your chosen investment for at least five years. If you buy the bond, then it is safe to assume that by mid-2005 you will earn 31¢—having received a stream of 6.1¢ per year for five years). Accordingly, during its five-year life the bond will return to you $1.31 (that is, the $1.00 principal plus the five interest payments). Given the bond's risk-free nature, it makes sense to buy the X Ltd stock only if there are strong grounds to believe that during the next five years it will return to you significantly more than $1.31.

How much more? That depends upon the 'risk premium' which you require (either consciously or not) before you will buy the share rather than the bond. Recall that the bond is in two senses a risk-free asset: its interest payments are both fixed and virtually perfectly predictable over time. (There are, however, other risks in making this type of investment.) In both of these senses common stocks are riskier: first, their earnings are variable (indeed, they may not eventuate at all), and second, their earnings are much less predictable than the bond's coupons. Therefore, given the prospect of an equivalent stream of earnings from a Commonwealth bond and a particular share, by how much must the share's yield exceed the bond's yield before you are prepared to buy the share? How much cheaper, in other words, must the share be relative to the bond?

Despite the conservative and stringent assumptions which we are making, there are nonetheless reasonable grounds to assume also that X Ltd will be able to return a total of at least $1.31 by 2005. These assumptions and their consequences are summarised in table 6.1, overleaf.

Decision-making rule 1

Our first assumption is that in 2001 X Ltd's coupon or earnings per share (EPS) will be 13.3¢. We assume, in other words, that any purchase at a price of $1.00 on 1 June 2000 will turn out to be equivalent to 7.5 times X Ltd's EPS in 2001. This assumption is conservative because value investors strive to purchase equity at lower price multiples (and hence higher earnings yields). If, for example, we resolve to purchase X Ltd at no more than five times its current (2000) earnings and are actually able to do so, then our purchase price of $1.00 per share implies that earnings per share for 2000 are 20¢. Our first decision rule is therefore very robust in the sense that it allows for the possibility that X Ltd's earnings will decrease by as much as 33 per cent during the next twelve months.

Table 6.1: a thumbnail evaluation of a typical 'value' investment

Year	Coupon (EPS)	Yield on $1.00 investment	Annual dividend (50% payout)	Shareholders' equity
2001	$0.133	13.3%	$0.067	$1.067
2002	$0.140	14.0%	$0.070	$1.137
2003	$0.147	14.7%	$0.074	$1.211
2004	$0.154	15.4%	$0.077	$1.288
2005	$0.162	16.2%	$0.081	$1.369
Totals	**$0.736**	**11.7%***	**$0.369**	**$1.369**

* Compound p.a.

Decision-making rule 2

Table 6.1 makes a second stringent assumption: the earnings per share of X Ltd, notwithstanding their growth in the past, will increase during the next five years at a virtually stagnant annual compound rate of no more than 5 per cent. Our decision rule, in other words, is to adopt a consciously pessimistic view of X Ltd's future operations. Clearly, a track record of sound operating results hardly guarantees that these results will continue. This point is particularly apposite during periods of strong economic growth such as that experienced in Australia since the mid-1990s. Our second assumption, then, is also robust, incorporating as it does the possibility that X Ltd's sound track record will subsequently deteriorate into mediocrity.

Decision-making rule 3

Thirdly, table 6.1 assumes that X Ltd's current per-share shareholders' equity (that is to say, its assets less its liabilities divided by the total number of shares issued) is $1.00 and that in the next five years it will return half its earnings to its owners as a dividend and retain the other half. The corresponding—and very Grahamite—decision rules are that we buy companies at no more than book value (which is not the same as intrinsic value) and which possess solid records and prospects of paying dividends.

SOME IMMEDIATE IMPLICATIONS
AND A MORE EXPLICIT CONCEPTION OF RISK

Our purposefully dour assumptions, if they actually prove to be accurate, have some startling implications.

The first implication is that in 2001 the yield on our investment in X Ltd (that is to say, its EPS divided by our purchase price of $1.00) works out at 13.3 per cent. This is more than twice the bond's yield of 6.1 per cent. Moreover, this yield increases modestly thereafter such that in 2005 it is almost three times the bond's yield. In other words, not only are each of X Ltd's five coupons significantly greater than the bond's corresponding coupon, but the extent of this disparity also increases over time. Accordingly, at the end of the fifth year cumulative earnings of 74¢ — *roughly two-and-one-half times greater than the risk-free bond's cumulative coupons of 31¢*—accrue to the owner of the X Ltd share. Indeed, in the sense that cumulative earnings of $1.08 are generated by 2007, this investment will 'pay for itself' within seven years. The purchase of X Ltd under conditions prevailing on 1 June 2000 would therefore clearly possess what Benjamin Graham called a 'margin of safety'.

The second implication is that if all unfolds according to these lacklustre plans, then during the 2000–2005 period, X Ltd will pay its owners a total of 37¢ per share in dividends. In order to match the bond's total return, in five years the owner of the X Ltd share would therefore have to be able to sell her X Ltd share for at least 94¢ (that is, $1.31 minus 37¢). Again, it can be seen that our decision rules are robust. If X Ltd's operations deteriorate further than our already pessimistic assumptions allow (or if for some other reason the market price of its shares stagnates) and the investor must sell the X Ltd share for 6¢ less than she paid for it, her stream of dividends—if they transpire according to our assumptions—still assures her a return equal to the bond's.

If, however, X Ltd's operating results do meet our conservative expectations, and if we are willing to assume that other market participants will by 2005 attach the same undemanding multiple (1.0) to its shareholders' equity that they do today, then we could reasonably expect that X Ltd's shares will sell for roughly $1.37. Under these conditions our compound return (including dividends) increases to 11.7 per cent per annum. If X Ltd's operating results during the next five years are comparable to those observed during the last five years, they will exceed our sober expectations; the shares' market quotation will be higher (again assuming that market participants will attach the same multiple to its shareholders' equity); and our compound return would be higher still. As a general rule, then, the value investor accepts the risk that inheres in a decision to invest only when its positives greatly outweigh its negatives—when the 'upside' seems to be more likely than the 'downside'. Given its past operations and current market price, X Ltd—unlike most blue chips and virtually all tech market darlings—seems to possess this characteristic.

SOME MORE FUNDAMENTAL IMPLICATIONS ABOUT RISK AND RETURN

Several more fundamental implications—each of which raises an important point about value investing—also follow from this analysis of the hypothetical company X Ltd. They reveal more about both value investors' conception of risk and the methods they use to mitigate it. They also indicate that in order to obtain higher investment returns the value investor need not accept higher risk. Quite the opposite: the stringent steps she takes to reduce risk can increase rather than decrease the eventual returns on her investment.

All investment decisions must necessarily rest upon an analysis of past operations and a set of assumptions about future developments. Hence the value investor juxtaposes good-to-excellent past operations and cautious-to-pessimistic assumptions about the future. This approach entails less risk (as I have defined it) than the other three alternatives. To take this approach is to incorporate into investment analysis the unpleasant but ever-present possibility that good business operations in the past will not continue into the future.

Table 6.2: level of perceived risk inhering in investment decisions

	Cautious assumptions about the future	Exuberant assumptions about the future
Excellent past operations	Lower risk	Medium risk
Mediocre past operations	Medium risk	Highest risk

As table 6.2 indicates, to assume that a company with a mediocre track record of operations will continue on a mediocre path is judged to be a medium risk—perhaps company-specific mismanagement, industry-specific economy-wide factors (to which mediocre compani~ be particularly prone) will at some point within th~ years turn a mediocre track record into a poor o~ that a company with a sound track record ~ such a path is also considered a medium~ quality management, bad decisions, u~ or other innumerable (and perh~ will turn a solid track record in~ all is the assumption that a comp~ record—or, as was usually the case ~

in the tech and dotcom areas, a company with no track record of any description—will henceforth produce stellar results. Rarely if ever is one's crystal ball clear enough to make this heroic assumption with any degree of confidence.

It is for this reason that (unless there exist very exceptional and compelling reasons to do otherwise) the value investor restricts attention to companies that have strong track records established over a period of five to ten years, and preferably longer, and that meet three criteria. First, these companies should generate growing 'real' profits (as opposed to 'accounting' profits). Second, their earnings must be high relative to the capital required to generate those earnings. (In our example, X Ltd's projected earnings are between 11 per cent and 13 per cent of its book value.) Third, the earnings which they retain must not be squandered or destroyed but should rather be used to generate higher earnings in subsequent years.

Very low initial (acquisition) price

Another fundamental implication of our evaluation is that, for value investors, a security's purchase price is as important as its soundness. Bargain price and sound business operations, like Siamese twins, are inextricably linked. It is axiomatic that investors should attempt to pay as little as possible for the income stream which they (cautiously) assume a given asset will generate. For each cent of X Ltd's earnings in 2001, for example, we strive in 2000 to pay 5¢, but assume cautiously that we will actually pay 50 per cent more; that is, 7.5¢. We therefore refuse to pay high prices, endeavouring always to pay a bargain price, but we are prepared to settle for a reasonable price if our cautious assumptions do not, alas, come to fruition.

Investors' attitudes towards securities are thus identical to their attitudes as consumers towards any good or service. Other things being equal, the lower the price, the greater the quantity consumers demand. If, for example, the price of a certain grade of beef mince decreases from $10.99 to

$7.99 per kilo and becomes cheaper relative to its alternatives (mutton, pork, chicken, and so on), consumers will tend to demand fewer of these substitutes and more beef mince. Many if not most participants in financial markets, however, seem to turn this axiom of human action on its head. They act as if financial assets are what economists call 'Giffen goods'. Giffen goods are goods for which demand increases as their prices rise. (They are named for nineteenth-century economist, Sir Francis Giffen, who reputedly observed that an increase in the price of potatoes during an Irish famine led to an increase in the consumption of potatoes.)

In chapter 5, it was established that it was on the basis of very generous assumptions that many market participants were willing, at the close of business on 1 June 2000, to pay 21¢ for each cent of BHP's estimated 2001 earnings, 22¢ for each cent of Telstra's, 29¢ for Solution 6's and no less than 46¢ for each penny of News Corp.'s. *In so doing, they revealed that they were prepared to pay between three and six times more for the earnings of these relatively risky assets than a Grahamite investor would be prepared to pay for the earnings of the less-risky X Ltd.*

As the information presented in table 6.1 implies, the rationale for buying a quality asset at a low price is simple: the lower the purchase price, the higher the yield, the larger the pile of earnings accumulated per dollar of capital invested, and the higher the investment's long-term compound return. As table 6.2 shows, to make cautious assumptions about a sound security is simultaneously to reduce the risks in any decision to allocate investment capital. This is a variant of Benjamin Graham's rule that investors should purchase quality assets whose current yield is more than twice that of a risk-free government bond. One of the ways the value investor copes with risk, in other words, is by constantly seeking to mitigate the chance that she will pay too much for sound assets.

The utter irrelevance of 'intermediate' market quotations

Another tenet of value investing is implicit in table 6.1: to the Grahamite investor, the 'performance' of an asset is measured primarily in terms of the size of the long-term stream of earnings it generates—and not at all in terms of short-term fluctuations in its market price. If all goes to plan and X Ltd earns 14¢ per share in 2002, for example, then the yield of those earnings, given the purchase price of $1.00, is 14 per cent. Volatility in the price of X Ltd stock during that year does not affect this result. Accordingly, except to the extent that they allow the value investor to buy greater quantities of a quality asset at an even cheaper price, short-term fluctuations in market quotations are irrelevant and investors are indifferent to them. *Indeed, from an investor's perspective, the best possible outcome in 2002 is that X Ltd's business operations exceed the sceptic's conservative assumptions and that the price of the company's shares decreases.* As long as our cautious expectations about X Ltd come to fruition, at some point its share price will recover strongly.

Since the late nineteenth century, many scholars have observed that on a day-to-day, week-to-week and even month-to-month basis the prices of stocks fluctuate largely randomly. Unlike market quotations, which are a will-o'-the-wisp, a company's earnings—and particularly its dividends—are tangible and meaningful. And of critical importance, over much longer periods (five to ten years and longer) a reasonably strong correlation exists between growth in earnings, shareholders' equity and market price. If all goes according to our cautious plans, and given X Ltd's sound track record, there are both logical and empirical grounds on which to believe that over the years the price of its shares will reflect the earnings that it has generated and retained on its owners' behalf.

Value investors therefore strive to ignore short-term noise (market price) and concentrate upon longer-term music (company operations). They devote considerable time to the study of a company's financial statements; they put forward cautious assumptions about its capacity to generate a stream of earnings; and they wait patiently until it or a similarly attractive asset becomes available at a sensible price. In so doing they liberate themselves from an obsession which is as pointless and distracting as it is ubiquitous: they do not presently have, never have had and never will have any inclination to issue forecasts about phenomena such as the price of 'their' shares at a particular point in the future, or the future level or direction of 'the market'. Value investors neither need nor utilise such predictions. They waste no time fretting about gloomy forecasts, and their purchases of quality assets at bargain prices are not deterred by such prophecies. Quite the contrary: because these forecasts can spook some market participants and make excellent businesses available at excellent prices, they sometimes offer value investors the chance to buy attractive securities which others dismiss as unfashionable, old-fashioned or otherwise out of favour. Finally, because they make no attempt to predict market movements they are able to ignore the mindless, short-term and self-defeating rat race of attempting to 'beat the market'.

Moderate diversification and buying-and-holding

It is clear that not all companies are 'sound' as that term has been defined. Equally clearly, very few become available at low multiples of their earnings or at a discount to their shareholders' equity. Another two implications thereby follow. The first is that, because attractive investment opportunities occur infrequently, value investors can investigate each opportunity thoroughly and act only when all the facts at hand seem to work in their favour. As a result, value investors' portfolios tend to include modest numbers of quality assets (in practice, the securities of approximately ten to twenty companies) and a relatively large allocation of cash.

Statistical simulations corroborate this stance.[1] They indicate that the benefits of diversification are real, but that an increase in the number of assets beyond twenty or so provides little added benefit. Common sense tells us that it is better to possess twenty excellent assets than a grab bag of twenty excellent and eighty mediocre ones. The greater the number of items in a portfolio, the less thorough is the research which precedes the purchase of each security; and after its purchase, the more cursory is the ongoing examination of the business that underlies the security. In Warren Buffett's estimation, concentrating efforts on a smaller number of assets actually *reduces* the overall risk that inheres in investment operations, as it forces investors to conduct more thorough and rigorous research. Value investors thus tend to cope with investment risk by placing their eggs in a select and manageable number of baskets—and then watching those baskets like a hawk.

The second implication is that because 'value' investments are so difficult to find, the value investor should retain them as long as their operations meet her stringent and sceptical criteria. In other words, the value investor buys quality assets at bargain prices and holds them indefinitely, unless she has compelling reasons to do otherwise, thus obtaining returns commensurate with the results of the underlying business's operations. Her focus, then, is upon the company and its ability to generate a stream of income—not upon the market and the cacophony of opinions, predictions and actions of other market participants.

THE POLICY OF REASONED SCEPTICISM

Most people are reasonably optimistic about the future and confident about their knowledge and abilities. In most respects this is a good thing: people with a positive mental attitude tend to be happier and are more focused, determined, virile and successful than those with negative outlooks. When making financial and investment decisions, however, optimism about the future and overconfidence about one's abilities can be distinct disadvantages. Time after time they lure investors into overestimating assets' future streams of earnings and paying too much for them. They also tempt market participants to buy and sell rather than buy and hold, and to trade on the basis of rumours, late-breaking news, tips, babble and other spurious prompts. Speculators typically think that they know more than can reasonably be known and often act on the basis of this 'knowledge'. As a result, on any given day a substantial proportion of the turnover on financial markets is pointless churning. Unfortunately, however, it seems that the higher market participants' level of optimism, degree of self-confidence and frequency of trading, the less rigorous and thorough is their research — and the lower the return on their investments (net of tax, brokerage, and so on).

The value investor's response to this general human bias towards hubris and the pretence to knowledge is a policy of reasoned scepticism. This means that the reasoning that underlies her investment operations must be made explicit and therefore that its errors and omissions may be more easily detectable. It also ensures that her assumptions incorporate a stringent discount for overconfidence. As this chapter and the previous chapter suggest, Aesop's fable of the tortoise and hare applies as much to investment as it does to other areas of human endeavour. There is good reason to believe that the returns from reasoned scepticism will over time surpass those generated by irrational exuberance. The value investor's objective, then, is not to allocate capital in order to obtain the gratification of immediately outperforming the market; rather, it is to mitigate risk whilst securing the prospect of reasonable long-term reward. The value investor does not attempt to surmount the imposing two-metre bars that everybody else is trying to leap. Both the height and the quantity and quality of the competition bode badly for her chances. Instead, she searches assiduously for the twenty-centimetre bars that others occasionally ignore — and, when she finds them, steps safely over. The likelihood of consistent success is far greater and the risk of embarrassment and permanent injury is much lower.

NOTES

1   An informative and readable overview appears in Robert Hagstrom, *The Warren Buffett Portfolio* (John Wiley & Sons, 1999).

Part II

◇◇◇◇◇◇◇◇◇◇◇◇◇◇◇◇◇◇◇◇◇◇◇◇

Three scourges

The improvements which, in modern times, have been made in several different branches of philosophy have not, the greater part of them, been made in universities ... The greater part of universities have not even been very forward to adopt those improvements after they were made; and several of those learned societies have chosen to remain, for a long time, the sanctuaries in which exploded systems and obsolete prejudices found shelter and protection after they had been hunted out of every other corner of the world. In general, the richest and best endowed universities have been the slowest in adopting those improvements, and the most averse to permit any considerable change in the established plan of education. Those improvements were more easily introduced into some of the poorer universities, in which the teachers, depending upon their reputation for the greater part of their subsistence, were obliged to pay more attention to the current opinions of the world.

Adam Smith
The Wealth of Nations (1776)

Chapter 7

◇◇◇◇◇◇◇◇◇◇◇◇◇◇◇◇◇◇◇◇◇◇◇◇◇◇◇◇◇◇◇◇

Ignore predictions about market and economic conditions

The further one gets away from Wall Street, the more scepticism one will find, we believe, as to the pretensions of stock-market forecasting or timing. The investor can scarcely take seriously the innumerable predictions which appear almost daily and are his for the asking.

Benjamin Graham
The Intelligent Investor (1949)

In March 2005, the Reserve Bank of Australia announced that it had raised the short-term rate of interest (the overnight cash rate) that it controls. On this occasion, as on others in the past, a flood of predictions about interest rates followed this decision. Some people forecast that during the next six to twelve months rates would rise further. Others predicted that they would remain stable and a few prophesied that they would fall. More generally, few days pass when investors are not bombarded with a variety of market and macroeconomic forecasts: the All Ordinaries Index will rise; inflation will climb; economic growth will decelerate; the dollar will depreciate; the current account deficit will balloon. Similarly, analysts and 'strategists' brandishing various predictions about corporate earnings and the prices of particular securities constantly beset investors. An enormous industry, populated by confident, articulate and well-paid people, exists in order to satisfy Australians' insatiable appetite for financial and economic predictions.[1]

The consumers of these predictions would benefit if they curbed their appetites. The time and effort devoted to pondering forecasts is wasted, and if these resources were turned towards other pursuits they would be deployed far more effectively. Part II of this book analyses three time and money wasters. Part III describes five sensible and remunerative activities.

IGNORING MARKET AND STOCK TIMERS

Investors pay no attention to market predictions. They take no notice of predictions about the future levels of (or movements in) overall financial markets, or of the prices of individual securities. Neither forecasts nor forecasters influence their investment decisions. In this respect they are very unusual. Since time immemorial, a few people have attempted to foresee the future, and the benighted have obsessed about the prophesies of these anointed seers. Also since the beginning of recorded history, the confidence of the many in the ability of the few to make accurate predictions has — to put it mildly — greatly exceeded their actual ability to do so. The inability to anticipate the level and direction of financial markets and the prices of securities with any reliable degree of accuracy is just one instance of a more general phenomenon: human beings' basic inability to foresee the future. This inability is absolute. And so too, it seems, is most people's obstinate and gullible refusal to recognise or accept this limitation. Prominent and otherwise formidably intelligent people are no exception.

The problem is that the higher the stock market rises, the greater the number of people who believe that accurate prediction is possible. At or near the peak, many are tempted to believe that their line of sight into the future is clear and unimpeded — the summit, of course, can only be discerned in retrospect. Suffering from this delusion, they happily pay prices that significantly exceed any reasonable conception of value. The trouble, then, is that people who believe that tomorrow is as clear as today discount or dismiss the margin of safety that necessarily underpins any investment worthy of the name. Forecasts may—and often do—reveal something about the states of mind of the people who produce and consume forecasts, but they seldom disclose much that is useful about the future.

To acknowledge that the future is largely unknowable is contrarian and perhaps even reprobate.[2] Forecasters, after all, often use formidably advanced statistical methods. They usually possess advanced degrees from prestigious academic institutions, and use words and methods well beyond the comprehension of people who consume their prophesies. Well-established and influential organisations employ forecasters. Confident, smooth-talking, photogenic soothsayers appear regularly in the news, and some of the government's most prominent institutions—such as the Reserve Bank and the Treasury—are to a significant extent forecasting organisations. Clearly, forecasters are influential people.

It is therefore hardly surprising that predictions appear prominently on the pages of most business publications, stock market newsletters and tip sheets. They also scream through internet chat rooms and over the back garden fences of suburbia. Much time and psychological energy is devoted to making and debating predictions of one type or another. During the next three months, for example, will the All Ordinaries Index rise or fall? By how much? What about over the next six months? And how about the price of residential real estate? Similarly, major investment institutions, financial planners and humble retail investors devote tremendous effort to the selection of individual stocks or managed funds, and to the identification of particular segments of the market (such as mining stocks, banks and retailers), whose prices are expected to rise more quickly or more significantly than the rest over some fairly short period in the future. Never mind the painful consequences of the Great Bubble: now as ever, 'hot funds', 'hot sectors' and 'hot stocks' sell magazines and attract clients.

However, pondering and acting upon predictions neither suits the temperament nor the needs of the true investor. Why? To obsess about predictions is first (and typically), as we have discussed, to emphasise movements of price. Second (if at all) it is to consider changes of underlying values. To do these things, as we have seen, is to speculate. Further, to devote otherwise intelligent minds to unintelligent activities is simply pointless. William Sherden, the author of a good, clear book about the perils of prediction, concurs.[3] Of the 108 stock market timing newsletters and tip sheets whose predictions he analysed, only one consistently published forecasts that corresponded even crudely and for a short time to subsequent events.

One in 108, it is important to emphasise, is little different to the success rate that would be expected to result from pure chance. Take flips of a coin as an analogy. In any group of 100 coin flippers, roughly one, on average, will be able to predict on seven consecutive flips whether his toss lands heads or tails. In a very wide variety of settings, chance and random factors usually play a much bigger role than we realise.

The unscrupulous have used this principle to entice the unsuspecting to pay astronomical amounts of money for tip sheets. You could, if you were dishonest, test this: collect the addresses of roughly 1,000 names and addresses from your local telephone directory. Post to each a brochure (together with an attractive photo) that extols your incredible and guru-like ability to predict whether the All Ords will rise or fall during the next week. To half of these people attach a cover letter predicting that the All Ords will rise next week; and to the other half attach a letter predicting that it will fall. One week later, write again *to the 500 people to whom you accurately 'predicted' the direction of the All Ords*. Again, send them your brochure; and once again send half of them (that is, 250 people) a cover letter predicting that the stock market will rise in the next week, and the other half a cover letter predicting that it will fall. Repeat this process for another couple of weeks. Before long, people who are convinced of your uncanny ability to 'predict' will send you hefty subscriptions in order to capitalise upon your 'genius'.

Sherden showed that 'market experts' (that is, people whose business is the prediction of prices and events) cannot consistently get things right—but that they can and do get things thoroughly wrong. In reality, market timers are seldom in doubt but virtually always in error. Benjamin Graham and Warren Buffett's names are not alone on the list of investors who disclaim any ability to predict financial markets' levels or directions in the future. Peter Lynch, one of the most prominent and successful funds managers of the last four decades, reckons that 'when it comes to predicting the market, the important skill ... is not listening, it's snoring'. Further, he says, market timers 'can't predict markets with any useful consistency, any more than gizzard squeezers could tell the Roman Emperors when the Huns would attack'.[4]

So much for tip sheets that purport to predict which stocks' prices will shortly rise and which will fall. Are analysts able to forecast companies' earnings more accurately? David Dreman reviewed almost 100,000 earnings forecasts made between 1973 and 1996.[5] He found that the average forecast erred by 30 to 60 per cent. Further, the odds are 1 in 130—less than 1 per cent—that an analyst can predict a company's profit to within 5 per cent of its true value four times in succession. Just as the speculator cannot predict future prices, the analyst cannot predict future profits. Not surprisingly, Dreman concluded that company earnings are 'utterly unpredictable' and warned that predictions of earnings are of 'not much value' (something of an understatement). William Sherden agrees. Despite their apparently advanced methods, (often) incomprehensible jargon and (almost invariably) high salaries, financial analysts are no better at predicting the future than astrologers.[6]

Ignoring mainstream and 'market' economists

Similarly, intelligent investors pay no attention to economists' forecasts about macroeconomic phenomena. They ignore predictions about exchange rates, interest rates, unemployment rates, the balance of payments, rates of growth of GDP and all the rest. They also disregard forecasts about particular prices—such as those of oil or wheat or iron ore—at some given point in the future. Why? You guessed it: economists' ability to foresee the future is at best tenuous. Even if they could forecast reasonably accurately, these forecasts would distract rather than inform investors.

Perhaps the most prominent forecaster of them all, and surely the most revered, seems to think so. According to Alan Greenspan, Chairman of the US Federal Reserve:

> despite extensive efforts on the part of analysts, to my knowledge, no model projecting directional movements in exchange rates is significantly superior to tossing a coin. I am aware that of the thousands who try, some are quite successful. So are winners of coin-tossing contests. The seeming ability of a number of banking organisations to make consistent profits from foreign-exchange trading likely derives not from their insight into future rate changes but from market making.[7]

Perhaps this is why Warren Buffett once said, '[If] Greenspan were to whisper to me what his monetary policy was going to be over the next two years, it wouldn't change one thing I do.'[8]

As mentioned above, William Sherden reviewed leading research about the accuracy of macroeconomic forecasts conducted since the 1970s. His findings can be summarised as follows:

- economists cannot predict turning points in the economy (that is, when boom turns to bust and vice versa)

- their forecasting skill is, on average, no better than the 'naive forecast' that the near future will continue to be pretty much like the recent past

- their ability to forecast accurately is, on average, neither better nor worse than guessing

- increased sophistication (such as vastly more powerful computers, much more arcane econometric models and ever-growing mountains of data) has not improved the accuracy of their forecasts

- there is no evidence that forecasters' skill has increased since the 1970s (if anything, their skill, such as it is, has deteriorated over time)

- 'consensus' forecasts (the combination of individual forecasts into a single forecast) are no more accurate than the individual forecasts which comprise them

- the further into the future economists attempt to see, the less accurate their forecasts become

- there are no individual economic forecasters who are consistently more accurate than their peers.

Sherden's first finding listed above is perhaps the most important. Even when Sherden gave economists the benefit of the doubt and used generous criteria to decide whether a particular prediction was accurate, he found that between 1980 and 1995 the US Federal Reserve—a very large and prestigious organisation that commands extensive resources and employs many of that country's best-trained mainstream economists—predicted only three of the six turning points in America's gross national product (GNP). It predicted neither of the two turning points in consumer price inflation.

The US Federal Reserve's analysis of others' predictions comes to a similar conclusion.[9] Economists in its Atlanta branch studied macroeconomic forecasts published in *The Wall Street Journal* between 1985 and 2001 and found that forecasters predicted particularly poorly at turning points in the business cycle—exactly, in other words, when sound advice about the future would have been most useful and unsound advice most damaging. The accuracy of forecasts was gauged on a scale from zero to 100 (where zero denoted the least and 100 the most accurate). In the middle of an economic expansion, when by definition the near future most closely resembles the recent past, scores tended to hover between sixty and eighty, but at turning points they utterly collapsed. At the start of the 1990s recession in July 1990, for example, the score fell to fifteen. In January 2001, just before the collapse of the Great Bubble, it fell to seventeen.

The second of Sherden's findings listed above is perhaps the most disconcerting. The econometric studies he cites show that econometric predictions are so prone to error—particularly of the vastly overoptimistic variety—that they are as worthless as witchcraft. Indeed, if you want to predict the future course of (say) interest rates, you might well decide to take rates for the past year, plot them on a piece of paper, draw a 'best fitting' line through the scatter of points and extrapolate the line into the next year. A pencil and ruler actually tend to be more accurate than the extremely complex methods used by prestigious organisations—including government treasuries and central banks—staffed with PhDs from world-class universities.

The weather and demographic change are somewhat more predictable, but not so most areas of private and public management. A generation ago, Peter Drucker wrote:

> forecasting is not a respectable human activity and [is] not worthwhile beyond the shortest of periods ... The future is unpredictable. We can only discredit what we are doing by trying [to predict] it.'[10]

The startling fact that child's play can outperform highly educated and intelligent professionals across a range of complex areas of human endeavour appears to be more than coincidental. That experts' conclusions, routinely accepted with little or no question, are often no better than those obtained by flipping a coin or making naive (or intuitive) guesses implies that the money paid to such experts is an utter waste.

The 'Maestro' himself provides proof of this point. 'There are several things that we can stipulate with some degree of certainty,' Alan Greenspan told the Fed's Open Market Committee on 21 August 1990. '[Most importantly,] those who argue that we are already in a recession ... are reasonably certain to be wrong.' Unfortunately for Mr Greenspan, the National Bureau of Economic Research, the official arbiter of measurements of the US business cycle, subsequently determined that the US had entered a two-year recession in July 1990. More recently, virtually all elite economic forecasters, including the International Monetary Fund, the Organisation for Economic Co-operation and Development and major international credit ratings agencies, were unable to foresee the Asian economic crisis of 1997. Once it had occurred, few if any domestic forecasters accurately predicted its impact upon the Australian economy.

Philip Fisher's conclusion, first uttered decades ago, thus remains sound:

> I believe that the economics which deals with forecasting business trends may be considered to be about as far along as was the science of chemistry during the Middle Ages ... The amount of mental effort the financial community puts into this constant attempt to guess the economic future ... makes one wonder what might have been accomplished if only a fraction of such mental effort had been applied to something with a better chance of proving useful.'[11]

WHY FORECAST, ANYWAY?

One is tempted to infer from the daily torrent of forecasts (as well as from the flood of newspaper articles dutifully reporting these predictions) that the prices of stocks and bonds depend upon economic conditions. Stocks, many market participants seem to assume, tend to rise when economic conditions are perceived to be strong and expected to remain robust. The quicker (or slower) the pace of economic activity, in other words, the more (or less) favourable is the investment climate and hence the bigger (or smaller) are the gains that investors can expect. To most people this is obvious. Indeed, it is so evident that the forecasting industry undertakes a constant, frenetic and expensive search for new and ever more arcane insights into economic and financial market conditions, the relation of one to the other, and their course into the 'foreseeable future'. Members of this industry—not to mention politicians and finance journalists—implicitly encourage people to believe that a strong and growing economy means favourable investing conditions.

Alas, there are ample grounds to question and reject this generalisation. A growing body of studies finds little evidence that supports it and much that contradicts it. Elroy Dimson, Paul Marsh and Mike Staunton, for example, studied movements in the economies and stock markets of sixteen countries during the past century.[12] In each country, they found that stock market returns were either unrelated to or inversely related with growth of GDP. The correlation is –0.27 for the period between 1900 and 2000 and -0.03 for the period from 1951 to 2000. (The correlation coefficient is a statistic that measures the direction of association—positive or negative—between variables.) Statistically, the rate of growth of GDP explained only about 7 per cent of the fluctuation of stock returns between 1900 and 2000, and this key summary measure of economic conditions explained less than 1 per cent of the variation of returns during the second half of the twentieth century.

Jeremy Siegel conducted another, much more detailed analysis, covering longer periods of time than research that had been done earlier, and reached the same conclusion. He found that between 1970 and 1997 the average correlation between stock returns and GDP growth was –0.32 in seventeen developed countries and –0.03 in eighteen emerging markets.[13] Jay Ritter, using the data assembled by Dimson et al., obtained a correlation of –0.42 for sixteen countries during the twentieth century.[14] If anything, then, the more robust a country's overall rate of economic growth, the *lower* its stock market's subsequent rate of return (as these things are conventionally measured). As a rough rule of thumb, rates of growth explain between 1 per cent and 18 per cent of the variation in stock returns in these countries during the past century.

Ritter adds a caveat. In the short run (which seems to be one year or less), *unexpected* changes in the rate of growth do influence the prices of stocks. Prices decline when market participants suddenly anticipate a recession (or discover that a recession has begun) and they increase when investors abruptly sense a recovery (or realise that a recession has ended). Ritter believes that these cyclical or business-cycle effects 'should rationally have an effect on equity valuations, but the effects should be largely transitory'. The effects associated with recessions 'are partly due to higher risk aversion at the bottom of a recession, but also due partly to an irrational overreaction'. In a passage that warms the heart of the Grahamite investor, Ritter says this 'irrationality' generates short-term volatility 'and mean reversion over multi-year horizons'. According to Ritter, then:

> whether the Chinese economy grows by 7 per cent per year or by 3 per cent per year for the foreseeable future is largely irrelevant for the future returns on Chinese stocks. There is also an asymmetry—if a country has negative growth, this is probably bad for stocks. But for positive rates of long-term growth, whether the growth rate is 3 per cent or 7 per cent shouldn't matter.

Why does economic growth (as it is conventionally defined and measured) not seem to benefit investors (considered as a group)? Indeed, why does robust growth seem to *depress* returns? Jeremy Siegel hypothesises that market participants tend to anticipate higher rates of growth by paying higher prices for each dollar of anticipated income. To do so is to lower realised returns because more money must be invested today in order to secure a given stream of earnings and dividends tomorrow. Hence the prescient headlines from *The Wall Street Journal*: 'Dow 10,000 Means It's Time to Prepare for the Hangover' (23 March 1999) and 'Forget the Party Hats: Why Dow 10,000 Should Be No Cause for Celebration' (10 December 2003).

Ritter provides another clue to this puzzle. In every country and at every point in time, certain industries are growing (indeed, some are expanding so quickly that they become regarded as the 'industries of the future') and others are declining. Some are declining in an absolute sense, and some are declining in a relative sense (that is, they are growing more slowly than the overall economy). In the US, for example, the twentieth century's 'growth' industries included motor cars, air transport, pharmaceuticals, computer hardware and software and biotechnology. Industries in decline included railways, steel and tobacco.

The airline industry has not made people rich; nor (during the past thirty to forty years) have auto manufacturers or biotech firms. Cigarette companies, on the other hand, have generated significant wealth for their shareholders (subject to the favourable settlement of unresolved lawsuits). So too have pharmaceutical firms. 'Growth industries', in other words, typically contain both successful and unsuccessful businesses; ditto declining industries. According to Ritter, companies earn profits only if entry into the industry is restricted and consumers and employees (including executives) do not expropriate these profits from owners and capitalists, and these factors are not related to industries' growth or decline. In summary, technological changes do not increase profits unless firms affected by them have enduring competitive advantages (which few do). Nations whose potential economic growth is high do not offer attractive opportunities for investment unless asset prices are low relative to values.

WHY DO 'EXPERTS' PREDICT SO POORLY?

There are three reasons why the so-called experts so frequently make poor predictions. The first is that the purpose of many forecasts is not so much to make accurate predictions as it is to sell things; that is, to persuade investors to make particular investments with particular investment firms. According to the Australian Reserve Bank's assistant governor, Glen Stevens, many people prophesy:

> with a view to selling a product, or a piece of advice … many forecasts made in the private sector are essentially of this variety. The forecaster has a story to tell in order to provide credibility to their employer's efforts to win business.[15]

Perhaps this is why these predictions tend to err systematically in an overoptimistic direction.[16]

The second reason that forecasts are so often wrong is that the options available to individuals—and therefore the choices they make—are subjective. As chapters 3 and 4 showed, value and risk are subjective. Different individuals with different perceptions, amounts and types of information of varying quality will therefore respond differently to particular market and economic events. Moreover, over time the same individual will perceive things differently and therefore make different choices even when faced with similar options. The forum in which they make these choices—the market—is not a machine; accordingly, markets and economies simply cannot be 'restrained' and 'stimulated' in the same way that water in a dam is shut off or let flow as an engineer opens and closes its sluices. Indeed, it is vital to keep in mind that 'the market' and 'the economy' do not exist: these phrases are simply a convenient shorthand used to talk about large numbers of individuals. Buying and selling in the market is of course subject to general laws of human action, and therefore to overall relationships of cause and effect, but the specifics of the individual person and time and place are so variable that they preclude anything approaching accurate prediction.

For this reason, the present is just as difficult to interpret as the future will be to predict. To explain what the buyers and sellers in a given market are doing today (to say nothing about what they might do tomorrow) is a herculean effort.

There are many buyers and sellers, and each will have a particular motivation to buy and sell. Accordingly—and as econometricians well know—it is very difficult and perhaps impossible to distinguish the short- and long-term shifts in the supply of and demand for a particular currency, commodity or security. There is no single, collective reason that prompts investors and speculators to buy and sell on any given day; consequently, there simply is no collective market mood or psyche. More than a few forecasters implicitly recognise this. One prominent commentator, in a moment of candour, said:

> I read stuff I wrote a year ago about which I can remember thinking, not necessarily that something would happen, but that something was a reasonable conjecture. And it turned out that something was completely wrong. It's disappointing but forecasts are about the future, and the future is inherently unknowable.[17]

The third reason why predictions tend to yield such inaccurate results is that the data underlying them are less reliable than most people seem to realise (despite the integrity and best efforts of their compilers). It is not a case of 'lies, damned lies and statistics'. Rather, most government statistics must necessarily be estimates that are based upon representative samples—if they were not, then they would take far longer to compile and would be much less accurate. Agencies revise these estimates as new and more complete information comes to hand. In some instances, economic statistics pertaining to a particular point in time undergo repeated revisions that require several years to complete. A significant amount of forecasting error is thus likely to stem from random sampling errors in the data themselves. To raise this point is not to criticise the Australian Bureau of Statistics (ABS) and like organisations: it is to recognise the limits of the data that they compile. Indeed, comparing the fine print and footnotes in ABS reports to forecasters' sound bites in the media, it is clear that the forecasters impute to them an unerring accuracy that the ABS does not claim. What Oskar Morgenstern wrote a generation ago thus remains true:

> textbooks on national income and macro-economics show little if any evidence of the awareness of their data's difficulties and limitations. In Great Britain, as in the US and elsewhere, national income statistics are still being interpreted as if their accuracy compared favourably with the measurement of the speed of light.[18]

The subjectivity of individual choice and the objective sampling error of survey data have a sobering consequence. Not only is the effort devoted to predictions wasted, but forecasts based upon extrapolations from imperfectly accurate data—which are routinely used by government policy makers, business executives, investors and consumers—can also produce incorrect, costly and potentially disastrous decisions.

Fundamentally important decisions have been made at least partially on the basis of wildly inaccurate extrapolations from erroneous data. The US Presidential election of 1992, at which Bill Clinton defeated George Bush, is an example. Two premises underlay Clinton's key message to voters ('It's the economy, stupid'): that economic growth was sluggish and that President Bush was responsible for its sluggishness. Yet at precisely the moment that Bill Clinton was assailing the Bush Administration's poor economic performance, the US economy was growing at a blistering annualised rate of 5.7 per cent. Unfortunately for Mr Bush, however, this fact was unknown during the election: not until 1994, halfway through President Clinton's first term of office, did US authorities complete their revisions to key economic indicators for the period between 1990 and 1993. When they did, they increased their estimate of real GDP by 25 per cent and that of real disposable income by a whopping 70 per cent.[19]

These problems are hardly confined to the US. Most Australian retailers, including the country's largest retailers, stated late in 1998 that the Christmas period would be one of their busiest ever. Economists thus predicted that official retail trade statistics for December would reflect retailers' enthusiasm. It then came as a great surprise when retail sales data for December showed one of the largest monthly decreases (in seasonally adjusted terms) for some years. The decrease was so great that it depressed the month-by-month trend in retail sales. Indeed, it depressed this trend so much that the new trend suggested that a sharp deceleration in retail trade — and, a few muttered, possibly a recession — was on the cards. This, in turn, caused consternation in financial markets and prompted the usual knee-jerk demands to cut interest rates. The December estimate decreased so much that the ABS felt obliged to remind the users of its statistics that its data are subject to sampling error. Given a roughly stable underlying number (whatever this number is), a low estimate is likely to be followed by a higher estimate. And so it proved: the ABS announced a record (5.2 per cent) seasonally adjusted increase in retail trade for January 1999.

WHAT IS THE INTELLIGENT INVESTOR TO DO?

Decisions that rely upon inaccurate forecasts will tend to be erroneous and costly. Rather than decrease uncertainty — which, presumably, is a key purpose of forecasts — they can actually amplify it. The automobile industry, for example, like many manufacturing operations, has long production cycles and lead times. If auto executives relied solely on economic forecasts to set their production plans, they would incur huge costs, adding new capacity and increasing inventories in response to rosy projections, and shutting plants and cancelling contracts with suppliers in response to gloomy projections. Instead of relying on forecasts — and as management guru Peter Drucker suggested as early as the 1950s — managers in this industry treat forecasts cautiously and embrace common sense by putting in place robust plans which remain viable under very different (and quickly changing) conditions.

Ignore predictions about market and economic conditions

Grahamite investors plan their investments in precisely the same manner. First, they keep firmly in mind that economics is not a quantitative science whose practitioners are capable of making accurate forecasts. For every economist or 'market strategist' promulgating a certain prediction, there will be another predicting the exact opposite—and their predictions, if they make predictions, are *both* likely to be wrong. Second, investors recognise that to disclaim any ability to divine the future with any useful degree of accuracy is not to ignore the future. Quite the contrary: as we saw in part I and will see again in part III, investors cope with an inherently uncertain future by considering scenarios—concentrating upon somewhat pessimistic scenarios—of what *might conceivably* happen (as opposed to predictions of what *will likely* happen). They then use these scenarios to structure their investment operations and portfolio accordingly, taking due care to leave a margin of safety and to 'protect the downside'.

Finally, investors focus their attention neither upon the macroeconomy nor upon financial markets as a whole. Instead, they concentrate upon the identification and valuation of individual companies and their securities. A small (and thus manageable) percentage of companies possess, on the basis of their operations during the preceding five to ten years, reasonably robust characteristics. Reasonable assumptions, carefully weighted on the dour or pessimistic side, can be made about their operations into the future. Most of all, investors keep uppermost in mind the fact that, since the 1930s, Benjamin Graham and his descendants have invested successfully by basing their investment decisions not upon forecasts but rather upon the thorough analysis of companies' financial statements. Given their track records and the future's inherently uncertain nature, it is difficult to find more useful role models.

Notes

1   The same is true of political predictions. What will the Budget contain? What form will changes to media law take? Will Iraq implode? Will Osama bin Laden reappear? Intelligent investors ignore these speculations. In Warren Buffett's words (quoted in Janet Lowe, *Warren Buffett Speaks*, p. 97), 'We simply try to focus on businesses that we think we understand and where we like the price and management. If we see anything that relates to what's going to happen in Congress, we don't even read it. We just don't think it's helpful to have a view on these matters.'

2   To recognise that the future is inherently uncertain is to acknowledge that there can exist no probability distribution and data that can 'model' it. Importantly, however, the future is not radically uncertain in the sense that radical subjectivists like the economist Ludwig Lachmann maintained. Like most Austrian School economists, value investors accept that one can know some things — most notably, historical market and economic data and relationships of cause and effect and (hence) the laws of economics — and therefore that to some limited (but not accurately foreseeable) extent, the past does project into the future. The past does cause the present, which causes the future; the trouble, however, is that humans do not understand the past and present well enough to anticipate the future: indeed, they often disagree about what has happened and what is presently happening. Looking to the future, value investors do not agree that *anything* can happen; but they are acutely aware — because they have learnt from repeated personal experience — that the unexpected can and often does happen. Hence they are cautious and humble. A readable discussion of this topic appears in Alexander Shand, *The Capitalist Alternative: An Introduction to Neo-Austrian Economics* (New York University Press, 1984).

3   William Sherden, *The Fortune Sellers: The Big Business of Buying and Selling Predictions* (John Wiley & Sons, 1999), pp. 102–110.

4   Peter Lynch, *One Up on Wall Street: How to Use What You Already Know to Make Money in the Market* (Fireside, 2000), pp. 83–85.

5   David Dreman, *Contrarian Investment Strategies: The Next Generation* (Simon & Schuster, 1998), chapter 4.

6   William Sherden, *The Fortune Sellers*, chapter 1.

7   Remarks by Chairman Alan Greenspan at the European Banking Conference 2004, Frankfurt, Germany, 19 November 2004.

8   Quoted in Robert G. Hagstrom, Jr., *The Warren Buffett Way: Investment Strategies of the World's Greatest Investor* (John Wiley & Sons, 1995), p. 56.

9   See Jon E. Hilsenrath, 'Economists' Forecasts Are Worst When They Might Be Most Useful', *The Wall Street Journal Online* (1 July 2002).

10   Peter Drucker, *Management: Tasks, Responsibilities, Practices* (Harper & Row, 1974), pp. 123–124. Incidentally, Drucker also wrote 'management science has been a disappointment. It has not lived up, so far, to its promise'. (pp. 507-508) That point, too, remains valid.

11   Philip A. Fisher, *Common Stocks and Uncommon Profits and Other Writings by Philip A. Fisher* (John Wiley & Sons, 1996), pp. 62–63.

12   Elroy Dimson, Paul Marsh and Mike Staunton, *The Triumph of the Optimists: 101 Years of Global Investment Returns* (Princeton University Press, 2002).

13   Jeremy Siegel, *Stocks for the Long Run: The Definitive Guide to Financial Market Returns and Long-Term Investment Strategies* (McGraw-Hill Trade, 2003).

14   Jay Ritter, 'Economic Growth and Equity Returns' (working paper, University of Florida, 1 November 2004), available at <http://bear.cba.ufl.edu/ritter/work_papers/EconGrowth.pdf>. See also Alan Wood's column in *The Weekend Australian* (17–18 July 2004).

15   See Ian Henderon, 'Forecasting is Not for the Faint-Hearted' (*The Australian,* 6 October 1999). On 8 April 2005, in a speech entitled 'The Changing Statistical Needs of Central Banks', Stevens added, 'where an entity which has a vested interest is releasing data, upon which they then base claims for advancing their own opinions or agenda, we should take care. Some private surveys one occasionally sees could only be described as crude advertising or propaganda ... These sorts of series don't deserve to be taken seriously.' Although Stevens conveniently neglects to mention it, exactly the same point applies to the 'vested interest' and 'crude advertising or propaganda' of the RBA.

16   David Dreman, *Contrarian Investment Strategies*, chapter 6.

17   See Gideon Haigh, 'Prophet and Loss' (*The Sydney Morning Herald*, 9 January 1999).

18   Oskar Morgenstern, *On the Accuracy of Economic Observations* (Princeton University Press, 1963), p. 6.

19   Paul Magnusson, 'Need an Economic Forecast?' (*Business Week*, 13 September 1993, p.38); 'Pick a Number' (*The Economist*, 13 September 1992); and William Sherden, *The Fortune Sellers*, pp. 77–81.

Chapter 8

◇◇◇◇◇◇◇◇◇◇◇◇◇◇◇◇◇◇◇◇◇◇◇◇◇◇◇◇◇◇◇◇◇

Reject efficient markets dogma (and the business schools that peddle it)

In forty-four years of Wall Street experience and study, I have never seen dependable calculations made about common stock values, or related investment policies, that went beyond simple arithmetic or the most elementary algebra. Whenever [calculus] is brought in, or higher algebra, you could take it as a warning signal that the operator was trying to substitute theory for experience, and usually also to give speculation the deceptive guise of investment.

Benjamin Graham
'The New Speculation in Common Stocks'
The Analysts Journal (1958)

Graham-style value investors are staunch individualists. The disagreement of others does not dissuade them from a course of action. Nor do they undertake something simply because others are doing it. As Graham emphasised, the intelligent and truly conservative investor derives satisfaction from the thought that her operations are diametrically opposite those of the crowd, rather than worrying about it. That is just as well, because since the 1970s, Grahamite value investors have stood further and further apart from the financial mainstream.

Indeed, as mainstream beliefs have hardened into ever stricter and more arcane orthodoxy, Grahamites have become more and more critical of the majority. This disapproval is mutual. The creators and protectors of conventional financial wisdom—the business schools of North American universities—have either ignored Grahamites or regarded them as persona non grata in terms of their research, hiring and teaching. To be a value investor, then, is to be sceptical about—if not hostile to—universities, and to reject the financial orthodoxy they propagate.[1]

THE 1970S WAS AN AWFUL DECADE BECAUSE ...

The Great Depression which followed the Crash of 1929 was the worst financial and economic disaster of the twentieth century. The second worst was the recession and bear market of the 1970s. As in 1929 and into the 1930s, so too in the 1970s: a ferocious bear market and severe recession were felt in all English-speaking countries. The recession began around 1973, and the bear market lasted until 1982 or thereabouts, depending upon the country in question and the definitions applied. Unlike the Crash, the funk of the 1970s did not begin on a single horrific day, nor were its effects as devastating. In Australia, attention was distracted from economic matters by an unprecedented political drama. Perhaps this is why, despite their much more recent occurrence, the recession and bear market of the 1970s do not evoke the same uniformly dreadful memories as the 1930s.

It was nonetheless an excruciatingly painful affair. Week after week and month after month (and, indeed, year after year) the prices of stocks and bonds fell. One of Benjamin Graham's employees and Warren Buffett's colleagues at Graham-Newman Corp. during the 1950s, William Ruane, managed funds throughout the 1970s. He recalled:

> we had the blurred vision to start the Sequoia Fund
> in mid-1970 and suffered the Chinese water torture
> of underperforming the S&P [for] four straight years.

130

We hid under the desk, didn't answer the phones and
wondered if the storm would ever clear.'[2]

Moods were bleak. There was not just a recession and rising
unemployment: interest rates and the Consumer Price Index
also soared into double digits. From the point of view of
mainstream economists, it was impossible and thus inexplicable
that these things should occur at the same time. The
phenomenon, dubbed 'stagflation', shocked the mainstream,
but economists of the Austrian School were able to explain
it.[3] In partial recognition of this fact, Friedrich Hayek, whose
comparatively free market views had been marginalised,
ridiculed or ignored since the 1930s, was awarded the Nobel
Prize in Economic Science in 1974. (This recognition was
grudging: much to Hayek's irritation, he shared that year's
prize with the unrepentant socialist Gunnar Myrdal.)

So severe was the financial damage and emotional despair that,
for the first time since the 1930s, funds managers, advisers
and individual investors began to question their principles
and methods. They sought answers, but they did not ask the
best student, most energetic colleague, and phenomenally
successful follower of the acknowledged founder of security
analysis. In the early 1970s, Warren Buffett could point
to an outstanding twenty-year track record of investment
management, based upon Graham's insights and methods,
and he took every possible opportunity to credit Graham for
his success. But Buffett had closed his partnership in 1969
and was concentrating upon the migration of capital from
poor businesses into more favourable ones. Those who knew
him revered him; alas, at that stage nobody anticipated how
he would remake Berkshire Hathaway and so he was not yet
universally known.

Nor did many people turn to Graham's ideas. He was
recognised and respected, and his articles 'Renaissance
of Value: Rare Investment Opportunities Are Emerging'
(*Barron's*, 23 September 1974) and 'The Future of Common
Stocks' (*Financial Analysts Journal*, September–October 1974)
cogently restated the case for sober and businesslike investing

during trying times. Graham reaffirmed timeless principles and presciently pointed the way ahead.[4] However, in the final years of his life (he died in 1976), his involvement and interest in financial matters was relatively slight. Instead, most advisers and institutional investors turned—a few of them consciously and enthusiastically, some desperately and a stalwart few with great reluctance—to a small number of academics responsible for a growing body of academic research that has collectively come to be called the 'efficient markets theory' (EMT). Among its most important strands are modern portfolio theory (MPT) and the capital assets pricing model (CAPM).

THE 1970S' STULTIFYING FINANCIAL ORTHODOXY

The efficient markets theory, in its strictest form,[5] builds upon several contentions:

- All market participants have the same information and expectations, and they react identically to new information.

- Price and value are synonyms.

- The prices of securities, which adjust so quickly to new information that they render 'excess' returns impossible and the analysis of businesses and securities superfluous, nonetheless bear a common relationship to an underlying base factor.

- The more volatile a security's price, the greater its risk.

- Risk and return are inextricably linked such that the greater the desired return, the greater the risk one must accept.[6]

The base factor for the prices of stocks—and hence the single greatest influence upon their fluctuations—is the general level of prices (represented by a price index such as the All Ordinaries Index). Accordingly, *if a given stock's price is more* volatile than that of the overall market, then it is a 'riskier' stock (and vice versa). Further, according to the theorists, a particular security carries two sets of risks. The first, 'systemic risk', inheres in any security whose price is subject to market fluctuations; and the second, 'unsystemic risk', is specific to the security. Recession, war, technological developments in an industry, scandal within the boardroom and unexpectedly bad (or good) management can exacerbate the price volatility of a stock and hence its unsystemic risk.

Whether for a single security or a portfolio of securities, a two-dimensional graph can be used to depict the relationship between risk and expected return. Expected return is measured on one axis and risk on the other, and the 'efficient frontier' is a line or curve drawn from the graph's bottom-left to its top-right. Each point on the line represents an intersection between a potential return and its corresponding level of risk. Modern portfolio theorists believe that the most 'efficient' portfolio is the one that generates the highest return that is consistent with a given level of risk; and an 'inefficient' portfolio exposes its owner to a level of risk that does not offer a commensurate rate of return. An investor's goal, according to this doctrine, is to select an efficient portfolio that corresponds to her desired level of risk. The most efficient portfolio is the market itself. No other portfolio with equal risk can offer a higher expected return; and no other portfolio with an equivalent expected return will be less risky. In practical terms, therefore, the most efficient portfolio for an EMT theorist is an 'index portfolio' that is composed of a representative sample of the securities that comprise its 'benchmark' index.

A portfolio's risk is not the average price volatility of the securities that comprise it. Rather, it is the extent to which each security's volatility is correlated with that of the others in the portfolio. The more prices move in the same direction, the greater the possibility that economic or political or other events will depress them simultaneously. Conversely, a portfolio that comprises securities likely to be judged 'risky' if considered individually might actually be conservative, if the volatility of the securities' prices is not correlated (that is, if they move in different directions in response to a given stimulus). Either way, diversification is a foundation of modern portfolio theory. An investor informed by MPT first identifies the extent to which she tolerates price volatility; then, given this level of acceptable risk, she constructs an efficiently diversified portfolio.

The originally disparate threads of the theories now known as EMT and MPT became tightly intertwined during the 1950s and 1960s. At that time, most professional and institutional investors ignored these academic developments, but during the early and mid 1970s—in a stampede reminiscent of the sudden elevation in the late 1930s and war years of John Maynard Keynes's *General Theory of Employment, Interest and Money* to unrivalled economic orthodoxy—institutional investors' indifference to academics was abruptly replaced by close attention and growing obedience to them.

The slump of American markets in 1973 and 1974 convinced one consultant to investment institutions, Peter Bernstein, that there had to be a better way, and he joined mass movement towards the new theory:

> Even if I could have convinced myself to turn my back on the theoretical structure that the academics were erecting, there was too much of it coming from major universities for me to accept the view of my colleagues that it was 'a lot of baloney'.[7]

By the 1980s, EMT and MPT had become an unquestioned orthodoxy within universities and were embraced on Wall Street. According to John Train, it 'has become so accepted in academia that, as Michael C. Jensen of the University of Rochester has said, we are dangerously close to the point where no graduate student would dare send off a paper criticising it. Nonetheless, many of the best investment practitioners, including Buffett, regard it as absurd.'[8]

These developments occurred quickly and without the knowledge of (and hence deliberation by) members of the general public. Accordingly, their implications have been less recognised and more profound than might appear at first glance. A major and enduring consequence of the Keynesian revolution—and one that has outlived orthodox Keynesianism—has been the concentration of huge amounts of power and other people's money in the hands of politicians and elite policy makers. These decision-makers are often advised by academics in prestigious universities. Similarly, a major consequence of the EMT revolution has been the concentration of vast resources and the authority to allocate them in the hands of a small number of institutional investors (also advised, directly or indirectly, by academics).

Neither politicians nor academics, it seems, trust individuals to be the primary arbiters of their own economic and financial destinies. Nor, apparently, can standards of living be allowed to depend upon the ability of capitalists and entrepreneurs to serve consumers. Instead, the fortunes of hundreds of millions and perhaps billions are owed to a small number of suitably pedigreed people in places like Martin Place, Sydney; Constitution and Pennsylvania Avenues, Washington DC; and Wall Street. The ideas that inform their decisions are those of the allegedly best and brightest at the most prestigious universities. Once upon a time, they were the obscure and safely ignored residents of ivory towers, but today elite academics are much more prominent and powerful. Indeed, in the US a few have become high priests of the economy and finance.

ORTHODOXY, ARROGANCE AND REIGNS OF ERROR

The concentration of enormous quantities of other people's money in the hands of politicians, bureaucrats, funds managers and their academic advisers—anybody, in short, other than the money's actual owners—is, from the point of view of a staunch individualist, a distinctly unwelcome development. In the days of our eighteenth, nineteenth and early-twentieth century forebears, individuals in Australia were free (subject to conscience and common law) to conduct their financial affairs as they saw fit. For the most part, those intelligent (or lucky) enough to accumulate capital also judged themselves to be competent enough to manage it. A few of their decisions were undoubtedly very shrewd, a few appallingly stupid and the remainder passable and adequate. On the whole, these many individual decisions formed a natural and stable balance. It was not the rigidly imposed 'balance' of a typical (that is, hideous) government building; rather, it was the ecological stability and symmetry of an ancient hedgerow.

Alas, one basis of a free society, namely the prominence and preponderance of self-employed and independent business owners, has weakened drastically over time. Those who make their own decisions about assets, prices and incomes are far fewer in number today than they were a century ago. Today's salary earners meekly and unthinkingly accept a degree of coercion that their pioneering and autonomous forebears would rightly have regarded as intolerable infringements upon conscience and liberty. Even worse, given that today's economic and financial elites are advised more and more by elite academics, decision-makers tend to think ever more alike. Given the exponential increase in the speed at which information is disseminated in recent years, these ever fewer and larger decision-making units are also tending to act more and more alike.

As a result, the economic boat that used to be manned by countless mice is now steered by a handful of elephants. Because they are herd-conscious elephants, at critical junctures the boat becomes wobbly and unbalanced, and because they are also arrogant elephants, their colossal blunders (whose consequences, to add insult to injury, are borne not by the anointed but rather by the masses) are never followed by restitution. Whether in business or government, to be an elite decision-maker is virtually never to apologise and atone for your appalling mistakes. To disperse decision making is to localise and thereby minimise the consequences of the gaffes that regularly and inevitably accompany human action. It is also to reap the benefits of trial and error, cautiously adopting and extending successes and pruning failures. Conversely, to concentrate power is to magnify the consequences (such as obfuscation, denial and cover-up) that typically accompany egregious error. In capital markets in recent years, centralised decision-makers and arrogant academics have often been wrong but never in doubt; and the damage their ideas have wrought has been considerable.[9]

Just as the recession and bear market of the 1970s tarnished the reputation of Keynesianism, the Crash of 1987 and the bursting of the Great Bubble have dented the stature of EMT. Indeed, the efficient market hypothesis crashed along with the rest of the market on 'Black Monday', 19 October 1987; however, not everyone noticed that its stock had crashed—which is curious, to say the least, given EMT's assumptions. Richard Brealey and Stewart Myers, for example, conceded in editions of their influential mainstream text published after 1987 that Black Monday posed 'some problems'. They reassured their readers that 'in an efficient market you can trust prices', but neglected to specify *which* prices—pre- or post-crash—were trustworthy. Prices 'impound all available information about the value of each security ... in an efficient market there are no financial illusions'. So you needn't fret: despite the Crash of 1987 and the Great Bubble and all the rest, the orthodoxy remains 'remarkably well-supported by the facts'.[10]

In response to these sharp rebukes from the real world, mainstream finance has retreated from unequivocal claims into ambiguity shrouded by ever more arcane mathematics. It is true that since the 1980s a new generation of academics, embracing insights from psychology and other disciplines, has created an emerging field of 'behavioural finance' which seems to challenge the assumptions and findings of EMT. Indeed, Burton Malkiel, a leading light of orthodoxy, says that he now treads a 'middle road' between EMT and behavioural finance. Still, many funds managers and their advisers—like the politicians, bureaucrats and business journalists who remain wedded to the crude Keynesianism abandoned long ago by academics—continue to parrot EMT and MPT as if nothing were amiss. Furthermore, the gulf between behavioural finance and orthodoxy is more apparent than real. According to prominent academic Andrei Shleifer, behavioural finance shows that financial markets are inefficient. As a result, 'tremendous opportunities for both research and intelligent discussion of how to make markets more efficient open up'.[11] The point, though, is not to impose government regulations such that financial markets conform to the 'efficient' ideal of ivory tower academics. Quite the contrary: it is to remove regulation such that markets serve flesh-and-blood consumers in the real world. And that, to put it bluntly, is a job for entrepreneurs, capitalists and investors — not governments and academic economists.

DIVERSIFICATION AND VALUE INVESTING

Despite their disasters, the concentration of decision making and the 'efficient' diversification of portfolios remain mantras of the contemporary financial mainstream. Few advisers would dream of recommending to their clients a portfolio of securities that had not been efficiently diversified by a prominent funds manager, and few managers construct portfolios without this attribute. (Whatever their labels, many funds managers are 'closet indexers': they tend to hold weightings of banks, major retailers, major miners and the like that conform closely to these securities' weights in major indexes. Somehow, though, they forget to charge index funds' lower management fees.) Adherents of MPT believe that the chance that one can minimise risk improves as the number of stocks in the portfolio grows. Hence a portfolio of ten securities is better than a portfolio with only one and a portfolio of one hundred is better than a portfolio of ten.

'Efficient' diversification limits the impact of severe fluctuations upon the 'performance' of individual securities' prices. Managers know what often happens when investors open their statements and notice that the capitalisation of their holdings has suddenly and unexpectedly fallen. Even investors who understand that such dips are hardly unusual may become grumpy and take their funds elsewhere. The more 'efficiently' diversified the portfolio, the lower the likelihood that the performance of any one security will influence the monthly statement. The better diversified the portfolio, in other words, the less the risk to the manager's career.

What is wrong with diversification? Up to a point, nothing. Where a portfolio contains around fifteen to twenty securities or thereabouts, diversification is indeed beneficial. Beyond this point, however, it greatly increases the chances that the buyer buys securities about which he knows (too) little. Philip Fisher wrote that far too few people consider the 'evils' of extreme diversification. 'This is the disadvantage of having eggs in so many baskets that a lot of the eggs do not end up in really attractive baskets, and it is impossible to keep watching all the baskets after the eggs get put into them.' Diversification has been 'so oversold' that their fear of having too many eggs in one basket has caused people to put far too few eggs into companies they thoroughly understand and far too many in others about which they know next to nothing. 'It never seems to occur to them, much less their advisors, that buying a company without having sufficient knowledge of it may be even more dangerous than having inadequate diversification.'[12]

Similarly, Warren Buffett says 'diversification serves as a protection against ignorance. [It] makes very little sense for those who know what they're doing.' Further, 'if you want to make sure that nothing bad happens to you relative to the market, you should own everything. There's nothing wrong with that. It's a perfectly sound approach for somebody who doesn't know how to analyse businesses.' If, however, 'you are a know-something investor, able to understand business economics and to find ... sensibly priced companies that possess important long-term competitive advantages, [then] conventional diversification makes no sense for you.'[13] To diversify far beyond fifteen to twenty securities in one's portfolio, then, is necessarily to lower one's standards and to buy less discriminately. To do so actually *increases* risk.

Clearly, then, value investors and advocates of EMT regard risk and diversification in mutually incompatible ways. To a value investor, investment risk has nothing whatever to do with price volatility and to equate the two produces absurdities. In 1974, for example, Berkshire Hathaway bought a substantial percentage of The Washington Post Company (TWPC). The price paid implied that TWPC, considered as a whole, would fetch $80 million if it were sold. Yet 'if you'd asked any one of 100 analysts how much the [entire] company was worth when we were buying it, no one would have argued with the fact that it was [actually] worth $400 million.' By Buffett's way of thinking, the price volatility of TWPC's shares enabled him at a propitious moment to buy them at a fraction of a businesslike assessment of their value. In effect, he was buying for 20¢ an asset widely acknowledged to be worth $1.00. According to the financial orthodoxy, the price volatility of TWPC's shares made their purchase a risky proposition—the greater these shares' price volatility and the lower their purchase price, the *riskier* the investment. As Buffett concluded incredulously, 'this is truly Alice in Wonderland. I never have been able to figure out why it's riskier to buy $400 million worth of properties for $40 million than $80 million.'[14] The market capitalisation of Berkshire's 'risky' stake in The Washington Post Company has subsequently fluctuated wildly—from $10.6 million in 1974 to $150 million in 1984, $419 million in 1994 and $1.4 billion in 2004.

Diversification: an 'Austrian' view

In sharp contrast to the mainstream's absurdity and obscurantism, the work of Frank Shostak is a deep breath of fresh air.[15] He uses concepts and reasoning, and derives conclusions, that Grahamites roundly applaud. According to Shostak, MPT implies that there is a sharp difference between investing in the stock market and investing in a business. However, as he points out, the stock market simply does not have a life of its own. The success or failure that stems from the purchase of a particular stock, in other words, depends upon the same factors that determine the success or failure of the underlying business. The purchase of some shares of X Ltd should therefore be regarded as an investment in X Ltd's business operations—and not as an investment in a 'stock'. By investing in a business, the purchaser of its stock has undertaken an entrepreneurial activity. She has, in other words, committed her capital with a view towards supplying consumers' most urgent needs.

In the real world, entrepreneurs and capitalists strive to invest such that their capital produces the goods and services (or produces the capital goods that in turn produce the consumer goods) that are most highly sought—and hence valued—by consumers. She who can best satisfy consumers' most urgent needs either directly or through more roundabout processes generates profits; and it is profit and profit alone that guides entrepreneurs. Investors thus strive to maintain and expand profits—and not, as EMH, MPT and the like assert, to minimise risk.

An entrepreneur's return on her investment is therefore determined not by how much risk she assumes; instead, it depends upon the extent to which she anticipates and serves consumers' wishes. According to Shostak, the fact that an entrepreneur invests in various businesses over time does not necessarily mean that she is attempting to reduce risk. She might diversify in order to boost her chances of earning profits. Indeed, the moment the reduction of risk rather than the attainment of the highest possible profit becomes the primary consideration underlying a series of investment operations, all manner of bizarre decisions tend to be made. Most notably, strictly following MPT, the 'investor' may deliberately buy an asset that loses money in order to reduce the portfolio's overall risk. Clearly, however, no sane investor deliberately does this. It is the emergence of conditions that have not been anticipated by the investor that leads to a bad investment.

Echoing Buffett and Fisher, Shostak notes that, in an attempt to minimise 'risk', practitioners of MPT tend to diversify their portfolios very widely. However, as we have discussed, increasing the number of entries in a portfolio necessarily leaves less and less time to analyse each component of the portfolio. In this sense, mainstream 'investment' is actually speculation of the type described in chapter 5. Shostak concludes:

> proponents of modern portfolio theory argue that diversification is the key to the creation of the best possible consistent returns. We argue that one must focus on the profitability of the investments in a portfolio before one considers their contribution to the portfolio's diversification. Consequently, whilst we agree with the general principle of diversification, we believe that the profitability of an individual investment should be the primary consideration for the investor.

BLOWING THE WHISTLE ON PROFESSORS AND POLITICIANS

What, ultimately, is wrong with the efficient markets hypothesis, modern portfolio theory and contemporary finance? Mainstream academics say—quite correctly—that market transactions are efficient; however, they are 'efficient' in a way that utterly escapes these theorists. Markets are efficient not relative to some abstract ideal, but because in the here-and-now they serve consumers better and more quickly than governments. Accordingly, and as a rough rule, the capitalisation of a company in a market that has not been corrupted by government intervention will not often deviate dramatically or for a long period of time from astute entrepreneurs' subjective estimates of its value. This is why the value investor is cautious and patient: precisely because Mr Market is so erratic, it pays to wait for him to offer you an attractively low quote. If he does not do so today, he will eventually. Alas, observing correctly that markets are *usually* efficient (by their abstract standard), the enthusiasts of EMT, MPT and all the rest conclude that markets are *always and constantly* efficient. In this instance, the difference between 'usually' and 'always and constantly' is the difference between night and day: 'strong form' efficiency is utterly absurd and 'weak form' efficiency was expressed much more coherently over a century ago.

The ultimate problem is that, like the mainstream economics that subsume and inspire it, EMT dismisses individuals, subjectivism and entrepreneurship to the sidelines.[16] To EMT's adherents, things like flesh-and-blood individuals, their inspirations, values, plans, passions, follies and the businesses they found, build and sometimes run into the ground—all of these things may just as well not exist. There are only aggregates, omniscient markets and benevolent governments, arid models, lifeless data and stylised behaviour. Mainstream academics study what is statistically measurable and 'model-able' rather than what is commercially meaningful. Hence there is no room for the inspired (or, for that matter, misguided) capitalists, investors and businesspeople whose behaviour does not conform to the straitjacket into which EMT tries to bind them. There is simply no room, in other words, for staunch individualists and mould-breakers like Benjamin Graham and Warren Buffett.

If the contemporary mainstream is correct then advanced mathematics and other technical expertise, computers and automatic pilots are essential—and historical perspective, qualitative judgment and cautious analyses of individual businesses, their operations and prospects are pointless. If the orthodoxy is correct then the confident 'rocket scientist' armed with a PhD is indispensable and the sceptical business owner–investor with skin in the game and a successful track record is superfluous. The mainstream attenuates the individual, the particular case, common sense and tacit knowledge, and accentuates the abstract, aggregate, technical and esoteric. In so doing, it encourages centralised decision making in the hands of a technocratic elite.

In a Keynesian world, elites of any stripe tend to be arrogant, error-prone and insulated from the consequences of their regular and occasionally mammoth blunders. As a result, the efficient markets theory, modern portfolio theory and the like actually encourage and facilitate risk-seeking behaviour, turmoil and the destruction of capital (as the Crash of 1987 and the Great Bubble amply demonstrated). Even elite decision-makers occasionally seem to agree. According to Timothy Geithner, president of the Federal Reserve Bank of New York (*The Wall Street Journal*, 15 April 2004), 'the same developments in financial technology that have improved the sophistication of risk management and the ability to transfer risk can ... at least for short periods of time amplify large moves in asset prices'.

We have finance academics to thank for EMT, business schools to thank for finance academics, universities to thank for business schools and politicians to thank for universities. Warren Buffett and his company's vice-chairman, Charles Munger, have for decades, and to various degrees, castigated them all. Buffett laments the fact that 'business schools reward difficult and complex behaviour more than simple behaviour, but simple behaviour is more effective'. Further, 'it has been helpful to me to have tens of thousands [of students] turned out of business schools taught that it didn't do any good to think.' Munger describes modern portfolio theory as 'a type of dementia that I can't even classify'.[17]

At the 2002 annual general meeting of Wesco Financial Corp., which he chairs, Munger intensified his fusillade, saying he believed that there was much wrong with universities, and that if he could he would disband everything but the hard sciences. Obviously, he is in no position to do so, and nobody else is going to do it, so these pernicious defects are likely to persist indefinitely. 'It's amazing how wrongheaded [the teaching is]. There is fatal disconnectedness. You have these squirrelly people in each department who don't see the big picture.' Generalising his point, Munger acknowledged that this perversity does not just occur within universities. Companies, too, are balkanised. 'Look at what happened at Arthur Andersen and Enron. They weren't all bad people, but their cultures were dysfunctional. It's easy to create such a culture, in which you have good people but terrible results.

Many areas of government are dysfunctional. Universities are complicit. They don't feel guilty about the product they're producing ...'[18]

The hordes of cookie-cutter MBAs and investment professionals who have swallowed efficient markets dogma make value investors' lives much easier than they otherwise would be. In any sort of contest—financial, mental or physical—it is a great advantage to have opponents who have been taught, in effect, that it is useless to think. In a game of bridge, you stand to benefit if the opposing team refuses even to look at its cards. In order to cement this advantage, Buffett and Munger have publicly pondered whether they should endow chairs to ensure the perpetual teaching of EMT and MPT.[19]

The value investor, then, is acutely aware that the financial world is rife with false, destructive and plainly crazy notions propounded by the great and the powerful. These ideas, whether expressed in their military, economic or financial variants, possess much in common: they strive to commandeer others' property, centralise decision making in elites' hands and generate interventionist policies. These elites' unspoken motto is 'we're smarter than you and we know better than you do what's good for you; so shut up, step aside, hand over your money and let us work our wonders'. Vastly overestimating their intelligence, underestimating the brains of the general public, flouting the laws of human action and lacking any meaningful feedback mechanism, these arrogant elites' policies almost always cause great damage.[20]

NOTES

1   In his 1988 'Letter to Shareholders', Warren Buffett denounced academic 'witch doctors' who peddled 'arcane formulae' and 'techniques shrouded in mystery'. To this day, scarcely any business school in the US (or Australia) uses Benjamin Graham's texts—or even mentions them to students. Buffett's scepticism

of philanthropy has been influenced by his jaundiced views about universities. One biographer noted, 'As [Buffett] saw it, [universities spent money] in ways that did not enhance the students' educations, and the professors had it rather easy. This soured him on higher education.' A colleague observed, 'Warren would rather choke to death than write a cheque to a university.' (See Roger Lowenstein, *Buffett: The Making of an American Capitalist*, Weidenfeld & Nicolson, 1996, p. 343).

2   Sequoia Fund, quarterly report, 31 March 1996, cited in Robert Hagstrom, *The Warren Buffett Portfolio*, p. 70.

3   Clear and concise analyses that appeared during the 1970s include Richard Ebeling's *The Austrian Theory of the Trade Cycle* (Ludwig von Mises Institute, 1978, 1996) and Murray Rothbard's *For a New Liberty* (Fox & Wilkes, 1973, 1996), chapter 9.

4   These and other articles have been reprinted in Janet Lowe, *The Rediscovered Benjamin Graham: Selected Writings of the Wall Street Legend* (John Wiley & Sons, 1999).

5   The efficient markets hypothesis (EMH) takes three forms. The 'strong' version holds that at any given time the market prices of securities are 'efficient'. A stock's price, in other words, always reflects all that is known about a company. If this were true, (among other things) 'inside' information would be useless and market regulators would be chasing their tails. Further, if the prices of stocks were unerringly 'correct' then debate about prices would be superfluous and people would consider their investments as 'safe' as demand deposits in a bank. The 'semi-strong' form asserts that prices fully reflect all *publicly available* information. If this were true, then conducting analyses and valuations of companies would be pointless. The 'weaker' versions of EMH posit that: (1) past prices (and 'performance') are not a reliable guide to future prices and performance (which is unquestionably true—otherwise the market truly would be efficient in the 'strong' sense); and (2) given the efforts of large numbers of market participants, facts about a public company's operations are 'rapidly' reflected in the price of its stock. The trouble is that many of today's proponents of EMH claim to support only 'weaker' versions—which say nothing that Austrian School economists did not already say much more insightfully more than a century ago—yet act as if the 'strong' version were true.

6   For clear introductions to this massive and arcane literature, see Burton G. Malkiel, *A Random Walk Down Wall Street* (W.W. Norton, 2004); Robert Hagstrom, *The Warren Buffett Portfolio*, chapter 2; and Roger Lowenstein, *Buffett: The Making of an American Capitalist*, chapter 17.

7   Peter Bernstein, *Capital Ideas: The Improbable Origins of Modern Wall Street* (The Free Press, 1993), p. 13.

8   John Train, *The Midas Touch: The Strategies that Have Made Warren Buffett America's Pre-eminent Investor* (Harper & Row, 1987), p. 50.

9   For very clear and informative elaborations of this fundamental point, see two excellent books by Roger Lowenstein: *Origins of the Crash: The Great Bubble and Its Undoing* (Penguin Press, 2004); and *When Genius Failed: The Rise and Fall of Long-Term Capital Management* (Random House, 2001).

10   See Richard Brealey and Stewart Myers, *Principles of Corporate Finance*, 2nd ed. (McGraw-Hill, 1984), pp. 266, 272–273; and also its 4th ed. (McGraw-Hill, 1991), pp. 297–300, 310.

11   Andrei Shleifer, *Inefficient Markets: An Introduction to Behavioral Finance* (Oxford University Press, 2000), p. 197.

12   Philip A. Fisher, *Common Stocks and Uncommon Profits and Other Writings by Philip A. Fisher* (John Wiley & Sons, 1996), pp. 108–109.

13   Quoted in Janet Lowe, *Warren Buffett Speaks: Wit and Wisdom from the World's Greatest Investor* (John Wiley & Sons, 1997) p. 160 and Robert Hagstrom, *The Warren Buffett Portfolio* (John Wiley & Sons, 1999), pp. 9, 32.

14   Warren Buffett, 'The Superinvestors of Graham-and-Doddsville' (reprinted in *The Intelligent Investor*, pp. 537–560).

15   Frank Shostak, 'Diversification: An Austrian View' (Ludwig von Mises Institute, Daily Article, 1 November 2000).

16   See in particular Frank Shostak, 'In Defense of Fundamental Analysis: A Critique of the Efficient Market Hypothesis', *Review of Austrian Economics*, vol. 10, no. 2 (1997), pp. 27–45 and EC Pasour, 'The Efficient-Markets Hypothesis and Entrepreneurship', *Review of Austrian Economics*, vol. 3, no. 1 (1989), pp. 95–107.

17   Janet Lowe, *Warren Buffett Speaks*, p. 94.

18   Source: notes taken at Wesco's 2002 annual general meeting, available at: <www.tilsonfunds.com/wscmtg02notes.html>.

19   Robert Hagstrom, *The Warren Buffett Portfolio*, p. 34.

20   See the reading list in chapter 14 for details.

Chapter 9

◇◇◇◇◇◇◇◇◇◇◇◇◇◇◇◇◇◇◇◇◇◇◇◇◇◇◇◇◇◇

Beware institutional and bureaucratic imperatives

[Groupthink is] a quick and easy way to refer to a mode of thinking that people engage in when they are deeply involved in a cohesive in-group [and] when the members' strivings for unanimity override their motivation to realistically appraise alternative courses of action ... Groupthink refers to a deterioration of mental efficiency, reality testing, and moral judgment that results from in-group pressures ...

Irving Janis,
Victims of Groupthink: A Psychological Study of Foreign-Policy Decisions and Fiascos
(1972)

As staunch individualists, Grahamite value investors are well positioned to resist what Irving Janis called 'groupthink' and to withstand what Warren Buffett has dubbed 'the institutional imperative'. This is the tendency, endemic within committees and small groups and often present in a milder form throughout organisations, to imitate others' behaviour—no matter how absurd or destructive it might be. This tendency is particularly marked during booms and busts. When they are members of teams, in other words, people do things that they would never countenance as individuals. To defy the institutional imperative is, when applied to the allocation of capital, to ignore the crowd and committee, embrace individual self-reliance and invest on the basis of reason and enduring value rather than emotion and current popularity.

OF LEMMINGS, TEENAGERS AND INVESTMENT-BY-COMMITTEE

Lemmings are mouse-like rodents that live in Arctic regions of North America and Eurasia. Depending upon the presence of predators, availability of food, vagaries of climate and other factors, their populations fluctuate enormously. Under ideal conditions (which occur every three to seven years), a local population of lemmings can increase ten-fold in a single year. These population explosions resemble the comparatively rare mouse plagues that occur in warmer climes. When the lemmings have exhausted the local food supply, they disperse—like moose, beaver and many other animals that inhabit their environment.

Their migration begins slowly and erratically. Small numbers move at night; larger groups, finding strength in numbers, roam during daylight hours. They do not form a continuous mass. Instead, they travel in 'convoys' with gaps of ten minutes or more separating each group. They tend to follow roads and natural paths, avoid water and seek land crossings, but if they must, they will swim. They can cross a 200-metre body of calm water, but most will drown in tides or winds. In the mountains of Scandinavia and the north slope of Alaska, large numbers of lemmings have been observed approaching a body of water, temporarily stopping and accumulating so densely along the shore that some are forced into the water. When they get wet to the skin, they quickly die.

This dramatic mass dispersal and accidental death is neither instinctive nor deliberate mass suicide.[1] Its true cause remains a mystery. After almost a century of research, scientists have clues why their populations occasionally fluctuate so wildly. Various factors (such as change in weather and climate and the availability of food, the density of predators, infectious diseases and sunspots) have been advanced; each, however, is at best a partial explanation of the phenomenon.

Many market participants, including major institutions, sometimes act like lemmings, though with one significant difference: the consequences of their movements tend to harm others more than themselves. Every several years, something causes many people to 'migrate' from one segment of the market towards another. More generally, and whether it occurs in an acute or chronic form, the underlying tendency of many market participants is to gossip incessantly, form groups and mimic the actions of 'leaders'; that is, to buy what market leaders are buying and sell what they are selling. In 1989, Warren Buffett recalled to his shareholders the most surprising thing he discovered after he had completed his studies and entered the real world was the pervasive importance of what he called 'the institutional imperative'. Initially, he was not only unaware of its importance, he did not even know that it existed. He assumed that managers were invariably intelligent and experienced, and therefore that their deliberations and decisions would automatically be based upon evidence and reasoning. He soon realised, though, that we do not inhabit this kind of world. 'Instead, rationality frequently wilts when the institutional imperative comes into play.'

In particular, Buffett uncovered four principles that influence the behaviour of individuals within large corporations. The first is a commercial counterpart of Newton's First Law of Motion: executives will resist any change of their companies' current direction. The second is a business extension of Boyle's Law: just as work expands to fill available time, corporate projects materialise to use up any and all available money. Thirdly, subordinates respond positively to any notion — no matter how obviously foolish — of senior executives. The bosses' desire to buy another company, for example, is almost invariably 'substantiated' by a seemingly rigorous study prepared by underlings. Finally, and to use another analogy, most business executives are not fundamentally different from angst-ridden and peer-conscious teenagers. Most notably, if a 'leading' company is acquiring, selling, merging, demerging, plunging into e-commerce (or whatever is the present fad), then other companies in its industry will often strive to imitate it.

Consequently, most executives, funds managers and other market participants are prepared to be wrong—indeed, they are quite happy to be wrong—in the company of others. Buying blue chips at inflated prices is not risky from the point of view of managers' job security and career prospects (even when the buyers suspect they are paying too much) *as long as most others are also buying them.* For managers, if not for the people whose money they invest, these companies are safe at any price. Few if any funds managers get the sack for buying Telstra. In sharp contrast, people are usually very reluctant to run the risk of being right alone. This is because the kudos that accrue to a funds manager who buys an unloved company that subsequently rises from the ashes is more than outweighed by the disapprobation that befalls him if this company falls further rather than rises. In business and funds management and many other pursuits, there is strength in numbers. Hence mediocrity loves company and conformity is safety.[2] As a species, lemmings are (often, it seems, unfairly) ridiculed, but no individual lemming is ever identified and lambasted. The rational thing to do, from the point of view of an individual member of a team or a group, is therefore to kowtow to the consensus—even if the majority is proposing or doing something silly.

The trouble, of course, is that within large companies most decisions tend to be made by teams or committees, and the larger the organisation the greater the tyranny of the committee. Teams and groups, in turn, encourage and insidiously enforce conformity to certain conventions of thought and behaviour; and in so doing they suppress individuality and creativity.[3] Within a closely knit group, standard practice (whether it is sensible or not) tends to be rewarded. Independent thinking that gainsays the consensus and challenges the group's cohesion is discouraged and sometimes punished (no matter how firmly justified by logic and evidence). What managers seem to fear most is not so much the possibility of being wrong but rather the possibility of being out of step. Given the perverse institutional incentives they face, for most funds managers the risk to their careers is more salient than the risk to their clients' money. To adhere closely to the consensus and thereby to fail conventionally is a rational and sensible route.

THE INSTITUTIONAL IMPERATIVE IN DETAIL

At some point, virtually everybody must become a member of a group or team. Perhaps on the assumption that two or more heads are better than one, people generally consider that groups will make better decisions than individuals. Accordingly, businesses, non-profit organisations and governments from local to national levels rely heavily upon teams and committees to make decisions. Yet people acting in small groups do not always make good decisions. Quite the contrary: they often make mediocre and occasionally disastrous choices. Juries, for example, not infrequently render verdicts that contradict the evidence presented. Political cabinets and civic groups regularly adopt nonsensical stances and obstinately refuse to acknowledge their ramifications; and boards of directors, military strategists and myriad other groups constantly concoct plans that are clearly ill conceived.[4]

A paradox also presents itself: powerful groups and committees having access to the best brains, information and other resources are disproportionately likely to make choices (including the decision to do nothing) leading to failure or even disaster. Examples include the attack on Pearl Harbour (from both American and Japanese points of view), the formulation and implementation of the Marshall Plan, the outbreak of the Korean War, the attack on Cuba at the Bay of Pigs and the Cuban missile crisis, the Vietnam War, various 'wars' on poverty, drugs and terrorism, Watergate, the Challenger space shuttle explosion and the attacks on the World Trade Center and Pentagon.[5]

Irving Janis (1918–1990), a psychologist at Yale University, analysed many of the abovementioned events. He was puzzled by the tendency of groups of seemingly accomplished, intelligent, energetic and well-resourced people to make poor and even ruinous decisions. One of the causes of this phenomenon, he discovered, was a condition he termed 'groupthink'. His book, *Victims of Groupthink* (1972), presented a series of detailed studies of American foreign-policy decisions. A feature of these decisions — and, more generally, of decision making within small groups — is the emergence of intense pressures upon a group's members towards conformity. These pressures seriously restrict the range of options considered, bias the collection and analysis of information and promote overconfidence, self-righteous stereotyping and the denigration of outsiders. These pressures distort decision making and generate poor decisions. In this research, which he continued until the end of his life, Janis also identified personality-based, organisational and political processes that can exacerbate groupthink.

The crux of groupthink is that members of 'in-groups' conform to certain attitudes and behaviour. Within these groups and wider organisations, a distinct way of 'thinking and doing things round here' tends to exist. In extreme situations, individuals surrender their individuality and become willing to make sacrifices in order to maintain their membership of and identification with the group. The implicit requirement that members alter their views and neuter their behaviour causes the group (often despite its individual members' better judgment) to make poor decisions.

Symptoms of groupthink

Janis organised the symptoms of groupthink into three categories. The first type is characterised by an overestimation of group members' power, intelligence and morality. Its symptoms include a feeling of invulnerability. This illusion creates excessive optimism among members of the group and encourages them to discount risks. Another symptom is an unquestioned faith in the morality of the group and its 'vision' or 'mission'. This belief encourages members to ignore the moral consequences of their actions and decisions—and to denounce outsiders who dare to question them. Committees that succumb to groupthink may enthusiastically plan and execute fiascos. Yet all the while, their members are serenely happy and confident; accordingly, they proceed boldly and with the unshakeable conviction that (damn the ignorant and malicious critics!) everything is working well and will conclude triumphantly.

The distinguishing feature of the second type of groupthink is closed-mindedness. Most noteworthy among this cluster of symptoms are committee members' strenuous efforts to ridicule, rationalise and discount warnings or other discordant information or reasoning that might lead to a reconsideration of their plans and decisions. During the Great Bubble, sceptics 'just didn't get it'. Members of groups deluded by groupthink believe that their plans have no flaws. Because 'Plan A' cannot go or has not gone awry—even if there is mounting evidence to the contrary—there is no need for any backup 'Plan B'.

Further, members of such groups respond to opponents not with logic and evidence but with a mixture of suspicion, hostility and derision. They are insulated to a considerable extent from external influences (and tend to bear little or no personal cost for their errors of judgment). As a result, members of these committees tend to adopt and rationalise ideas that flatly contradict reality. Other symptoms of this second type of groupthink also include stereotyped views of 'opposition' leaders and members. 'Enemies' are too misguided or malevolent to warrant genuine attempts to negotiate; or they are too weak or decadent or stupid to counter or even understand the committee's plans, actions and decisions. Disdain for those who are not members of the group, and an absence of creativity spurred by influences from and interactions with other groups, are characteristic of groups within which groupthink prevails.

Finally, the hallmark of the third type of groupthink is the pressure towards uniformity that each member of the committee imposes upon the others. Members of such committees:

- self-censor any deviation from the consensus and are inclined to minimise the importance of whatever doubts they might privately possess or counterarguments that they or others might mount

- overestimate the extent of the group's consensus, majority or unanimous view (this misjudgment results partly from each member's self-censorship and partly from the false assumption that the silence of others means consent by others)

- pressure any other member who questions any of the group's stereotypes, illusions or commitments

- make it clear to any dissenter that any difference with another member is disloyalty towards all members (or to the organisation as a whole)

- strive to 'protect' other members of the group from adverse information that might weaken these members' confidence about the effectiveness and morality of the group's attitudes and decisions.

Self-censorship occurs when group members do not share their own ideas with the rest of the group because they fear that their ideas will be rejected. The resultant illusion of unanimity within such groups explains why silence is often interpreted as agreement, and why each member is reluctant to challenge the group's 'consensus'. Through self-censorship, the imposition of pressure and the veiled threat of sanctions upon dissenters, the group develops the facade of unanimity.

Consequences of groupthink

Clearly, the more cohesive the group the greater is the resultant risk of groupthink; and the greater the risk of groupthink, the higher is the resultant probability of poor processes and bad—even catastrophic—decisions. In a cohesive group, members become increasingly reluctant to say or do anything that goes against the grain. Under these conditions, the number of internal debates and the extent of contingency planning—which are essentials of good decisions—decrease. Groupthink is also disproportionately likely to afflict privileged groups. The anointed members of such groups attempt to isolate themselves from, and regard themselves as morally and intellectually superior to, non-members. Elites tend to associate only with fellow elites. Their backgrounds and educations are similar; they tend to congregate in the same suburbs; they send their children to the same schools; and they socialise together. As a result, their biases and prejudices are alike and tend to reinforce one another.

Further, when members of a unified group must deal with tight deadlines and financial constraints, or carry out their work under other similar pressures, the risk of groupthink rises. In response to such pressures, members often alleviate their discomfort by choosing a plan of action that minimises debate and dissent. In their discussions, members then rationalise this course of action by exaggerating the likelihood that it will have positive consequences, underplaying the possibility that it will have bad or unintended consequences, concentrating on minor details and studiously ignoring larger risks and issues. Members of such a group no longer think clearly. Their specification of objectives and survey of alternatives tend to be incomplete; their acquisition and consideration of information is selective; they neither examine the risks of options nor reappraise initially rejected alternatives; and they fail to devise contingency plans.

In short, when a group succumbs to groupthink its members commit themselves prematurely to a faulty plan of action—and do not waver from it. According to Janis, when a group demonstrates many or all of the symptoms of groupthink, its members perform their collective tasks enthusiastically but ineffectively; and as a result of their desire to achieve consensus, they usually fail to attain their collective objectives.

This, then, is the explanation for the nearly uniformly positive—and greatly mistaken—assessments by 'experts' of dotcoms, BHP, News Corp. and Telstra, and a variety of other financial matters, during the past several years. It is the groups, teams and committees that pervade most investment institutions; their relatively homogenous and consciously 'expert' and 'elite' composition; the intense pressure towards uniformity faced by their members; these members' confidence about their intelligence and self-assurance about their morality; their apparent closed-mindedness to other—particularly conflicting—ideas, premises, arguments and evidence; and the time, financial or other pressures imposed by the 'boom' of the late 1990s and the 'bust' of the new century.

Antidotes to groupthink

Irving Janis proposed several ways to combat groupthink. Suitably modified, five apply directly to investors and investment operations:

1. It is very useful to have an irascible and pain-in-the-backside partner who airs objections, doubts and generally plays the role of an 'abominable no-man'. Benjamin Graham had his Jerome Newman and Warren Buffett has his Charles Munger. The success of this division of labour depends upon one partner's willingness to accept constructive criticism from the other and to voice rather than mute disagreement. It also succeeds in direct proportion to the extent that both partners hate losing money.

2. Each partner should also assess the feasibility and effectiveness of alternatives independently of the other. Only when each has reached a tentative conclusion should they talk (preferably via telephone rather than face to face) in order to consider any

differences with respect to an appropriate course of action. During such discussions, one of the two should consciously adopt the role of devil's advocate.

3. Each partner should regularly ask: 'In this situation, and given the information to hand, what would Graham have done? What would Buffett do?'

4. Value investors work independently, but they must not become hermits. That is, they should read voraciously from a wide variety of sources and maintain contact with a wide variety of acquaintances, discussing matters of general interest and encouraging others constructively to challenge their views. Like all of us, value investors make mistakes; but unlike many of us, they analyse these mistakes and try to learn from them so that over time they become less likely to repeat them.

5. After reaching a preliminary conclusion about a particular course of action, investment partners should hold a 'second chance' (tele)conference at which each expresses as frankly as possible any residual doubts and rethinks the entire issue before making a final choice.

The institutional imperative, it bears repeating, is the tendency to imitate others' behaviour — no matter how demonstrably silly or self-destructive it might be. This tendency is virtually always present, if not prevalent, within large organisations, and is particularly marked during extreme or pressure-laden times. In an investment setting, pressured times are typically booms or busts. The cause of groupthink is the abandonment of individuality to a group, team or committee. Hence its antidote is not more intelligence or training. Nor is its conquest a matter of access to complex mathematical models, larger amounts of statistical data and forecasts generated from them. The antidote to groupthink is decentralisation, individuality and the cultivation of a particular temperament. The investor who recognises that much of what she hears and reads is noise, but strives to find and separate wheat from chaff, one who ultimately takes her own counsel and recognises that prominent and powerful people can have soft minds and clay feet, is the investor who is well-equipped to withstand the institutional imperative.

For these reasons and more besides, Graham-style value investors, unlike most market participants (particularly major institutional participants), are staunch individualists. They work with one or a handful of others and virtually never within large organisations. Given their individualist bent, they seek and analyse primary sources of information (such as companies' financial statements) and discount secondary sources (such as gossip and media reports). They also draw a sharp distinction between the rationality and the popularity of a proposed course of action. In sharp contrast to committees afflicted with groupthink, investors tend to make decisions by acquiring information, weighing alternatives, debating costs and benefits, asking questions, entertaining and retaining doubts, seeking countervailing information and soliciting feedback and criticism. Like Ralph Waldo Emerson, so too the value investor: 'It is easy in the world to live after the world's opinion ... but the great man is he who in the midst of the crowd keeps with perfect sweetness the independence of solitude.'

NOTES

1   In 1958, as part of its *True Life Adventure* series, Walt Disney produced 'White Wilderness'. Filmed in Alberta (not a lemming habitat) with rodents transported from Manitoba, it featured a segment that described lemmings' alleged compulsion to mass suicide. According to a 1983 investigation by the Canadian Broadcasting Corporation, the suicide scenes were faked. The lemmings supposedly killing themselves by leaping into the ocean were actually thrown from a cliff by members of the film crew. (Alberta, by the way, is a landlocked province.) The epic mass-

suicide scene—the source of an enduring urban myth—was staged using careful editing, tight camera angles and a few dozen lemmings running on a snow-covered lazy-Susan style turntable. I believed in the mass suicide of lemmings myself until Anthony Stone of John Wiley & Sons Australia brought it to my attention that this was a myth. This story provides a salutary lesson: investment research that takes conventional wisdom for granted and thus does not dig sufficiently deeply can lead to embarrassment, financial loss and other undesirable outcomes.

2   A politician (of course) expressed what is probably the ultimate position on this point. Defending an allegedly mediocre man whose appointment to the bench was being considered, Senator Roman Hruska (Republican, Nebraska USA, who beat a certain Howard Buffett, father of Warren, to the post) said 'even if he were mediocre, there are a lot of mediocre judges and people and lawyers. They are entitled to a little representation, aren't they, and a little chance?' Quoted in Lawrence Baum, *The Supreme Court* (Congressional Quarterly Press, 1981), p. 47.

3   'Groupthink and You', (Daily Article, Ludwig von Mises Institute, 23 August 2001) by Karen de Coster and Brad Edmonds is an excellent summary of the baleful influence of 'teamwork' upon business school curriculums and students. More generally, apart from the King James Bible, it is very doubtful whether any formally constituted committee has ever contributed anything of lasting significance to English-speaking civilisation. Yes, the Constitutional Convention of 1787 and its associated committees helped to produce the US Constitution. But that document owes most to two individuals—Charles Pinckney and James Madison—who separately prepared draft constitutions before the Convention. Furthermore, the Constitution has not endured: Abraham Lincoln mortally wounded it; it has probably been a dead letter since the presidency of Woodrow Wilson; and it has certainly been so since Franklin Roosevelt's New Deal (see the references in chapter 14). America has not had a great president—that is, a stalwart defender of the Constitution—since Grover Cleveland; and it has not had a tolerable president—one who grudgingly respected the Constitution—since Warren Harding and Calvin Coolidge. Grover Cleveland avoided committees; bad presidents have tended to embrace them.

4   Clearly, the actions of mobs led by silver-tongued shysters can have calamitous consequences—see John Mackay's classic *Extraordinary Delusions and the Madness of Crowds* (Templeton Foundation

Press, 1999). Yet large numbers of individuals acting in free and unfettered markets regularly derive solutions that individuals acting alone cannot. See in particular James Surowiecki, *The Wisdom of Crowds: Why the Many Are Smarter than the Few and How Collective Wisdom Shapes Business, Economies, Societies and Nations* (Doubleday, 2004).

5   These examples hardly imply that governments possess a monopoly on calamity: a very lengthy list of private sector catastrophes could be assembled with ease. In 2002, AOL–Time Warner alone generated losses that competed in magnitude with America's monthly deficit of external trade; and past losses by News Ltd have surpassed Australia's monthly deficits.

Part III

Five blessings

Chairman:

When you find a special situation and you decide, just for illustration, that you can buy for ten and it is worth thirty, and you take a position, and then you cannot realise it until a lot of other people decide it is worth thirty, how is that process brought about — by advertising, or what happens?

What causes a cheap stock to find its value?

Graham:

That is one of the mysteries of our business, and it is a mystery to me as well as to everybody else. [But] we know from experience that eventually the market catches up with value.

Benjamin Graham
Testimony to the Committee on
Banking and Commerce,
US Senate
(11 March 1955)

Chapter 10

◇◇◇◇◇◇◇◇◇◇◇◇◇◇◇◇◇◇◇◇◇◇◇◇◇

'Base rates' and regression to the mean

As a protection against financial illusion or insanity, [historical] memory is far better than law. When [in the early 1970s, late 1980s and late 1990s] the memory of the 1929 disaster failed, law and regulation no longer sufficed. For protecting people from the cupidity of others and [themselves], history is highly utilitarian. It sustains memory and memory serves the same purpose as [government regulators] and, on the record, is far more effective.

John Kenneth Galbraith
The Great Crash of 1929 (1997 edition)

The introduction to Benjamin Graham's autobiography states that he 'came to his convictions after long, searching and realistic meditations about history, garnered from extensive reading and daily immersion in the intricate values-testing of Wall Street'. His student and colleague, Warren Buffett, spends many hours reading a variety of publications and massive quantities of financial statements. Buffett's vice-chairman, Charles Munger, told his biographer:

> both Warren and I learn more from the great business magazines than we do [from] anywhere else … If

165

> you get into the mental habit of relating what you're
> reading to the basic structure of the underlying ideas
> being demonstrated, you gradually accumulate some
> wisdom about investing. I don't think you can get to
> be a really good investor over a broad range without
> doing a massive amount of reading.'[1]

Value investors read in order to accumulate a reliable base of historical background information. Good decisions require hard facts. One way to acquire them is to conduct one's affairs by trial and error and, over the years, learn from one's inevitable mistakes. However, hardly any of today's investors have directly experienced the full range of conditions, from boom to bust and exuberance to despondency, that have occurred since (say) the 1920s. Fortunately, there is a quicker and less painful way to acquire wisdom. Diligent study of the historical record, and of approaches to business and investment that pass the stiff test imposed by that record, provide the best indirect substitute for lack of direct experience.

Critical reading also helps to inculcate a healthy scepticism in dealing with the large amount of information, misinformation and outright falsehood that we all encounter during the course of our normal daily activities. Making justifiable decisions in the face of uncertainty requires caution, disbelief and a basic sense of humility. Wide reading, says Richard FitzHerbert, provides 'the necessary background and historical depth to facilitate unemotional judgments of the various ideas, advice, opinions and "recommendations" with which investors are bombarded ... The most important lesson of history is that investors who fail to study history are ill-equipped for their task.'[2]

ODDS ARE, YOU HAVE NO IDEA WHAT THE ODDS ARE

When considering options and making decisions, people often immerse themselves in the details of the particular and present situation and neglect the general characteristics of large numbers of similar past situations. These general characteristics and past experiences can help to guide particular choices in the present.[3] In practice, however, decision-makers often overlook them.

Imagine that you have just moved into a suburb close to a large university. You have not yet met your next-door neighbour, Robert, but you have met others who know him. They tell you that he is thirty years of age and describe him as shy, kind and helpful, fastidious and meticulous. Which is more likely to be Robert's occupation: retail salesperson or librarian?

Given the paucity and the unknown accuracy of the information about Robert, what should you do? The answer is that you should discount the information you have been given (or perhaps even ignore it) and concentrate upon more reliable general information. Most notably, at the 2001 Census there were more than 750,000 people employed in retail sales but only about 8,500 librarians in Australia. The words that a single neighbour uses to describe Robert conform to many people's stereotypical conception of a librarian. A range of experiments has shown that most people do in fact take these words as their cue and therefore decide that Robert is more likely to be a librarian. Statistically, however, an Australian selected at random is *eighty-eight times* more likely to work in retail sales than in a library. Given the small amount and unsubstantiated nature of our specific information about him (the 'case rate'), and the much more reliable generalisation that sales workers are far more numerous than librarians (the 'base rate'), the base rate should figure heavily in any decision about Robert's occupation.

Ignoring statistical and historical generalisations and focusing upon unusual and memorable events and vivid images in the present greatly increases the likelihood that resultant decisions—including investment decisions—will be poor. The next time somebody tries to praise the merits of a particular 'biotech' firm, for example, the sensible response—unless you are a specialist in the field—is to zip your wallet and run. Why? Consider two relevant base rates. First, since the first biotechnology company was listed on the New York Stock Exchange in the 1970s, in the US alone more than US$100 billion has been ploughed into this sector. Second, this tsunami of capital has wrought a cumulative net loss of more than US$40 billion and a rate of loss that has accelerated over time.[4] Yes, it is possible that a randomly selected *individual* biotech will be an excellent investment; in general, however, *biotechs as a class* do not generate profits. Biotechnology has no doubt dispensed benefits, but the recipients of these benefits have not, by and large, included biotech firms' shareholders.

Similarly, do not remind Warren Buffett about the airline industry. In particular, do not remind him about his investment in USAir in the 1980s. From the moment in 1903 when Wilbur Wright first flew a heavier-than-air machine at Kitty Hawk, North Carolina, the air transport business in the US has made no money. Its cumulative loss has also run into the tens of billions. 'If there had been a capitalist at Kitty Hawk, the guy should have shot down Wilbur. [His triumph] was one small step for mankind and one huge step back for capitalism.'[5] Does this mean that you should never buy a biotech or airline? No. It just means that doing so is, in effect, swimming against a strong tide.

Initial public offerings or 'IPOs' are another case in point. When considering an IPO, certainly study the company's prospectus, but also ask yourself, based upon the historical record, how likely is an investment in an IPO to fare well? The answer to this question will likely sour you against the vast majority of floats. The same is true of most mergers and acquisitions. Only when you have grounds to conclude that a case rate comprehensively trumps a base rate does such an investment make sense. By their very nature, these instances are few and far between.

HEREDITY AND VALUE INVESTING

Sir Francis Galton (1822–1911), a cousin of Charles Darwin, was keenly interested in heredity and not at all in business and finance. Yet his studies of 'the average ancestral type' uncovered a statistical regularity that provides a basis for Grahamite value investing. In an analysis of the heights of parents and their children, he found that tall parents tended to bear tall children and that short parents tended to bear short children. Heredity clearly plays an important role in determining a child's potential height, but it does so in a counterintuitive way: on average, Galton noted, the offspring of tall parents were not as tall as their parents; and the offspring of short parents were not as short as their parents. These and other experiments led him to formulate a principle that has become known as *regression to the mean* (or *reversion to the mean*). According to Galton, 'reversion is the tendency of the ideal mean filial type to depart from the parental type, reverting to what may be roughly and perhaps fairly described as the average ancestral type'. If this process did not exist—if, for example, sweet pea plants grown from large peas produced ever-larger peas and pea plants grown from small peas produced ever-smaller offspring—the world would eventually comprise naught but midgets and giants. (Sweet pea plants were the focus of another of Galton's studies.) With every passing generation, nature would produce fewer average and more extreme specimens.[6]

Regression to the mean occurs in financial markets.[7] It occurs at both individual and aggregate levels; that is, with respect to both individual securities and markets as a whole. Using data for the period 1926 to 1982, Werner De Bondt and Richard Thaler studied the securities of companies whose prices had either increased or decreased more than the market average over a three-year interval. They found that significant movements in the opposite direction subsequently followed these extreme movements of price. If investors are either unduly optimistic or pessimistic about a particular company's securities, and if that company's fundamentals remain unchanged, then after some decent interval the investors' stance was likely to reverse.[8]

Very fashionable stocks and market segments thus become less exalted, and highly unfashionable companies and sectors return to average favour. 'Many shall be restored that are now fallen and many Shall fall that are now in honour.' This line, from the Roman poet Horace's *Ars Poetica*, appeared opposite the title page of Benjamin Graham's seminal text *Security Analysis*. Graham gave it such a prominent place, I believe, because the crowd's exaggerated reactions occasionally offer tremendous opportunities to investors prepared to stand apart from the group. If a sound company's stock is savaged by pessimists such that its price falls considerably below a cautious estimate of its value, *as long as the company's operations and prospects remain sound*, the price of its securities will tend eventually to recover. Conversely, if a company's shares rise well above a reasonable estimate of value, *even when its operations and prospects remain unchanged*, at some point they will fall from their exalted status. As with children and peas in a pod, so too with companies: it cannot be otherwise. If it were, then the economic and financial landscape would comprise companies with either colossal or microscopic market capitalisations but virtually no medium-sized enterprises.

The simple and powerful notion of regression to the mean underpins many sound decisions, and for good reason: there are few situations in which large things continue without interruption to become infinitely large and small things become infinitesimally small. Trees grow upwards but never reach the heavens. Accordingly, when we are tempted—as we so often are—to extrapolate trends from the recent past into the indefinite future, we should recall Horace and Sir Francis's humble sweet peas.

Of course, a strong dose of caution is also necessary. If regression to the mean is so pervasive, then why is forecasting such a frustrating (and ultimately useless) activity? I believe it is because the forces at work in nature are not the same as the forces at work between people's ears. The accuracy of most financial forecasts depends more upon decisions made by people than the laws of nature; and nature, with all its vagaries, is much steadier than Mr Market or than committees trying to reach a consensus.

'Base rates' and regression to the mean

There are three reasons why regression to the mean can be a fallible and frustrating guide to investment decisions. First, regression can proceed at an unexpectedly and unpredictably slow pace. Second, the regression may be so forceful that matters do not come to rest once they regress to the mean; rather, they 'overshoot' before—eventually—fluctuating erratically around the historical average. Finally, and perhaps most importantly, the mean itself may be subject to slow (evolution) or sudden (revolution) change. In other words, a new base rate that we cannot anticipate and hence presently know little or nothing about may supplant yesterday's base rate.

SOME BASE RATES FOR VALUE INVESTORS

Bearing previous caveats in mind, the intelligent investor can use these two essential concepts—base rates and mean regression—to derive a series of expectations to assist her investment operations. The first batch of base rates investors should keep in mind is summarised in table 10.1, overleaf.

I have already noted that the value investor has two objectives. The first is to preserve her wealth—that is, to protect the purchasing power of her capital. To do this, she must compound this capital more quickly than the rate of consumer price inflation. The second objective is to build wealth—that is, to invest her capital in a portfolio of securities whose rate of return (given cautious assumptions) can reasonably be expected to exceed that offered by a benchmark such as a five-year Commonwealth Government bond. When attractive securities are difficult to locate, she accumulates cash until securities become available at attractive prices.

What is a reasonable ('benchmark') investment result? That depends upon the investor's time frame. Let's consider the best, worst and average total returns of Standard & Poor's 500 Index (S&P 500), a commonly used American index, between 1925 and 2004, using figures reported by Vanguard Investment Group.[9] (These returns have been measured conventionally and thus comprise dividend income plus unrealised capital gain while ignoring the effects of price inflation.) Vanguard's analysts found that the results achieved during any one-year period were quite volatile. The S&P 500's best result was +54%; its worst was −43%; and the average was 12.4%. The greater the time span, the lower the volatility of results and the greater the likelihood that they were positive. Comparing each consecutive five-year period (that is, periods from 1925 to 1929, 1926 to 1930 and so on, through to 2000 to 2004), the best result was a compound return of 28.6%; the worst was −12.4%; and the average was 10.6%. Considering each rolling ten-year period, the worst result was a compound return of −0.8% and the average was 11.2%. In no twenty-year period since 1925 — including the period encompassing the Great Depression — has a negative result been obtained. Volatile short-term results, then, regress towards a relatively stable historical average. On the basis of these figures, investors might choose to use as a rough yardstick the approximate rates of return set out in table 10.1.

Table 10.1: Base rates for S&P 500 returns, (consecutive periods, rounded to nearest five per cent)

	Best	Worst	Average
1 year	55%	−45%	10%
5 years	30%	−10%	10%
10 years	20%	0%	10%
20 years	20%	5%	10%

It follows that the longer the period *in* the market, the less volatile the average annualised result *from* the market, and (as we will shortly see), thanks in no small part to inflation, the more likely this nominal result will be positive. (The result is nominal as it has not been adjusted for the effects of inflation.) Investing, then, is not gambling. From one month to the next in the stock market and from one night to the next at the roulette wheel, in other words, results can and will vary widely. However, over longer periods of time, the expected results from these two activities grow ever easier to distinguish. In particular, investing is a 'positive net present value' activity: the longer your time frame, the sounder your investment principles and the greater the control you have over your emotions, the more likely it is that you will enjoy a positive nominal result. If this were not so, then savers would not forgo consumption today in return for the expectation of greater consumption in the future.[10] This high probability of success comes with a critical caveat, though: there is no reason to expect average long-term compound returns of more than—and considerable reason to expect short-term results less than—around 10% per annum.[11]

What is a reasonable investment result? The answer also depends upon the type of security you purchase. Vanguard's analysts compared the average results achieved by conventional categories of asset over the very short term (the twelve months to 30 June 2004) and the very long term (the half-century to 30 June 2004).[12] Their data confirmed that short-term results tend to be volatile. Compared to most years, the year to 30 June 2004 was abnormally good for most shares, bonds and real estate. The data also demonstrated that medium-term (that is, five-year) results need not be positive. Yet the long term (that is, the past twenty, thirty and fifty years) has been kind to Australian investors. Anyone who purchased a representative portfolio of Australian stocks on 30 June 1984 and held it for twenty years would have earned an averaged compound return of 13.2% (versus 12.7% for listed property trusts). The study's findings also corroborated those of the historical research we discussed previously, showing that, given the different results from one type of asset to another, and as a very rough rule of thumb, investors should not expect nominal long-term compound returns of more than 10% to 12% per year. Table 10.2, overleaf, sets out approximate historical base rates for the various asset classes.

Table 10.2: base rates of return for various asset categories to 30 June 2004 (nominal and rounded to the nearest 2.5 per cent)

	2004	1999–2004	1994–2004	1984–2004	1974–2004	1954–2004
Australian shares	22.5%	7.5%	10.0%	12.5%	15.0%	12.5%
International shares	20.0%	–2.5%	7.5%	12.5%	12.5%	n.a.
Australian bonds	2.5%	5.0%	7.5%	12.5%	10.0%	7.5%
Australian listed property	17.5%	15.0%	12.5%	12.5%	n.a.	n.a.
Australian cash	5.0%	5.0%	5.0%	10.0%	10.0%	7.5%
Australian CPI	2.5%	2.5%	2.5%	5.0%	7.5%	5.0%

SOME MORE BASE RATES FOR VALUE INVESTORS

The trouble with the figures set out in tables 10.1 and 10.2, as relevant as they are, is that they encourage a fixation upon outcomes. Interestingly, investors who achieve superior results are those who first establish a superior process of decision making. They concentrate, in other words, upon inputs and premises—and then let the outcomes of this process take care of themselves. With this insight in mind, we can derive additional premises that underpin value investors' activities. This additional batch of base rates appears in table 10.3.

CPI and inflation

It is essential to recognise that the Consumer Price Index and 'inflation' are related but distinct things. Like value and price, they eventually regress towards one another; but at any given point in time they may diverge (sometimes by a wide margin). Very few people recognise the fundamental difference between CPI and inflation (just as very few make the distinction between value and price). The word 'inflation' is invariably used by the Reserve Bank of Australia (RBA) — and by economists, politicians and market commentators and participants — to describe increases in the prices of particular raw materials, finished products and wages. Using this definition, the 'headline' rate of inflation in Australia (a close relative of consumer price inflation, which is, for practical purposes, synonymous with CPI), averaged roughly 2% per annum between January 1990 and December 1999, and has remained below or within the Bank's target range of 2% to 3% since early 1996. The mainstream thus defines inflation in terms of its several possible *consequences* rather than its single and definitive *cause*. Inflation, in other words, rarely if ever refers to an increase in the supply of money. Attention is thereby distracted from monetary expansion — and the RBA's sole responsibility for this expansion.

Table 10.3: more essential base rates for Australian investors

Item	Unit of measurement	Base rate
Consumer Price Index	Average percentage growth per year	2%–6%
Inflation (properly conceived)	Average percentage growth of money supply per year	6%–8%
Money rate of interest (five-year)	Long-term mean	9.4%
Natural rate of interest	Long-term mean	12.5%–17.5%
Nominal rate of growth of stocks' coupons	Average percentage growth per year	7%–9%
'Real' rate of growth of stocks' coupons	Average percentage growth per year	1%–3%
Real investment results (stocks)	Long-term average per year	0.5%–4.5%

As Ludwig von Mises demonstrated, this is no matter of mere semantics:

> The semantic revolution which is one of the characteristic features of our day has also changed the traditional connotation of the terms *inflation* and *deflation*. What many people today call inflation or deflation is no longer the great increase or decrease in the supply of money, but its inexorable consequences, the general tendency toward a rise or a fall in commodity prices and wage rates. This innovation is by no means harmless. It plays an important role in fomenting the popular tendencies towards inflationism [policies that encourage prices to rise].[13]

And so it has proved. Depending upon one's definition of the money supply (which is a notoriously slippery concept and thus very difficult to measure), inflation in Australia averaged closer to 6% to 7% per year during the 1990s and has averaged as much as 10% since 2000. The RBA's measure of 'broad money' for this period provides a good illustration. ('Money' can be defined in a narrow sense that excludes certain types of money, or in a broad sense that includes other types. The broadest definition encompasses notes and coins held by individuals and businesses plus deposits with banks and deposits held outside the banking sector.) Broad money grew from $257 billion at the beginning of 1990 to $472 billion at the beginning of 2000; that is, at an annualised compound rate of growth of 6.3%. Moreover, in recent years, inflation in Australia has accelerated: broad money grew 10.6% during 2002, by 9.4% during 2004 and has been growing at an annualised compound rate of 8.1% since January 2000. Other measures of money supply produce still higher estimates of inflation. Clearly, then, if inflation is properly seen as an increase in the money supply, then it is presently—and has long been—much more pronounced than central bankers, politicians, economists and investors recognise.

From this distinction follows a series of sobering insights. First, it is not just the prices of goods and services that eventually rise as a consequence of inflation: so too do the prices of stocks, bonds and real estate. Market participants rejoice when the prices of securities rise, but few recognise that these increases are to a significant extent a consequence not of business and investment acumen but of central banks' insidious debasement of the money supply. Second, inflation sometimes begets bull markets and at other times puts a fire under the prices of goods, services and wages. From one era to the next, in other words, the river of inflation can follow different channels. In the early 1970s, it produced relatively high food prices and low stock prices, but since the mid-1990s, it has produced comparatively low food prices and high stock prices.

This point helps to reconcile something that is otherwise difficult to comprehend: the coexistence in recent years of a growing economy (as conventional national accounts measure it) and a quiescent CPI (quiescent, that is, by the standards of the 1970s). Inflation usually causes the prices paid by consumers to increase, but it need not always or immediately do so. If technological improvements or organisational efficiencies or a flood of imports or good old-fashioned discipline exert a downward influence upon prices, but an increase in the money supply exerts an upward influence, only a small overall increase in prices may occur. During times of high inflation (properly understood), wages and prices may increase modestly or not at all. According to Friedrich Hayek, Wilhelm Röpke and Murray Rothbard, precisely such a situation occurred in Europe and the US during the Roaring Twenties.[14] It seemed to recur after 1990.

The lesson, then, that the value investor should derive from the data presented in the first two rows of table 10.3 is the importance of paying attention to what the Reserve Bank of Australia *does* over the years (that is, manufacture inflation) and ignore what it *says* from day to day. It is conceivable that today's CPI will eventually regress towards its historical base rate. The RBA's debasement of money, in other words, ultimately makes itself felt in the rising prices of goods, services and wages (compare the table's long-run measures of CPI with the average rate of inflation). It is therefore wise to ask under what circumstances today's CPI might rise towards the historical base rate of inflation. If it does, and given that the value investor's first objective is to preserve the purchasing power of her capital, she must have no illusions about the inclement weather the financial markets of the future might bring.

Money interest rates and natural interest rates

It is also vital to recognise that 'natural' rate of interest and the 'money' rate of interest are two distinct things. Interest reflects individuals' time preferences; that is, how much more they value consumption today than they do consumption in the future. The natural rate of interest (also known as the 'pure rate') indicates the extent to which individuals are willing to forgo consumption today in the expectation of greater consumption tomorrow. The greater their willingness to postpone consumption, the lower the natural rate (and vice versa).[15] Yet in the modern world the natural rate rarely prevails; it is actually the money rate of interest—the short-term rate of interest available on the market, manipulated by central and commercial banks—which is paramount. If the money rate is set lower than the natural rate, which it usually seems to be, then the pace of credit creation quickens: when the cost of credit is much less than what can be earned from the proceeds of credit, it pays to borrow, and businesses and individuals have a big night on the town. To finance it, they demand loans. In recent years the inflation created by central banks has made its presence felt most forcefully in markets for loans—particularly home loans.

In chapter 3, I described the chain or 'structure' of production that proceeds from higher order goods (such as raw materials and capital goods) to lower order or consumer goods. When not upset by banks, the structure of production at any particular time tends to be just long enough to exhaust the fund of savings generated by the natural rate, but the future is unknowable, entrepreneurial error is inevitable and a perfect match between the rate and the structure is highly unlikely. If the structure is too short relative to the rate, unused capital will be available for deployment on more marginal projects. If the structure is too long, then the available capital will be expended before production has been completed. This latter situation can best be illustrated by analogy: imagine a builder who has built the foundations of a house and belatedly discovers, once much of the superstructure has been raised, that there are insufficient bricks and tiles to complete it. To finish such projects, and reassured by the apparent boom, entrepreneurs borrow more at subsidised market rates of interest. Sooner or later, however, either commercial banks (worried about the increasing pace and declining quality of credit) or the central bank (fearful of incipient or actual increases of the prices of goods, services or wages, which it mistakenly calls 'inflation') will halt the boom by intervening in the various markets for loans. The central bank will increase the short-term money rate of interest it controls (in Australia, this is the rate banks charge one another to lend excess reserves overnight), and commercial banks will impose higher money rates and stiffer terms upon borrowers.[16]

Looking at inflation and interest rates from this perspective has profound implications for value investors. First, the relevant questions to ask about prices and credit relate not so much to their *stability* but rather to their *integrity*. Stability can and historically has masked distortions introduced by easy money. Hence intelligent investors regularly ask themselves: given governments' pervasive meddling in credit and financial markets, do the prices of assets and money rates of interest convey accurate signals and sensible information? Acting on them, would individuals make reasonable choices? Or would they make 'malinvestments' that must be liquidated when the boom inevitably ends? These days many obsess about the ambiguous but soothing words spoken by Alan Greenspan and RBA chief Ian Macfarlane, but nobody, it seems, recalls the bracing and crystal clear words of the Weimar German central banker Hjalmar Schacht. In 1927, with the coming bust already on the horizon, he protested, 'Don't give me a *low* rate. Give me a *true* rate; and then I shall know how to put my house in order.'

Another implication of looking at inflation and interest rates in this way is that additional savings and capital goods are what is needed for sound economic and investment conditions—and not more credit and consumption. The boom in recent years in some parts of Australia is therefore to a significant extent illusory. Much more so than in the past, today's Australians are subsisting on borrowed money; accordingly—given a proper definition of interest and inflation—they are also living on borrowed time. 'Investment' encouraged by subsidised rates of interest can continue only so long as central and commercial banks connive to make credit available at artificially low rates. It is this margin between the subsidised and the natural rate that misleads entrepreneurs and gives their investments the false appearance of profitability. It also hoodwinks consumers and gives their shopping sprees the false appearance of sustainability. When the boom ends, it does not *cause* difficulties: it *reveals* problems that inhered all along in inflation and artificially low rates of money interest. The defining feature of booms, then, is not that they are periods of good business; rather, they are irrationally exuberant times when capital is squandered on bad investments.[17]

What, then, should the value investor glean from the data set out in table 10.3 (see page 175)? Overall, the information presented indicates that today's artificially low rates of money interest may eventually rise towards their historical average.[18] If so, and given that the value investor's second objective is to invest her capital in a portfolio of securities whose rate of return (given cautious assumptions) can reasonably be expected to exceed those offered by a five-year Commonwealth Government bond, she must have absolutely no illusion that the results obtained during the recent past from investing in stocks can continue without interruption into the indefinite future.

Earnings growth

Value investors know that companies' earnings (considered as a whole) cannot grow more quickly than the overall economy. In fact, earnings must grow slightly more slowly than GDP.

If they consistently outpaced economic growth, then returns would migrate from labour to capital, which is great for owners of stocks and bonds but not so swell for employees. If, on the other hand, earnings grew much more slowly than the economic pie for extended periods, then returns would migrate from capital to labour. However, when it is understood that prosperity cannot exist without capital and a reasonable return on capital, it is obvious that this migration cannot continue indefinitely. Hence the returns to both capital and labour fluctuate in the short term, but over longer periods regress towards long-term averages. Indeed, except during the Great Depression, when they disappeared, and during occasional booms (like that we have been experiencing since 2001) corporate earnings in Australia have remained a roughly constant percentage (4% to 7%) of an economic pie growing slowly but steadily at an average of 3.3% per year between 1900 and 2000. During the twentieth century, and net of inflation, corporate coupons in this country grew at an average annual rate of 2.3% per year.[19] Hence coupons' nominal base rate of growth, including inflation, is 7% to 9% per year.[20]

Yet analysts ignore this historical norm and unabashedly and consistently predict that corporate earnings will grow into the future at an impossibly rapid rate. The analysis of Telstra in chapter 5 is but one of a large number of examples. During the ten years from 1985 to 1995, for example, American analysts estimated that the earnings of companies comprising the S&P 500 would grow at nominal rates of between 10.8% and 12.1% per year. Expectations rose steadily, to a rate of 14.9% per year, by the end of 1998. They then peaked at 18.7% in August 2000. Analysts, urged (or at least unhindered) by their institutional and retail clients, ignored the ineluctable limit upon the growth of profits that is imposed by the structure of production.

When the Great Bubble burst in 2000, analysts began to restrain their wildly optimistic projections. By the end of 2002, consensus expectations about long-term earnings growth for the S&P 500 had fallen from the all-time peak to a nominal

THE INTELLIGENT AUSTRALIAN INVESTOR

rate of 'only' 12.8% per year. The reversal in the tech sector of the S&P 500 was even more dramatic: growth expectations fell from the 2000 peak rate of 28.7% to 16% at the end of 2002. American businesses, it is important to recognise, were not significantly more profitable in 2004 than they were in 2001; yet analysts' reassessments of their prospects remained ridiculously overconfident. And so it goes in Australia: in early July 2004, the analysts of a major international brokerage house were 'optimistic about the coming reporting season, expecting an average (nominal) 17.7% rise in earnings compared with the previous period'. Clearly, then, analysts' collective ('consensus') forecast of long-term earnings growth is severely and seemingly permanently biased in an overly sanguine direction. If so, then so too are their assessments of most stocks' 'fair value'. In Grahamite terms, these improbably optimistic expectations encourage investors to disavow margins of safety and buy stocks at excessively high prices.

Why are analysts' estimates of earnings skewed so heavily towards overoptimism? One reason is that caution generates less attention—and business—than either unqualified buoyancy or unmitigated gloom. Another is that analysts tend to extrapolate the potential earnings growth of 'their' companies in 'their' industries. Few wish to cover laggard companies and industries, and so attention is concentrated upon 'winners'. A common problem, perhaps a bit less prevalent today than it was a few years ago, is that a 'winner' tends to be defined as a company with which the analyst's firm has or seeks business. If so, then the long-term outlook with respect to these companies is likely to be overly rosy, and overconfident outlooks with respect to individual companies will beget unrealistically bullish consensus outlooks.

BASE RATES AND REASONED SCEPTICISM

Value investors read widely and critically in order to:

- inform themselves of long-term norms and disabuse themselves of unrealistic expectations

- identify economic, business and financial principles that pass the test of logic and historical experience

- protect themselves generally against fads, chaff, ephemera and nonsense.

Armed with valid tools and reliable evidence, the humble and sceptical value investor can respond dispassionately to the daily deluge of information, part-information and outright falsehood. With that purpose in mind, this chapter has provided some sober benchmarks against which investors might restrain their premises and better appreciate their results. It has provided some specific numbers—namely, base rates—with which to implement the policy of reasoned scepticism introduced in chapter 6.

I have also suggested a general policy: the greater the complexity and uncertainty that attaches to a potential investment, the less the emphasis the value investor should place upon the case rate and the greater the weight she should accord to the base rate (if, indeed, she considers the investment at all, which is doubtful). The value investor knows that it is pointless to research a potential investment exhaustively. It is impossible to collect and analyse all information; further, what is collected will probably include strands that are contradictory, irrelevant, erroneous and difficult to evaluate. In sharp contrast, it is much more feasible—this is not the same thing as easy—to gauge the long-term record of success or failure of situations or courses of action like the one at hand.

For the value investor, the rule is therefore not to collect as much information as possible, but rather to collect enough reliable information to ascertain with reasonable confidence which general past situation encompasses the present particular situation. The information about the particular case will always be complemented and probably supplanted by reliable statistical evidence about the general results that have occurred in similar situations.

Notes

1   See Benjamin Graham, *Benjamin Graham: The Memoirs of the Dean of Wall Street* (McGraw-Hill, 1996); Roger Lowenstein, *Buffett: The Making of an American Capitalist* (Random House, 1995); Janet Lowe, *Damn Right! Behind the Scenes with Berkshire Hathaway Billionaire Charlie Munger* (John Wiley & Sons, 2000), p. 231.

2   Richard FitzHerbert, *BluePrint for Investment: An Approach for Serious Long-Term Investors* (Wrightbooks, 1994), p. v (see in particular chapter 2, 'The Lessons of History').

3   See Daniel Kahneman and Amos Tversky, 'On the Psychology of Prediction', *Psychological Review* 80 (1973), pp. 237–251.

4   David Hamilton, 'Biotech's Dismal Bottom Line: More than $40 Billion in Losses' (*The Wall Street Journal*, 20 May 2004).

5   Janet Lowe, *Warren Buffett Speaks*, p. 143.

6   More generally, 'regression to the mean' refers to an inverse correlation among roughly normally distributed observations that are made repeatedly over time. An extreme observation at one point in time ('outlier') tends to be followed by a less extreme observation; extremes, in other words, revert or regress over time towards mean or average measurements. A student's test scores provide another example. If the student's scholastic aptitude remains constant, then an extreme score at one point will probably be followed by ('regress towards') a result that is much closer to the student's average. All else being equal, an abnormally high score is likely to be followed at the next test by a lower score; and an abnormally low score is likely to be followed next time by a higher score. For a readable overview, see Peter Bernstein, *Against the Gods: The Remarkable Story of Risk,* (John Wiley & Sons, 1996), chapters 9 to 11.

7   It is important to distinguish regression from the mean from something commonly called the 'gambler's fallacy'. This is the tendency to impute 'patterns' from random occurrences. It manifests itself in the mistaken belief that because (say) five tosses of a coin have produced five heads, the next toss is likely (assuming a fair coin) to produce something other than fifty/fifty odds of a head. Some people will say a tail is 'due' and so will expect one on the next loss; others might say the flipper has a 'hot hand' and so will expect another head. The laws of probability give us

a long-term base rate: if you flip a coin five times and repeat this 'experiment' a very large number of times, the average number of heads will regress towards 2.5.

8   Werner De Bondt and Richard Thaler, 'Does the Stock Market Overreact?' *Journal of Finance* 40 (1985), pp. 793–805.

9   Vanguard Investment Group, <https://www.travelerslife.com/ pdfs/prospectuses/Vanguard-VIF-Total-Stock-Market-Index-Portfolio.pdf>.

10   In sharp contrast and with few exceptions, speculating and gambling are 'net present value negative' pursuits. They are a 'loser's game' in the sense that the longer you gamble or speculate, the more certainly the odds assure that you will lose everything you wager.

11   A very few investors have generated results over the decades that greatly exceed this benchmark. (Warren Buffett is the most obvious example.) However, logic and evidence concur that over the decades their number will be small. Many investors who produce better than average results will tend in subsequent periods to regress to the long-term average. Indeed, and much as Warren Buffett has warned, Berkshire Hathaway's average result since 1999, which is far lower than its average since 1965, may be an example of this.

12   Vanguard Investment Group; *Australian Financial Review* 13 October 2004.

13   See in particular Ludwig von Mises, *Human Action* (4th rev. ed., Fox & Wilkes, 1996), chapter 17.

14   See in particular Wilhelm Röpke, *Economics of the Free Society* (Libertarian Press, 1937, 1994), chapter 4; and Murray Rothbard, *America's Great Depression* (Richardson & Snyder, 1963).

15   For full details see Mises, *Human Action*, chapters 18 and 19; Murray Rothbard, *Man, Economy and State* (Ludwig von Mises Institute, 1993), chapter 6; and Hans-Hermann Hoppe, *Democracy, the God that Failed: The Economics and Politics of Monarchy, Democracy and Natural Order* (Transaction, 2002). Over the years, in various contexts in Australia and Canada ranging from classrooms of MBA students to conferences of senior executives, I have asked people to envisage the opportunity to receive $100 in exactly

one year's time. I have asked them to suppose that the receipt of this money is absolutely guaranteed. How much is the average MBA and executive willing to pay today in exchange for the absolute guarantee of $100 in a year's time? The answer is $85. They are prepared to pay no more than $85, in other words, for a guaranteed 'coupon' of $15 and the return of their $85. This implies a natural rate of interest of 17.6 per cent. On the one hand, as I have emphasised, valuation is a subjective matter that will vary from one person to the next and from one occasion to the next. On the other hand, this response should nonetheless be utterly astounding: the very same people prepared to accept a non-guaranteed yield of (say) 5 per cent on 'investment' real estate and stocks will decline a guaranteed (albeit hypothetical) yield that is much greater. For other imaginative ways intelligent people devise to drain money from their pockets, see Gary Belsky and Thomas Gilovich, *Why Smart People Make Big Money Mistakes and How to Correct Them: Lessons from the New Science of Behavioral Economics* (Simon & Schuster, 2000).

16   In this context it is quite significant that during 2004 and into 2005, central banks in English-speaking countries mouthed concern about 'inflation', but even more significantly, they have somehow forgotten to mention that their policies—and their policies alone—have created it.

17   See in particular James Grant, *The Trouble with Prosperity: A Contrarian's Tale of Boom, Bust, and Speculation* (Times Books, 1998).

18   The figure in table 10.3 is the average yield of a five-year Commonwealth Government bond between January 1972 and April 2005.

19   See in particular William J. Bernstein and Robert Arnott, 'Earnings Growth: The Two Percent Dilution', *Financial Analysts Journal* (September–October 2003). A passage from David Dreman (*Contrarian Investment Strategies*, p. 103) is also quite relevant: 'the remarkable conclusion of the present study is that the careful estimates of security analysts ... performed little better than those of (past) company growth rates.' American analysts could have prophesied better by simply assuming that earnings would continue to expand near the long-term rate of 3% to 4% annually.

20   Investors should be forewarned: when most Wall Street firms talk about earnings they mean 'operating earnings'—a non-standard,

non-official definition that excludes write-offs and expenses that companies claim are not central to their operations. It is generally far better to analyse earnings reported under Generally Accepted Accounted Principles (as Australians usually do), mostly because they are typically much lower.

Chapter 11

<><><><><><><><><><><><><><><><><><><><>

Analyse individual businesses, buy only when the price is right, make time your friend

Benjamin Graham:

They used to say about the Bourbons that they forgot nothing and they learned nothing, and I'll say about Wall Street people, typically, is that they learn nothing and they forget everything. I have no confidence whatever in the future behavior of the Wall Street people. I think this business of greed—the excessive hopes and fears and so on—will be with us as long as there will be people ... I am very cynical about Wall Street.

Harman Butler:

But there are independent thinkers on Wall Street and throughout the country who do well, aren't there?

Benjamin Graham:

Yes. There are two requirements for success in Wall Street. One, you have to think correctly; and secondly, you have to think independently.

Harman Butler,
'An Hour with Mr Graham'
Financial Analysts Journal (1976)

ANALYSING A BUSINESS

Brokers, financial advisers and commentators are usually optimistic. In contrast, since the late 1990s the world's most accomplished investors have tended to be cautious and in some cases gloomy. In the face of these contradictory signals, what should an intelligent investor do? One way to proceed is to compare a 'risky' security to a benchmark 'risk-free' security or group of securities, as we did in chapter 5. Simple reasoning can help to ascertain whether the risky option is likely to be a better or worse investment than the so-called risk-free option. When their respective coupons are compared—that is, the money that each generates (or can reasonably be expected to generate) over time—the risky security is judged more attractive when its yield continuously exceeds by a significant margin that of the risk-free alternative (and vice versa).

This comparison obliges the investor to ascertain whether the market price and assumed rate of growth of the risky security's coupon are reasonable. Graham's injunction is to buy quality stocks whose current yields significantly exceed those of government bonds. Over time, then, the investor's objective—through successive comparisons and detailed analysis—is to accumulate a portfolio of assets whose coupons can reasonably be expected to exceed by a significant margin the risk-free coupons of government bonds.

This chapter shows how the intelligent investor might think through these issues. As an illustration, it looks in detail at Telstra Corp. Ltd. (Note, however, that the processes outlined in this example are by no means purported to replace the systematic investigation of a company's operations and the thorough scrutiny of its financial statements.)

A tale of two Telstras

When its first 'tranche' was listed on the ASX in 1997, Telstra was the subject of a great deal of media hype, but by

2002, shareholders'—and analysts' and politicians'—naive expectations of unbridled growth had been dashed.

> We didn't say anything about Telstra that was untrue and nobody in our situation associated with [a] privatisation of that kind can be held to account for subsequent fluctuations in the share price ... I mean, that is the nature of the beast, you buy shares, you make a decision based on investment advice, you either make a profit or incur a loss.

These words, uttered by John Howard in *The Weekend Australian Financial Review* (4–5 May 2002), speak volumes. Alas, neither the misery of hundreds of thousands of Australians nor the implications of our preliminary analysis end where chapter 5 left them. Table 11.1, overleaf, summarises an analysis of Telstra under the conditions and typical assumptions prevailing in mid-2001. It shows Telstra's actual and projected coupons for the ten-year period from 1996 to 2006, making calculations based on both exuberant and chastened assumptions.

The table's second column shows that Telstra's actual coupons grew at a rate of 13.5 per cent per annum from 1996 to 2001. Judging from their enthusiasm during these years, the vast majority of investment professionals analysing Telstra expected the growth that had occurred in this five-year period would continue at this rate and probably even more rapidly over the next five years. Whether the 1996–2001 period was an historical aberration was something that, in the midst of a sharemarket boom, very few seemed willing to consider. Analysts either ignored or disbelieved the possibility that this rapid case rate might regress to something closer to a historical base rate. An implication of this exuberant assumption was that between 2001 and 2006, Telstra's coupons would grow at a compound rate of 17 per cent per annum. This assumption was widely accepted and therefore raised few eyebrows in 1999 and 2000. The data illustrating this exuberant projection are set out in the third column of table 11.1, overleaf.

Table 11.1: another simple 2001-vintage extrapolation of Telstra's coupons

Year	Actual growth (13.5%)	Exuberant assumptions of 1999 (17% growth)	Chastened assumptions of 2001 (7.5% growth)
1996	$0.17	–	–
1997	$0.22	–	–
1998	$0.23	–	–
1999	$0.27	–	–
2000	$0.31	–	–
2001	$0.34	$0.34	$0.34
2002	–	$0.40	$0.37
2003	–	$0.47	$0.39
2004	–	$0.54	$0.42
2005	–	$0.64	$0.45
2006	–	$0.76	$0.49

More chastened assumptions about the rate of growth of Telstra's coupons began to gain limited currency among some market participants in 2001. For example, one *Weekend Australian* columnist[1] noted in mid-June 2001 that if Telstra were going to retain the favour and confidence of market participants, the company would have to increase its earnings before interest and tax at a compound rate of at least 10 per cent per year during the next several years. This columnist also implied that there was a strong likelihood that it would do so. Indeed, he went so far as to declare that:

> the long outlook for Telstra is now looking better than it has been for some time ... The underlying value in the stock has never been better and institutions and individuals that have a long-term view are going to accumulate the stock at around these levels [$5.65 per share].

If it is assumed that Telstra had to pay tax during this interval (because if it had not, it would surely have disappointed the Australian Taxation Office) and also that it had to pay interest on the roughly $7 billion of long-term debt that it owed at that time (because if it had defaulted, it would have disappointed its bondholders), this columnist's statements implied that Telstra's earnings (after interest and tax, and ignoring hefty depreciation and amortisation charges) would increase at a compound rate of approximately 7.5 per cent. Data illustrating the implications of this belief are set out in the fourth column of table 11.1.

The contrast between the projected outcomes of the exuberant and chastened assumptions is marked. The exuberant assumption that raised no eyebrows in 1999 implied that by 2006 Telstra's coupon would grow to 76¢. Compare this estimate to growth implied by the chastened assumption, culminating in a coupon of 49¢: the former is 55 per cent greater than the latter. Similarly, the exuberant assumption implied that Telstra's coupon would be 47¢ in 2003; under the chastened assumption, however, this level of earnings would not be expected until 2006.

It is important—indeed, imperative—to note that none of the data set out in table 11.1 suggest that either Telstra or the Australian telecommunications market had fundamentally changed or would change during these years. Rather, credulous brokers, financial advisers, journalists and funds managers were simply seized by the euphoria of the late 1990s. Sadly, a stubborn and uncooperative reality subsequently saw their heady expectations about Telstra's coupons give way to a comparatively dour outlook. Only tangentially, in other words, has the hefty fall of Telstra's market capitalisation since 1999 had anything to do with factors such as changes in the Australian telecoms industry, Telstra's management and operations, its hybrid state-private ownership, or the vigour (or lack of vigour) of economic conditions in Australia. This is greatly embarrassing to the army of advisers, analysts, brokers and journalists who usually sing joyfully from the same script. It might thereby explain their strenuous and imaginative efforts since 1999 to devise various cover stories to distract attention from their cumulatively monumental error.

Let us extend the analysis to conditions prevailing more recently. Accordingly, assume that you can buy one of the following:

- one share of Telstra at $4.20 (the average closing price for these shares during the bear market prevailing in the early months of 2003)

- a hypothetical five-year Commonwealth bond at a price of $4.20 and a yield of 5.1 per cent (the average yield prevailing in May 2003 for Commonwealth bonds maturing in August 2008).

Between mid-1999 and mid-2003 the price of the Telstra share roughly halved (from $8.20 to $4.20) and yields of 'risk-free' government bonds fell 20% (from 6.4% to 5.1%). As before, assume that whichever you choose you are a long-term investor; that is, you will hold your investment for five years. If you purchase the bond, by late 2008 it is virtually certain, given the miniscule possibility of default, that you will earn $1.05 in coupons (that is, 21¢ per year for five years) and upon redemption will collect total proceeds of $5.25 (that is, $4.20 of principal plus $1.05 of coupons).

Table 11.2: a simple 2003-vintage evaluation of Telstra

Year	Coupon	Cumulative coupons	Yield on $4.20
2003	$0.29	$0.29	6.9%
2004	$0.30	$0.59	7.1%
2005	$0.31	$0.90	7.4%
2006	$0.31	$1.21	7.4%
2007	$0.32	$1.53	7.6%
2008	$0.33	$1.86	7.9%

If the Telstra share purchased in 2003 at $4.20 is going to be a better investment than the bond, then it must return at least $5.25 by mid-2008. Again, however, there is no guarantee that the Telstra share can be redeemed for $4.20 at that point; nor can we know the value of the coupons that Telstra will generate during this interval. Let us therefore adopt a dour assumption: the company's coupons will grow without interruption, but at a rate of no more than 2.5 per cent per year during the five years to mid-2008—that is, at one-third of the rate assumed by commentators in 2001 and below the base rate given in chapter 10. In other words, we are assuming that Telstra's coupons are virtually static and thus resemble those of a bond. Table 11.2 sets out Telstra's projected coupons under this assumption. If this projection is accurate, at the end of the period, a cumulative coupon of $1.86—*77 per cent more than the bond's cumulative coupon*—would accrue to the Telstra shareholder as dividends, retained earnings or some combination of the two. Note that from the first year of ownership Telstra's yield of 6.9 per cent exceeds that of the bond, which is only 5.1 per cent. (This presents a sharp contrast to the situation analysed in chapter 5, in which the bond seemed by far the superior alternative.)

Recall Benjamin Graham's rule of thumb: a share is generally the more sensible investment when its yield is and can reasonably be expected to remain significantly greater than that of a comparable bond; conversely, a bond is more attractive when its yield is equal to or greater than that of a comparable stock. The situation prevailing in mid-2003 is quite unlike the one we examined in mid-2000 in chapter 5: most importantly, the owner of the Telstra share purchased in 2003 does not have to wait for the share's yield to match the bond's yield.

Further, given that its coupon is projected to grow to 33¢ in 2008, in five years the Telstra share must trade at any multiple of its coupon greater than 6.47 in order to match the bond's yield. To see this, recall that the bond's yield is 5.1% or 0.051. Given an asset whose coupon is 33¢, at what price does the asset yield 5.1%? The answer is 0.33 divided by 0.051, which equals a multiple of 6.47 times its coupon.

In other words, in order to match the results guaranteed by the bond in 2003, Telstra's fortunes needed only to meet rather undemanding (dour) assumptions, rather than the challenging assumptions of 1999 and 2000. The greater the extent to which Telstra is able to meet or exceed these dour assumptions, the more attractive the share will prove relative to the bond; and the greater the relative attractiveness of the share, the lower its risk relative to the bond. Given the circumstances prevailing in 1999 and 2000, if Telstra was going to be a more lucrative investment than the Commonwealth bond, then we had to expect either that our ambitious assumptions would prove to be conservative or that Telstra's share price would increase even faster than its coupons. In 2003, neither of these demanding conditions applied. In 1999 and 2000, the results of an investment in Telstra could not reasonably be expected to surpass by a wide margin those available from a risk-free Commonwealth bond. Although legions apparently did so, it made little sense to purchase Telstra shares at prices remotely close to $8.20. To buy at an exuberant price and on exuberant assumptions is not to allocate capital rationally: it is to gamble that the market price of the shares in question will continue to increase and become even more detached from the company's operations, and that it will be possible to sell these shares at an even more inflated price. To buy under 1999 conditions, in other words, was clearly to speculate rather than invest.

TIME IS MONEY

'Remember that time is money' Benjamin Franklin once advised a young tradesman whom he befriended. Time is the enemy of the poor business, but it is the friend of the good business purchased at a sensible price. If you have invested in a sound business that yields 15 per cent, time is your friend, but if you have put your money into a business on a less sound footing that yields only 5 per cent, time is your enemy. The investor always seeks to harness time such that the purchasing power of her capital is maintained. The investor's portfolio, in other words, must generate a stream of income that over time is sufficient to maintain her standard of living. Once this primary goal has been achieved, the investor's secondary goal is to increase the purchasing power of her capital; that is, to generate a stream of income that over time augments her standard of living.

As I noted earlier, Graham's injunction is to buy quality stocks whose current yields significantly exceed that of government bonds. A much more challenging but rewarding objective is gradually to acquire a portfolio whose stream of earnings matches or surpasses a much stiffer threshold; that is, the natural rate of interest.

Investment return and the payback period

If time is money, it follows that the return on an investment can—indeed, should—be measured in terms of time as well as money. It is important to recognise that even when a variable stream of coupons (such as those from a stock) cumulate to the same amount as a fixed stream of coupons (such as those from a bond), an investor is unlikely to regard them as equivalent.

As an example, consider two occupations. Occupation A pays $50,000 every year whilst the salary of occupation B depends upon the flip of a coin: if the coin comes up heads it pays $20,000; tails, it pays $80,000. In purely mathematical terms the expected value of each occupation is $50,000 per year, but in psychological terms it is likely that you would require a higher expected income from the occupation with variable pay in order to make it equally attractive to the occupation with fixed pay. The additional increment of income that you require from the variable stream vis-a-vis the guaranteed one in order to render the two streams equally attractive is a 'risk premium'. The risk premium, like value and risk, is subjective: it will differ from person to person and from one occasion to another. Yet in a sane world stocks would always have higher yields than corporate bonds; and corporate bonds would have higher yields than government bonds that would otherwise be comparable in terms of their duration to maturity.

We have already seen that the degree of risk that inheres in a given investment operation varies with the individual's expectation about its coupons and the probability that principal will be repaid. It should also be noted that perceived risk also differs according to the estimated 'payback period' required to recoup an initial investment.

The 'payback period' of the Telstra share under the exuberant assumptions prevailing in 1999 was approximately twelve years, and that of the Commonwealth Government bond to which it was compared was slightly more than sixteen years.

Table 11.3 shows why. If we accept that Telstra's purchase price is $8.20 and that its coupons will grow at 17 per cent per year, twelve years must pass before the cumulative coupons will meet or exceed the asset's purchase price. Twelve years, in

Table 11.3: comparing 1999 stock and bond payback periods

| Year | Telstra share at $8.20, coupon growth of 17% | | Government bond, coupon fixed at 6.35% | |
	Coupon	Cumulative coupon	Coupon	Cumulative coupon
1	$0.27	$0.27	$0.51	$0.51
2	$0.32	$0.59	$0.51	$1.02
3	$0.37	$0.96	$0.51	$1.53
4	$0.43	$1.39	$0.51	$2.04
5	$0.51	$1.90	$0.51	$2.55
6	$0.59	$2.49	$0.51	$3.05
7	$0.69	$3.18	$0.51	$3.56
8	$0.81	$3.99	$0.51	$4.07
9	$0.95	$4.94	$0.51	$4.58
10	$1.11	$6.05	$0.51	$5.09
11	$1.29	$7.34	$0.51	$5.60
12	$1.52	**$8.86**	$0.51	$6.11
13	–	–	$0.51	$6.62
14	–	–	$0.51	$7.13
15	–	–	$0.51	$7.64
16	–	–	$0.51	**$8.15**

other words, is required—*assuming that the coupons eventuate according to this trajectory*—for the Telstra share to 'pay for itself'. Analogously, slightly more than sixteen years are required for the bond to pay for itself.

What is an appropriate payback period? First, note in general that the longer the time required to recoup an investment, the riskier—according to the Grahamite conception of risk—that investment becomes. The longer the payback period, the more a decision to invest depends upon the reasonableness and sturdiness of its underlying assumptions. Accordingly, the longer the estimated payback period, the more imperative it becomes that those assumptions correspond at least roughly to reality. For each additional year the payback period rises, the greater the chances are that unforeseen or uncontrollable factors will affect the yearly coupon and perhaps prolong the payback period even further.

These factors range from recessions to technological breakthroughs, regulatory changes to corporate scandals. Note that a natural rate of interest of 12 per cent to 15 per cent and a constant stream of coupons implies a payback period of six to eight years. For these reasons, the Telstra share's relatively short payback period of twelve years (versus the bond's sixteen years) does not make it attractive in an absolute sense. Both payback periods greatly exceed that implied by the admittedly crude but cautious estimate of the natural rate of interest in Australia. Measured by this absolute, venerable and more challenging yardstick (one that is, sadly, virtually unknown these days), neither of these investments is compelling.

In *Poor Richard's Almanac* in 1757, Ben Franklin observed:

> God helps them that help themselves ... At twenty years of age, the will reigns; at thirty, the wit; and at forty, the judgment ... Dost thou love life? Then do not squander time, for that is the stuff life is made of.

He added for good measure that 'an investment in knowledge pays the best interest'. Grahamite value investors agree that time is precious stuff, and insist on building dour and stringent assumptions about time into their calculations before they can be persuaded to exchange cash for a security.

To illustrate the value investor's approach, let's start by assuming that we can purchase a particular security (say, a stock of X Ltd) for $1.00, and that its coupon in the first year of ownership is 10¢, thereby generating a yield of 10 per cent. Assume, too, that its coupon can reasonably be expected to grow at a rate of 10 per cent per year. If these assumptions prove correct, our payback period is approximately seven years. These projections are set out in the left half of table 11.4, overleaf.

For the purposes of comparison, let's assume next that we can purchase this same investment at a yield of 15 per cent—1.5 times the yield originally assumed. As shown in the right half of table 11.4, our payback period falls to approximately 5.5 years. Clearly, the higher the initial yield is, the shorter the payback period will be. Logically, if the return *of* the investment is quicker, risk is reduced and the return *on* the investment will be greater.

An increase of both initial yield *and* the coupon's rate of growth further decrease the payback period. This is shown in the right half of table 11.5 (see page 203). *Note, however, that the yield at which an asset is purchased is at least as important as (and probably more important than) its coupon's rate of growth.* Compare the right half of table 11.4, where the initial yield is 15% and coupon growth is 10%, with the left half of table 11.5, where the initial yield is 10% and coupon growth is 15%. In the first instance the payback period is a little more than five years; in the second it is slightly more than six years. A 50% increase in the coupon's rate of growth (that is, from 10% to 15%) is unable to surmount the advantage imparted by a 50% advantage in initial yield. In a rational world, then, value trumps growth.

Table 11.4: payback periods under two sets of assumptions

Year	Assumption			
	10% initial yield, 10% growth of coupon		15% initial yield, 10% growth of coupon	
	Coupon	Cumulative coupon	Coupon	Cumulative coupon
1	$0.10	$0.10	$0.15	$0.15
2	$0.11	$0.21	$0.17	$0.32
3	$0.12	$0.33	$0.18	$0.50
4	$0.13	$0.46	$0.20	$0.70
5	$0.15	$0.61	$0.22	$0.92
6	$0.16	$0.77	$0.24	$1.16
7	$0.18	**$0.95**	$0.27	**$1.43**

True return on investment is tangible, and the intelligent investor must be able to justify the yardstick she uses to determine whether one investment is preferable to another. To adopt time (that is, payback period) as a measure of return is to gauge one's investment results in tangible terms. Income that is either retained or paid to the investor is another sensible unit of measurement; again, because it is tangible. The vast majority of market participants in Australia and in many other countries take the opposite approach, measuring virtually all investment vehicles in terms of their 'performance'; that is, changes in their market prices from one point in time to another. Adherence to this cult of performance, with its short-term focus, has many injurious consequences.[2] Alas, those beholden to the cult of performance and unrealised capital gain — that is, nearly all market participants, including Australia's biggest institutional investors — delude themselves. As we saw in chapter 3, a security's current market price represents the current *perception* of its value held by a very small number of market participants (namely its most eager buyers and most eager sellers). However, market price is not actual or intrinsic value, because there is simply no such thing as intrinsic value.

Table 11.5: payback periods under two further sets of assumptions

Year	Assumption			
	10% initial yield, 15% growth of coupon		15% initial yield, 15% growth of coupon	
	Coupon	Cumulative coupon	Coupon	Cumulative coupon
1	$0.10	$0.10	$0.15	$0.15
2	$0.12	$0.22	$0.17	$0.32
3	$0.13	$0.35	$0.20	$0.52
4	$0.15	$0.50	$0.23	$0.75
5	$0.17	$0.67	$0.26	$1.01
6	$0.20	$0.97	$0.30	$1.31
7	$0.23	**$1.20**	$0.35	**$1.66**

By definition, performance is neither tangible nor necessarily enduring. This is painfully obvious to the many Australians who have repeatedly witnessed abrupt up-and-down movements of a stock's price even where no material change in the company's operations or profitability has occurred. It is vital to remember that a market is not an arbiter of objective or intrinsic value; rather, it is a forum wherein individuals and organisations exchange subjective, sometimes justifiable and occasionally crazy judgments about value. These judgments can be as fallible as the people who make them. As a result, the fluctuations of assets' market prices are not an appropriate measure of investment results. Sometimes they reflect a sober assessment of a company's operations and prospects and hence the value of its securities, but many times they do not.

In summary, how, then, to gauge the return on one's investment? A good way is to look at its annual coupon and the time required to recoup one's initial outlay (that is, the return *of* the investment). Invstors must seek a combination of the highest plausible yield and the shortest possible payback period. If you spent $4.20 per share on Telstra's stock and if in your first year of ownership its coupon was 30¢, the return on your investment for that year would be 7.1 per cent (that is, 30¢ ÷ $4.20). You are repaid fully when Telstra generates $4.20 in cumulative per-share net income—measured from the time you bought it. *In the interim and between any two points in time, the stock's 'performance' is utterly irrelevant.* Perhaps it rallied 30 per cent during your first year of ownership; perhaps it sank 20 per cent; or maybe it changed little. No matter: unrealised capital gains and losses have nothing to do with an investment's tangible return.

A final point: according to the assumptions set out in table 11.3, Telstra's payback period is 12.5 years and that of the Commonwealth Government bond to which it is compared is twenty years. Between 1999 and 2003, then, Telstra became more attractive relative to the bond; however, in an absolute sense, and despite the fact that its price halved since late 1999 and the yields of government bonds fell, in terms of its estimated payback period the Telstra share was not much more attractive—and fixed-coupon bonds were much less attractive—in 2003 than in 1999. Similarly, it is true that from 2002 to 2005 many other Australian blue chips became more attractive relative to government bonds; however, a sober assessment of their payback periods makes it clear that they have not become more attractive to Grahamite value investors. It is for this reason that during the past couple of years value investors have generally found it very difficult to locate quality businesses at low prices. In the final two chapters, we will look at the strategies they employ to build portfolios under these and more general circumstances.

NOTES

1   *The Weekend Australian* (16–17 June 2001).

2   See in particular Richard FitzHerbert, *Blueprint for Investment: An Approach for Serious Long-Term Investors,* (Wrightbooks, 1994).

Chapter 12

<><><><><><><><><><><><><><><><><><><><><><><><><>

'Manage' risk by balancing competing risks

Is it more serious to convict an innocent man or to acquit a guilty one? That will depend on the consequences of the error. Is the punishment death or fine? What is the danger to the community of released prisoners? What are the current ethical views on punishment? From the point of view of mathematical theory, all that we can do is to show how the risk of the errors can be controlled ...

J. Neyman and E. Pearson
'On the Problem of the Most Efficient
Tests of Statistical Hypotheses'
Philosophical Transactions of the Royal Society (1933)

As shown in chapter 4, virtually all market participants, including institutions, brokers, advisers, journalists and commentators, define investment risk in terms of the short-term ups and downs of a security's market price, relative either to comparable securities or the market as a whole. As a result, the practice of 'investment risk management' is conventionally understood as an attempt to keep the short-term variability of a portfolio's market capitalisation — particularly its downward variability — within acceptable bounds. This chapter describes the Grahamite approach to risk management — one which generates results that are disconcerting from a mainstream point of view.

THE NATURE OF INVESTMENT RISK

As we have established, to invest is to exchange one asset (such as cash) for another (such as a common stock, a bond or title to real estate). The ownership of an asset confers the right to receive the stream of earnings that the asset is expected to generate. The investor must therefore make a series of decisions. Is it reasonable to expect that asset A (which Bloggs owns) will produce a larger or more secure stream of earnings than asset B (which I own)? Does it make sense to sell B to Bloggs? To buy A from him? At what price? These decisions necessarily rest upon analyses of A's and B's past and present ability to produce earnings and upon assumptions about their ability to generate earnings into the future. However, premises can be inappropriate, logic invalid and evidence unreliable. Consequently, analyses of the past and present are necessarily imperfect. Further, the future is inherently uncertain and only crudely foreseeable. Whether their magnitude is small or large, investors will inevitably make mistakes. The correspondence between the results the investor expects to achieve in several years' time on the basis of her assumptions and her actual results is frequently slight and at worst non-existent.

These statements apply not just to decision-makers considered in isolation: they are equally true of their interactions with one another. Participants in the market exchange assets because they expect over time to accrue greater benefit from what they receive than from what they must give in return. Trade occurs, in other words, only if each party to the exchange perceives that the (subjective) value of what is received exceeds the (objective) price that is paid. Clearly, however, these perceptions may be mistaken. Risk thereby unavoidably accompanies any decision to invest. Stripped of its complexities, risk is the probability that a decision will not yield its expected results ('good things') and instead produces undesirable, unforeseen and unintended consequences ('bad things'). Investment risk is the likelihood that an investment made today will cause a particular bad thing—namely, relative or absolute financial loss—to occur at some point in the future.

The Grahamite approach to risk clearly has nothing to do with the volatility of an investment's market price. Rather, it is analytic, in that it seeks to estimate probability; empirical, because it demands close observation of outcomes; and normative, evaluating these outcomes as desirable or undesirable. Grahamites see the potential to overestimate an asset's ability to generate a certain stream of earnings as one risk; paying too much for those earnings is another. There is also a chance that an investor will somehow combine both of these two errors. Where this occurs, a portfolio's rate of return will tend to fall below its owner's time preference or 'natural' rate of interest (see chapter 10 for a discussion of these concepts).

It follows that the key to an appreciation of risk—and thus to the ability to make well-founded decisions in the face of uncertainty—is the ability to:

- partition total risk (the overall likelihood that bad things of one kind or another might occur) into a set of specific risks (the individual bad things that might occur)

- prioritise these specific risks.

These specific risks typically 'compete' with one another. To sell all of one's shares and bury the cash proceeds in the back garden, for example, eliminates the likelihood that one type of bad thing will occur—namely the bankruptcy of the underlying businesses, evaporation of their stream of earnings and total loss of capital. To take this decision, however, necessarily creates the possibility that other bad things may occur—the money could be stolen, for example, or you may find over time that the pile of cash generates a smaller stream of earnings than it would have if you had invested it in a portfolio of common stocks. The challenge, whether one is investing or making any other decision with imperfect information, is to estimate the total risk at hand and then to choose a tolerable level of the most salient risk among a set of competing risks.

Frequentist and subjectivist probabilities

If risk is the probability that bad things occur (either individually or collectively), how does one estimate these probabilities? Some risks can be calculated with reasonable, and in some fields very high, degrees of retrospective accuracy. Their calculation depends upon the existence of uniform and thus very similar events, large amounts of valid and reliable data and long periods of comparable past experience. Their calculation also presupposes agreement with respect to certain auxiliary assumptions and mathematical techniques. Notable examples are the incidence of property theft and of injury, mortality and morbidity—the bases of life, property and casualty insurance rates. Indeed, the very existence of these lines of insurance presupposes the existence of large numbers of statistically comparable events such as deaths and motor vehicle crashes. 'Frequentist probabilities', based upon mathematical reasoning about the objective frequency of the past occurrence of large numbers of comparable events, are the bread and butter of the actuarial and insurance industries.

Other risks, however, can either be estimated only with far higher degrees of subjectivity or cannot be calculated at all. Several reasons underlie this difficulty: the events under consideration may be regarded as unique rather than general and comparable; they may be difficult to observe and record accurately; or they may occur very rarely. For these or other reasons, valid and reliable data from long periods of past experience may not be available. Further, consensus on auxiliary assumptions and appropriate mathematical models with which to calculate the probabilities of loss may not exist. Earthquakes and corporate bankruptcies are examples.

This is why it is much easier to insure your life against loss than it is to insure your business against bankruptcy. In the absence of frequentist probabilities, 'subjective probabilities' must suffice.[1]

The Law of Large Numbers

The Law of Large Numbers, which links theoretically derived frequentist probabilities to their actual frequency of occurrence in the real world, is a pillar of statistical theory. It tells us that in an infinitely large number of repeated, independent trials of a given event, the frequency with which we observe the event will coincide with the theoretical frequency of its occurrence. If, for example, our 'event' consists of 500 tosses of a fair coin and we repeat this event a very large number of times under identical conditions, the average observed frequency of heads per event will approach 250, the average observed percentage of heads will approximate 50 per cent, and the long-run probability of observing heads will approach 0.5. Further, the greater the number of comparable tosses which comprise an event and the greater the number of times we repeat the event the more closely our observed results will approximate their frequentist probabilities.

This law has two key implications. First, if one repeatedly takes 'bad risks', plays unfavourable games or undertakes unethical or illegal practices, then—although the result on any given occasion is uncertain and need not produce a loss—it is likely that a 'bad' outcome will eventually be incurred. The second implication is that if one repeatedly takes 'good' risks or undertakes 'good' practices, then over time desired results will be achieved and the losses borne along the way will tend to be relatively small.

The assessment of risk is to a significant extent a subjective matter. This does not mean that it is arbitrary. Instead, it means that different individuals will impute different probabilities of loss to a particular course of action. For this reason, and also because their goals differ and change over time, they will choose different options and therefore accept dissimilar levels of risk. To say that risk is subjective also implies that some people may possess a particularly well-developed ability to make decisions they can justify in light of uncertainty. More generally, the long-term results of Grahamite investors indicate they understand that if one repeatedly takes good risks, undertakes good practices, avoids bad risks and eschews bad practices, then one is likely to achieve good results and mitigate the impact of bad events.

The futile hunt for 'minimum risk'

Given the information to hand at a particular point in time, the overall risk which inheres in a series of decisions cannot be minimised or even reduced. In this critical respect, risk cannot be 'managed'. Moreover, poor choices borne of faulty premises, reasoning and evidence can increase total risk and thereby magnify the likelihood of loss. With the information at her disposal, the best the investor can do is to exchange a specific risk that is regarded most undesirable for another regarded as less intolerable. It is only in this limited respect that risk can be managed. Not just objective consequences but also subjective and ethical considerations are thus bound inextricably into the investor's decisions.

Consider an individual who is accused of a serious criminal offence and undergoes trial by jury. Clearly, this person is either guilty or innocent. Seldom, however, can complete and incontrovertible evidence be brought to bear in order to decide a criminal matter. As a consequence, members of the jury must evaluate imperfect and incomplete information that is put to them indirectly by the prosecution and defence. Influenced by such evidence, they must then deliberate and render a judgment about the defendant's guilt or innocence. Innate uncertainty, together with incomplete and imperfect nature of the information available and the possibility that this information is presented and interpreted erroneously, thereby ensures that some percentage of juries' verdicts—despite their best intentions—have always been, are presently and will always be mistaken.

Setting aside mistrials, hung juries and the like, in any given trial the jury must either convict or acquit. Four possible outcomes therefore present themselves. These are set out in table 12.1. Two outcomes are usually regarded as good: a guilty defendant is convicted and an innocent defendant is acquitted. The third, in which a guilty party is acquitted, is usually regarded as bad. The fourth, in which an innocent person is convicted, is regarded as even worse, because of the presumption of innocence which underlies the Anglo-Saxon trial by jury. Two specific risks thus inhere in any jury's verdict. The first is the possibility that it may acquit a guilty defendant (thereby leaving a crime unpunished and its perpetrator free to commit further offences). The second is the possibility that it may convict an innocent defendant (thereby depriving the defendant unjustly of his or her liberty and leaving the culprit at large to commit further offences).

Table 12.1: the jury process—four possible outcomes and two inherent risks

	Jury convicts	Jury acquits
Defendant is guilty	Outcome 1 Good	Outcome 3, Risk 2 Bad
Defendant is innocent	Outcome 2, Risk 1 Worst	Outcome 4 Good

Consider now a thought experiment in which one jury tries 100 individual defendants in a series of 100 trials (that is, one trial for each defendant). Let us say that you are perfectly omniscient, are not a member of the jury and have no contact with its members. You know which of the 100 defendants is guilty and which is innocent, but you cannot give jury members the benefit of this knowledge. Let us also say that fifty defendants are guilty and fifty are innocent, that (by sheer coincidence) the jury's conviction rate across the 100 trials is 50 per cent and that it is able to ascertain the guilt or innocence of any particular defendant with 75 per cent accuracy. The results of your and the jurors' decisions, if they were repeated over a large number of experiments, each involving 100 jury trials, would approximate those set out in table 12.2. As an omniscient observer, your 100 per cent accurate decisions would correctly identify each of the fifty guilty defendants and 'convict' them; similarly, you would correctly identify each of the fifty innocent defendants and correctly 'acquit' them.

Table 12.2: expected risks arising from 100 jury trials with a 50:50 conviction rate

	Jury convicts	Jury acquits	True totals
Guilty defendants	50 (100% accurate)	0 (100% accurate)	
	37.5 (75% accurate)	12.5 (75% accurate)	50
Innocent defendants	0 (100% accurate)	50 (100% accurate)	
	12.5 (75% accurate)	37.5 (75% accurate)	50
Jury's total	50	50	100

The jury's 50:50 conviction rate (as set out in the bottom row of table 12.2) corresponds exactly to the true numbers of guilty and innocent defendants. Unfortunately for the individual defendants, however, the members of the jury are fallible: they convict the right *number* of people, but not always the right individuals. Either because perfect and complete information is not put to the jurors, and they are therefore prone to misinterpret it, or because they let biases prejudice their judgment (or due to some combination of these and other factors), they make mistakes. Given the jury's accuracy rate of 75 per cent, on average it will correctly convict 37.5

of the 50 guilty defendants but erroneously acquit the other 12.5. Similarly, on average it will accurately acquit 37.5 of the 50 innocent defendants but mistakenly convict the other 12.5. As a result, the two undesirable outcomes—risks—actually occur: one-quarter of the defendants (12.5 plus 12.5) are either wrongly convicted or wrongly acquitted.

Table 12.3: expected risks arising from 100 jury trials with a 40:60 conviction rate

	Jury convicts	Jury acquits	True totals
Guilty defendants	50 (100% accurate)	0 (100% accurate)	
	30 (75% accurate)	20 (75% accurate)	50
Innocent defendants	0 (100% accurate)	50 (100% accurate)	
	10 (75% accurate)	40 (75% accurate)	50
Jury's total	40	60	100

Assume now that another series of 100 jury trials, using the same jury, takes place. Before the first trial begins, however (perhaps on the basis of new evidence, a confession or some other development), one or more of the wrongful convictions in table 12.2 comes to light and is overturned. The jury, being human, is chastened. It cannot know with absolute certainty which of the 100 new defendants is guilty and which is innocent, but in order to lessen the likelihood that it wrongfully convicts an innocent person, it decides to raise the bar against wrongful conviction by reducing its willingness to convict. Assume that it lowers its overall conviction ratio from 50:50 to 40:60. All else, however, remains equal: you are omniscient, fifty of the defendants are guilty and the jury's accuracy rate remains at 75 per cent. The results of your decisions and the jury's, if taken in accord with these assumptions over a large number of sequences of 100 trials, would approximate those set out in table 12.3. As an omniscient observer, you continue correctly to identify each of the fifty guilty defendants and convict them; similarly, you identify each of the fifty innocent defendants correctly and acquit them.

Again, however, the members of the jury are not omniscient, and when trying the individual defendants, they continue to make mistakes. Given their 40:60 conviction rate, they convict 40 defendants. If their accuracy rate is 75 per cent, 30 of the 40 people they convict are accurately identified as guilty. They thereby correctly convict 30 of the 50 guilty defendants — and erroneously acquit 20 others. Analogously, they correctly acquit 40 of the 50 innocent defendants but mistakenly acquit 10 guilty ones.

The lower conviction rate, in light of an unchanged number of guilty and innocent defendants, thus has two consequences. First, it causes the sum of the two risks — average total risk — to increase from 25 (12.5 plus 12.5, as illustrated in table 12.2) to 30 (10 plus 20, as illustrated in table 12.3). It also causes the distribution of the two risks to change. The jury tends to convict fewer innocent defendants wrongfully — 10 in the second round of trials versus 12.5 in the first — and thereby mitigates the extent of risk 1 (the worst outcome identified in table 12.1). At the same time, however, it tends wrongfully to acquit more guilty defendants — 20 in the second round of trials versus 12.5 in the first — and thus exacerbates the extent of risk 2 (the bad outcome in table 12.1). *The jury, in other words, makes a subjective trade-off whereby one risk which many people regard as more ethically undesirable is 'exchanged' for another which many regard as less undesirable. This exchange, however, comes at the cost of a greater number of mistaken jury verdicts.*

In conclusion, it can be seen that over the longer term, the only means by which jurors — and decision-makers more generally — can reduce the total risk that inheres in their decisions is to increase the average accuracy of their decisions.

This would require at least one, or a combination of, the following factors:

- an increase in the quality and quantity of the information to which they have access

- an improvement in their ability to interpret this information

- a reduction in the psychological biases which mar their judgment.

Some of the implications this approach to risk management would have in an investment setting are already obvious. It is not surprising, for example, that Grahamite value investors tend to be voracious consumers of primary information (such as raw statistical data and company financial statements) and either discount or ignore secondary information. Just as jurors could do without lawyers (in so far as they act as brokers and possibly unwitting distorters of primary information), value investors seek primary source material and eschew that which has been mediated by brokers, advisers, analysts and journalists. The next chapter applies this framework and its conclusions to an investment setting.

NOTES

1   It is no accident that Berkshire Hathaway's astounding success over the years stems to a significant extent from the ability of its senior executives, such as Warren Buffett and Ajit Jain, not only to calculate these subjective probabilities of loss accurately but also to price them profitably.

Chapter 13

Constructing and managing portfolios

In the old legend the wise men boiled down the history of mortal affairs into the single phrase 'this too shall pass'. Confronted with a like challenge to distil the secret of sound investment into three words, we venture the motto 'margin of safety'.

Benjamin Graham, *The Intelligent Investor* (1949)

As we saw in the previous chapter, when all the the information available at a particular point in time has been weighed up, the overall risk present in a series of decisions cannot be minimised or even reduced; but poor choices can increase total risk and thereby magnify the likelihood of loss. Without access to better information or improved ability to interpret existing facts, the best that the investor can do is to 'exchange' the risk regarded as most undesirable for one regarded as less undesirable. Obviously, then, subjective and ethical considerations are bound inextricably into the construction and management of an investment portfolio.

INVESTING: FOUR POSSIBLE OUTCOMES
AND TWO INHERENT RISKS

Following the analogy of the jury trials, imagine that you are a one-person 'jury' and that you must evaluate a security as a potential addition to your portfolio. It either will or will not generate the stream of earnings that your assumptions and analysis ascribe to it; and either is or is not available at a sensible price. Accordingly, it either is or is not suitable for your purposes. Clearly, however, evidence from the past and present never shed incontrovertible light upon the results that a potential investment will achieve in the future. Adding to the difficulty is delayed feedback—only in several years' time will its suitability or unsuitability become apparent. You must therefore decide using imperfect and incomplete information about the past and present and make assumptions about an inherently uncertain future. Despite your best intentions, it is virtually certain that some of your investment decisions (and mine) will be mistaken.

Let us assume that in five years it will be apparent whether a particular investment opportunity in front of you today is sound. The trouble is that you must decide today whether to act upon it. Four possible outcomes therefore present themselves. These are set out in table 13.1. Two are usually regarded as good outcomes: a sound investment opportunity is grasped and an unsound one is avoided. The third outcome, in which a sound opportunity is not grasped, is bad. The fourth, in which an unsound investment is purchased, is even worse. Table 13.1 therefore shows that two types of risk inhere in every investment decision. The first is a 'sin of omission'—the possibility that a sound opportunity is declined. The second is a 'sin of commission'—the possibility that an unsound investment is grasped and a loss eventually incurred.

Thought experiment 1

Consider now a thought experiment in which you and I face 100 potential investments, each of which we must accept or reject individually. Let us say that you are perfectly prescient: you can gaze into your crystal ball and see five years into the future to determine with perfect precision which of the opportunities are (for my purposes) sound and unsound. Unfortunately for me, you do not give me the benefit of your knowledge. Assume that fifty opportunities are sound and fifty are unsound, that my 'accuracy rate' is 50 per cent (that is, my assumptions and analysis can ascertain the soundness or otherwise of each opportunity with 50 per cent accuracy) and that my 'acceptance rate' is also 50 per cent (that is, given an assessment of a sound opportunity, the likelihood that I act upon it is 50:50).

Table 13.1: the investment process: four possible outcomes and two types of risk

In five years' time it is apparent that the investment opportunity was ...	Today, a decision was made ...	
	To invest	**Not to invest**
Sound	Outcome 1: a good decision	Outcome 3, Risk 2: a bad decision
Not sound	Outcome 2, Risk 1: a very bad decision	Outcome 4: a good decision

If our investment decisions were repeated over a large number of experiments, our results in five years' time would approximate those set out in table 13.2. As an omniscient observer, your 100 per cent accurate decisions would correctly identify each of the fifty sound assets and enable you to purchase them; similarly, you would correctly identify each of the fifty unsound assets and refrain from buying them.

Table 13.2: expected risks arising from a series of investment decisions with a 50:50 'acceptance rate' and a 50:50 'accuracy rate'

Today it is apparent that the investment opportunity was ...	Five years ago a decision was made ...		True totals
	To invest	Not to invest	
Sound	50 (100% accurate)	0 (100% accurate)	
	25 (50% accurate)	25 (50% accurate)	50
Not sound	0 (100% accurate)	50 (100% accurate)	
	25 (50% accurate)	25 (50% accurate)	50
Investor's total	50	50	100

But my decisions, remember, are fallible. At the aggregate level, the true numbers of sound and unsound assets (set out in the fourth column of table 13.2) correspond exactly to the total numbers that I actually buy and decline to buy. However, when making individual investment decisions, I make mistakes. Given that, on average, 50 per cent of my decisions are accurate, I will tend to purchase twenty-five of the sound investments but erroneously decline to purchase the other twenty-five. Similarly, on average I will accurately decline to purchase twenty-five of the fifty unsound investments but mistakenly buy the other twenty-five. As a result, the two investment risks come to fruition: one-half of the assets (25 plus 25) are either wrongly purchased or wrongly declined. My investment results under these circumstances are no different from those that would occur if I simply tossed a fair coin.

Constructing and managing portfolios

Thought experiment 2

Assume that five years later I am faced with another series of 100 investment decisions. Given the results in table 13.2, I am chastened. I cannot be certain which of the 100 new opportunities is sound and which is unsound. During the past five years, however, I have learnt that if the 'acceptance rate' is reduced then the expected number of dud investments in a portfolio (and the magnitude of the investment capital lost) can be reduced. Let us say that I lower this rate from 50:50 to 20:80. I have also realised that one can reduce the total risk in a series of investment decisions by increasing the average accuracy of each decision. I have therefore: increased the quality and quantity of the information that I use to make decisions; improved my ability to reason through and interpret this information; and reduced the extent of the psychological biases that mar my judgment. Let us say that these improvements have increased my average accuracy from 50 per cent to 75 per cent. Otherwise all else remains equal: you are omniscient and fifty of the 100 investment opportunities are sound.

The results of many decisions, if taken under these assumptions, would approximate those set out in table 13.3. As an omniscient observer, you will continue to identify each of the fifty sound investment opportunities and to act upon them; similarly, you will continue to identify each of the fifty unsound investments and to avoid them.

Again, I am not omniscient. At the aggregate level, my 20:80 acceptance rate no longer corresponds to the true numbers of sound and unsound investments, but I continue to make mistakes. Given my more stringent acceptance rate, I act upon just twenty opportunities; and given my 75 per cent accuracy rate, fifteen of these twenty are assessed correctly. I thereby invest correctly in fifteen of the fifty sound investments—and mistakenly forgo thirty-five others. On the other hand, I correctly avoid forty-five of the fifty unsound opportunities and mistakenly accept the other five.

Table 13.3: expected risks arising from a series of investment decisions with a 20:80 'acceptance rate' and 75% 'accuracy rate'

Today it is apparent that the investment opportunity was ...	Five years ago a decision was made ...		True totals
	To invest	Not to invest	
Sound	50 (100% accurate)	0 (100% accurate)	
	15 (75% accurate)	35 (75% accurate)	50
Not sound	0 (100% accurate)	50 (100% accurate)	
	5 (75% accurate)	45 (50% accurate)	50
Investor's total	20	80	100

Under the assumption of a much lower 'acceptance rate' and a higher 'accuracy rate', in other words, I will tend to accept far fewer unsound investment opportunities and thereby commit far fewer sins of commission (five in this second round of investment decisions, versus twenty-five in the first round). I will also tend to forgo more sound opportunities (thirty-five in the second round as opposed to twenty-five in the first) and thus commit more sins of omission. The distribution of the two competing investment risks thus changes substantially: there is a decrease in the occurrence of real financial losses and an increase in the forfeiture of hypothetical financial benefits. *In consequence, the ratio of sound to unsound investments in my portfolio increases from 1:1 (that is, 25:25) in the first round of investments to 3:1 (that is, 15:5) in the second round of investments.* At the same time, however, given better standards of analysis and more stringent criteria for decision making, total investment risk—that is to say, my total number of erroneous investment decisions (25 plus 25 in table 13.2, 5 plus 35 in table 13.3)—falls from fifty to forty.

GRAHAMITE RISK MANAGEMENT

As with jury decisions, so too with investment decisions: the major difference between the scenarios summarised in tables 13.2 and 13.3 is that a subjective trade-off of risks has occurred whereby fewer dud investments are purchased but more sound investments are overlooked and foregone. This is the value investor's approach: one risk which she regards as completely intolerable is willingly traded for another she regards as undesirable but nonetheless bearable. The 'acceptance rate' and the 'accuracy rate' are fundamentals of a Grahamite investment strategy. The acceptance rate denotes the extent to which investors prioritise their options and act only upon those which appear to have the shortest odds of achieving their intended long-run consequences. The accuracy rate indicates the total percentage of successful decisions—the extent to which the investor can ascertain whether a particular security's price is significantly lower than a subjective but justifiable estimate of its value.

Grahamite value investors strive to use logic and evidence to identify discrepancies between prices and values, acting only upon the widest discrepancies, and thereby increasing their decisions' overall accuracy rate. Conveniently, to concentrate their portfolios upon the most egregious of these discrepancies is also to reduce their acceptance rate. Value investors' assumptions (including their conception of risk), their analyses and their behaviour thereby tend cumulatively to create what Benjamin Graham called a *margin of safety*. This is the essence of Grahamite investing.

The acceptance rate, concentration and diversification

Grahamite investors are selective investors. Graham's employees at Graham-Newman Corp., such as Warren Buffett, William Ruane and Walter Schloss, often recounted the number of times they put investment proposals to Graham and the number of times he rebuffed them. Each employee agreed that the number rebuffed was a high percentage of the number proposed: Graham accepted few of the 'opportunities' that came his way.

Value portfolios are concentrated in the sense that they consist exclusively of assets that possess a healthy margin of safety. Yet value portfolios are also diversified, tending as they do to contain a heterogeneous group of assets. Moderate diversification and a hefty margin of safety go hand in hand. Even if a particular investment opportunity possesses a healthy margin of safety, it may nonetheless end badly. The margin implies only that the opportunity has a better chance for profit than for loss: it hardly guarantees that loss is impossible. However, as the number of such seemingly favourable investments rises, the more likely it is that the results of correct choices will exceed the results of poor ones. As a rough-and-ready rule of thumb, Graham concluded that the probability of a positive result under 'fairly normal conditions' was good, if such a margin were built into each of a diversified list of twenty (or more) stocks.[1]

In summary, Grahamite value investors are a relentlessly logical and analytical lot. They strive to maximise the accuracy rate of their investment decisions, that is, the extent to which they are able consistently to ascertain whether a security's price is significantly lower than a cautious estimate of its value. To do so they follow three strategies:

- They strive to increase the quality and quantity of the information to which they have access. In practice they tend to be voracious consumers of primary information (raw statistical data, company financial statements and so on) and either discount or ignore secondary information which has been mediated by brokers, advisers, analysts and journalists.

- They seek constantly to improve their ability to interpret this information.

- They attempt to identify and to reduce the psychological biases that mar their judgment.

Graham emphasised that the concept of the margin of safety rests upon simple and definite numerical reasoning from statistical data. 'Thus,' he concluded, 'in sum we say that to have a true investment there must be present a true margin of safety. And a true margin of safety is one that can be demonstrated by figures, by persuasive reasoning, and by reference to a body of actual experience.'[2]

NOTES

1   *The Intelligent Investor*, p. 515.

2   *The Intelligent Investor*, p. 520.

Chapter 14

◇◇◇◇◇◇◇◇◇◇◇◇◇◇◇◇◇◇◇◇◇◇◇◇◇◇◇◇◇◇◇◇◇◇

Learn from the giants who preceded you

He who lets the world, or his own portion of it, choose his plan of life for him has no need of any other faculty than the ape-like one of imitation. [Conversely,] he who chooses his plan for himself employs all his faculties. He must use observation to see, reasoning and judgment to foresee, activity to gather materials for decision, discrimination to decide, and when he has decided, firmness and self-control to hold to his deliberate decision.

John Stuart Mill
On Liberty (1859)

Throughout this book, I have emphasised that value investors read voraciously. They read in order to accumulate a reliable base of historical information—what we have called 'base rates'—from which to form their decisions. They also read in order to develop a healthy scepticism towards their subject matter. Making reasonable judgments in the face of uncertainty requires not just caution but also humility. Armed with these virtues, the value investor can respond calmly to the daily deluge of sense, part-sense and nonsense that bombards her. She is also able to react dispassionately to her inevitable mistakes and to Mr Market's abrupt changes of emotion.

To read Australian business and trade publications and the business section of the daily newspaper critically is occasionally to discern a valuable insight or bit of information, but little of what one reads is worth retaining; indeed, only a small number of writings repay careful study. If a sound education in business, finance and investment had to rely upon a single book, economic philosopher Adam Smith's *The Theory of Moral Sentiments* (1759) or *The Wealth of Nations* (1776) would be strong contenders, but perhaps the strongest would be the King James Bible (1611), the most engagingly written distillation of human experience in existence.[1]

The investor must peruse widely, focus upon what is worth reading, study it carefully and apply its lessons to her investment operations. To study investment from this point of view is to experience the epiphany that the 'eminent dead' ably refuted some of the most important and perennial fallacies of their day. It is also to realise that, no matter how comprehensively they have been disproved, the same old myths constantly reappear in new and deceptively authoritative guises. Fallacies about investment, finance and economics are just as prevalent today as they were in Adam Smith's day. Selective reading and sustained thought can thus reveal more about the crazy world we inhabit than the babble emanating from today's universities, governments and mass media—and guide us sensibly into the future.

This chapter suggests some reading materials. Books and resources marked with a double asterisk (**) are available over the internet. Leithner & Co.'s website, <www.leithner.com.au> provides links to these and other online sources of interest on its 'Links to Other Sites' page.

BIOGRAPHIES

No man is perfect, but Benjamin Graham's students and employees (and investors at large) maintain that his positive characteristics vastly exceeded his defects. Each day, he sought to do something wise, something generous and something whimsical; on his birthday, he gave presents to his closest friends. Graham asked his students, 'Have you ever seen a human being mentioned in a corporate business plan?' and beseeched them to 'always remember that you are dealing with people and their hard-earned savings'. Even more than his approach to investment and financial matters, these aspects of Graham's ethics deserve emulation.

Further, in a field that has usually attracted narrow and technical minds, Graham cultivated broad and deep interests. Upon his graduation from Columbia University he was offered academic posts in three departments. For decades he taught part-time in Columbia's Business School, but he was also a life-long scholar of classics, languages, literature, mathematics and philosophy, and eventually retired in order to pursue these passions. He commended to his grandchildren 'the incomparable richness of intellectual endeavour—for its own sake, independent of material acquisition'. For several years during the Great Depression, in a field where avarice and sharp practice are perceived to be more prevalent than generosity and plain dealing, Graham declined any salary until his investors' losses had been recouped. Further, in a line of work where 'growth' is worshipped, for years he withstood the temptation to increase the bulk of Graham-Newman Corp. Instead he concentrated upon maximising its profitability—and therefore the returns to its owners. These insights and more emerge in Graham's autobiography, *Benjamin Graham: The Memoirs of the Dean of Wall Street* (McGraw-Hill, 1996).

By far the best biography of Graham's most celebrated student, employee and torchbearer, Warren Buffett, is Roger Lowenstein's *Buffett: The Making of an American Capitalist* (Weidenfeld & Nicholson, 1996). Also well worth reading are Lowenstein's other books: *When Genius Failed: The Rise and Fall of Long-Term Capital Management* published by Random House in 2001 and *Origins of the Crash: The Great Bubble and Its Undoing* published by Penguin Press in 2004.

The most relevant Australian biography from a value investor's point of view is *Frank Lowy: Pushing the Limits* by Jill Margo (HarperCollins Australia, 2001). At the other end of the spectrum, the most gruesomely readable compendium of Australian corporate catastrophes is Trevor Sykes's *The Bold Riders* (Allen & Unwin, 1994). (Reading about what *not* to do can be salutary: that is why Charles Munger constantly exhorts people to 'invert, always invert'.)

GRAHAM'S MAJOR WORKS

Throughout his life, Benjamin Graham freely shared his insights. Warren Buffett, in a tribute published shortly after Graham's death, emphasised his generosity; and more than one student has recounted how the lessons learnt on any given day in Graham's class could be applied with immediate practical benefit. Graham thus sought not just to apply the principles of value investing: he sought as well to communicate their application clearly and widely. His major books appeal to beginners as well as seasoned investors.

Introductory

- *The Interpretation of Financial Statements: The Classic 1937 Edition* (Harper Business, 1998)

Good Australian books that cover similar terrain include Trevor Sykes's *The Numbers Game* (Allen & Unwin Australia, 2003) and Martin Roth's *Analysing Company Accounts: A Guide for Australian Investors* (Wrightbooks, 1995).

Intermediate

- *The Intelligent Investor: A Book of Practical Counsel* (HarperBusiness Essentials, revised edition with preface and appendix by Warren Buffett and commentary by Jason Zweig, 2003)

Advanced

- *Security Analysis: The Classic 1940 Second Edition* (David Dodd, co-author, McGraw-Hill, 1996)

Several of Graham's hard-to-find articles and lectures** have been reprinted in *The Rediscovered Benjamin Graham: Selected Writings of the Wall Street Legend* by Janet Lowe (John Wiley & Sons, 1999).

ANALYSING STOCKS AND BONDS LIKE GRAHAM

How can you best learn the specific methods that Benjamin Graham used to estimate the subjective value of particular securities? By reading, studying and rereading his major works—particularly *The Intelligent Investor*. Once you have digested it, you can proceed to updates, extensions and elaborations of his methods. The three books listed below are the pick of the crop.

Introductory

- Janet Lowe, *Value Investing Made Easy: Benjamin Graham's Classic Investment Strategy Explained for Everyone* (McGraw-Hill, 1996)

Intermediate

- Bruce Greenwald et al., *Value Investing: From Graham to Buffett and Beyond* (John Wiley & Sons, 2001)

Advanced

- Thomas P. Au, *A Modern Approach to Graham and Dodd Investing* (John Wiley & Sons, 2004)

GRAHAM'S MOST CELEBRATED
AND SUCCESSFUL TORCHBEARER

Warren Buffett, Chairman of Berkshire Hathaway, Inc., has inherited Graham's desire to disseminate widely and in plain language the fundamentals of good investment. For decades, Buffett has acknowledged Graham's profound influence upon his thinking and actions. So don't waste your time and money on an MBA (or if you already have, try to forget what has been stuffed into your head): Buffett's annual letter to Berkshire's shareholders** is much more insightful and far better attuned to the real world. And it is far better written than anything on a business school curriculum. So too are the letters to Wesco Financial Corp. shareholders.** Their author, Charles Munger, is Berkshire's vice-chairman and Wesco's chairman. Other must-reads include the notes taken at Berkshire's and Wesco's AGMs**. Among the best of the many secondary sources about Buffett and his approach to investment are the following three books by Robert Hagstrom.

- *The Warren Buffett Way: Investment Strategies of the World's Greatest Investor* (John Wiley & Sons, 1994)

- *The Warren Buffett Portfolio: Mastering the Power of the Focus Investment Strategy* (John Wiley & Sons, 1999)

- *The Essential Buffett: Timeless Principles for the New Economy* (John Wiley & Sons, 2002)

THE LAWS OF HUMAN ACTION

Intelligent investing requires a solid knowledge of—and healthy respect for—the laws of economics. If you have never studied the dismal science, rejoice—this means it is less likely that you will have to unlearn the myths and nonsense that pervade the contemporary mainstream. You can also exult because Austrian School economics is grounded in clarity, common sense and verbal logic rather than mathematical and graphical mumbo jumbo. Essential sources include the titles listed on the next page.

Learn from the giants who preceded you

Introductory

- Gene Callahan, *Economics for Real People: An Introduction to the Austrian School* (Ludwig von Mises Institute, 2002)

- Henry Hazlitt, *Economics in One Lesson*** (Laissez Faire Books 50th Anniversary Edition, 1996)

- Thomas Sowell, *Basic Economics: A Citizen's Guide to the Economy* (Basic Books, 2000)

Advanced

- Murray Rothbard, *Man, Economy and State: A Treatise on Economic Principles* ** (Ludwig von Mises Institute, 1963, 1993)

Very Advanced

- Ludwig von Mises, *Human Action: A Treatise on Economics*** (Fox & Wilkes, 1949, 4th rev. ed., 1996)

The Great Depression
AND THE INTELLIGENT INVESTOR

Perhaps because we are generations removed from it and the images it evokes are so unpleasant and discomfiting, the Great Depression seldom intrudes into our thoughts. At the same time, however, and in ways that are rarely recognised, important beliefs that most people presently hold dear were moulded during the 1930s. Views about what caused and ended the Depression and beliefs about the proper role, alleged benevolence and supposed efficacy of governments have all been strongly influenced, if not determined, by ideas and actions which gained currency between 1929 and 1945. Unfortunately, much of what we think we know about the Depression is false and many of the lessons we have learnt from it are mistaken. Central banks and governments, in short, created a slump; their policies extended and deepened this slump, bringing about the Depression; and the Second World War did not end it. The following is a list of the best of studies available.

- Benjamin Anderson, *Economics and the Public Welfare* (Liberty Press, 1949, 1979)

- Thomas DiLorenzo, *How Capitalism Saved America* (Crown Forum, 2004)

- Garet Garrett, *Salvos Against the New Deal: Selections from* The Saturday Evening Post, *1933–1940* (Caxton, 2002)

- Jim Powell, *FDR's Folly: How Roosevelt and His New Deal Prolonged the Great Depression* (Crown Forum, 2003)

- Murray Rothbard, *America's Great Depression*** (Richardson & Snyder, 1963)

- Gene Smiley, *Rethinking the Great Depression: A New View of Its Causes and Consequences* (Ivan R Dee, 2002)

Australian books about investment that take history seriously include Richard FitzHerbert's *Blue Print for Investment: An Approach for Serious Long-Term Investors* (Wrightbooks, 1994) and Trevor Sykes's *Two Centuries of Panic* (Allen & Unwin, 1998).

'SMART MONEY' CAN BE APPALLINGLY STUPID

The intelligent investor is humble because she knows that 'smart money' is often arrogant money and that arrogant money is eventually dumb money. Warren Buffett emphasises that successful investment does not require a stratospheric IQ, brilliant insights or 'inside' information. It does, however, require a sound intellectual framework and the discipline to prevent one's emotions from eroding that framework. An amusing but profound item on the Dow Jones Newswire (15 May 2001) confirms Buffett's point. An article by Eleanor Laise, entitled 'If We're So Smart, Why Aren't We Rich? The Inside Story of How a Select Group of the Best and the Brightest Managed to Bungle the Easiest Stock', profiled an investment club whose 'recent record has been nothing short of a fiasco'. This club's investments fell by more than 40 per cent in 2000. One of its members lamented 'we can screw up faster than anyone else'. Another described its investing strategy as 'buy low, sell lower'. From 1986 to 2001, it returned an average of 2.5 per cent a year (versus the S&P 500's 15.3 per cent).

Clearly, this group needs an intelligent investing strategy, which is ironic, given its membership. This is the Mensa Investment Club—that's right, Mensa, the organisation whose admission requirement is an IQ higher than that of 98 per cent of the population. This organisation, once dubbed 'a dating service for dorks', has one of the sorriest investment clubs you will ever see. Why are allegedly intelligent people able to act so stupidly for so long? Books which will help you ponder this question are listed below.

Introductory

- Gary Belsky and Thomas Gilovich, *Why Smart People Make Big Money Mistakes and How to Correct Them: Lessons from the New Science of Behavioral Economics* (Simon & Schuster, 2000)

- Thomas Gilovich, *How We Know What Isn't So: The Fallibility of Human Reason in Everyday Life*, (The Free Press, 1993)

- Three very readable books by John Allen Paulos: *Beyond Numeracy: Ruminations of a Numbers Man* (Vintage Books, 1992); *A Mathematician Reads the Newspaper* (Anchor, 1996); and *Innumeracy: Mathematical Illiteracy and Its Consequences* (Hill and Wang, 2001)

Intermediate

- Massimo Piattelli-Palmarini, *Inevitable Illusions: How Mistakes of Reason Rule Our Minds,* (John Wiley & Sons, 1996)

Predatory politicians
and the catastrophes they wreak

Intelligent investors know that governments inevitably make an appalling mess of far more than agriculture, commerce and industry. Investors are their own worst enemy, but politicians run a close second. Compelling demonstrations of this fundamental point include:

- Thomas Fleming, *The Illusion of Victory: America in World War I* (Basic Books, 2003)

- Thomas Fleming, *The New Dealers' War: FDR and the War Within World War II* (Basic Books, 2001)

- John T. Flynn, *The Roosevelt Myth* (Fox & Wilkes, 50th Anniversary Edition, 1998)

- Garet Garrett, *Defend America First: The Antiwar Editorials of The Saturday Evening Post, 1939–1942* (Caxton, 2003)

- Robert Higgs, *Crisis and Leviathan: Critical Episodes in the Growth of American Government* (Oxford University Press, 1987)

- Hans-Hermann Hoppe, *Democracy, The God that Failed: The Economics and Politics of Monarchy, Democracy and Natural Order* (Transaction, 2002)

- Charles Murray, *Losing Ground: American Social Policy, 1950–1980* (Basic Books, 1995)

- Jim Powell, *Wilson's War: How Woodrow Wilson's Great Blunder Led to Hitler, Lenin, Stalin, and World War II* (Crown Forum, 2005)

- Llewellyn H. Rockwell, *Speaking of Liberty* (Ludwig von Mises Institute, 2003)

- Murray Rothbard, *Wall Street, Banks and American Foreign Policy*** (Centre for Libertarian Studies, 1995)

- Eric Schansberg, *Poor Policy: How Government Harms the Poor* (Westview Press, 1996)

- Thomas Sowell, *The Vision of the Anointed: Self-Congratulation as a Basis for Social Policy* (Basic Books, 1995)

NOTES

1   Subservience to God (if you are devout) and service to others (whether you are devout, agnostic or atheistic) requires mastery of oneself. The study of Scripture reveals the foibles of human nature and the possibility of redemption; it inspires the defeat of misfortune; and it cultivates a disciplined way of life that inculcates peace of mind. See also Thomas Woods, *The Church and the Market: A Catholic Defense of the Free Economy* (Lexington Books, 2005) and Michael Novak, *Business as a Calling: Work and the Examined Life* (The Free Press, 1996). The trouble, of course, is that these days most clergy, Catholic and Protestant alike, are economic illiterates.

Afterword

Despite Benjamin Graham's eminence, despite the results of Graham-Newman Corp. from 1926 to 1956 and despite the results obtained by Graham's former students and employees since the 1950s, Grahamite value investors have seldom comprised more than a small minority of market participants. Many people ritually praise Graham, but very few bother either to study or practice what he taught. Warren Buffett and Charles Munger discuss their principles openly—but no matter: surprisingly few people are really interested in their many insights. Instead, what most people want desperately to know is what Berkshire is presently buying.

In his 'Superinvestors of Graham-and-Doddsville' speech (which is available online, and also appears as an appendix in recent editions of *The Intelligent Investor*), Buffett concluded that 'the secret has been out for fifty years ever since Ben Graham and Dave Dodd wrote *Security Analysis*, yet I have seen no trend toward value investing in the thirty-five years I've practised it. There seems to be some perverse human characteristic that likes to make easy things difficult. The academic world, if anything, has actually backed away from the teaching of value investing over the last thirty years. It's likely to continue that way. Ships will sail around the world but the Flat Earth Society will flourish. There will continue to be wide discrepancies between price and value in the marketplace and those who read their Graham and Dodd will continue to prosper.'

I hope that you become one of them.

Chris Leithner
Toowong, Queensland
July 2005

Index

~~~~~~~~~~~~~~~~~~

Note: An italicised *n* following a page reference indicates that the reference appears only in the chapter endnotes.

Index